THE SOUTHERN POETRY ANTHOLOGY

VOLUME III

CONTEMPORARY APPALACHIA

Copyright © 2025 by TRP: The University Press of SHSU
All rights reserved
Printed in the United States of America
First Edition Copyright © 2010

SECOND EDITION, 2025

Requests for permission to reproduce material from this work should be sent to:

> Permissions
> TRP: The University Press of SHSU
> P.O. Box 2146
> Sam Houston State University
> Huntsville, TX 77341-2146

Series cover design by Chad M. Pelton
Volume cover design by Miranda Ramírez
Cover Photo by Chad M. Pelton

Library of Congress Cataloging-in-Publication Data is on file at
The Library of Congress, Washington, DC

THE SOUTHERN POETRY ANTHOLOGY

VOLUME III

CONTEMPORARY APPALACHIA

William Wright, *Series Editor*

J. Bruce Fuller, Jesse Graves, & Paul Ruffin *Volume Editors*

PREVIOUS VOLUMES

William Wright, Series Editor

Volume I: South Carolina
Edited by Stephen Gardner and William Wright

Volume II: Mississippi
Edited by Stephen Gardner and William Wright

Volume III: Contemporary Appalachia
Edited by J. Bruce Fuller, Jesse Graves, Paul Ruffin, and William Wright

Volume IV: Louisiana
Edited by Paul Ruffin and William Wright

Volume V: Georgia
Edited by Paul Ruffin and William Wright

Volume VI: Tennessee
Edited by Jesse Graves, Paul Ruffin, and William Wright

Volume VII: North Carolina
Edited by Jesse Graves, Paul Ruffin, and William Wright

Volume VIII: Texas
Edited by Paul Ruffin and William Wright

Volume IX: Virginia
Edited by J. Bruce Fuller, Jesse Graves, Amy Wright, and William Wright

Volume X: Alabama
Edited by Taylor Byas, J. Bruce Fuller, Adam Vines, and William Wright

CONTENTS

xiv Series Editor's Preface
xvi Preface to the Second Edition
xviii Introduction

GILBERT ALLEN
1 Stairways to Nowhere
3 Some Week
4 Late Garden

MAGGIE ANDERSON
5 Long Story
7 House and Graveyard, Rowlesburg, West Virginia, 1935
8 Mining Camp Residents, West Virginia, 1935
8 Spitting in the Leaves
9 Street Scene, Morgantown, West Virginia, 1935

DARNELL ARNOULT
10 Medicinal
10 Lake Michael

JOSEPH BATHANTI
11 House-Hunting at Four Thousand Feet
12 Wall at Second Manassas
13 The Vilas Flood
14 Running

LAURA TREACY BENTLEY
16 Closet Appalachians
17 Gas Station

NICKOLE BROWN
18 Self-Portrait as Eastern Wood Rat
20 Parable

KATHRYN STRIPLING BYER
22 Drought Days

WAYNE CALDWELL
27 Fence Posts
27 Peeper Frogs
28 Bird Tree

SHULY XÓCHITL CAWOOD
29 Inheritance
30 Another Poem for Donna on a Crowded Saturday Afternoon in Kroger

FRED CHAPPELL
31 Stopping by the Old Homestead
31 All the Good Times Are Past and Gone
32 A Glimpse of the Traveler
33 Halloween Moon over Huddle Knob Graveyard

CATHERINE PRITCHARD CHILDRESS
34 Polysemy
35 Portrait

MICHAEL CHITWOOD
36   Those Dying Generations
39   Heat
39   The Great Wagon Road...
42   Transport in Early Spring
43   Woodpile
43   Black Locust
44   Hatchet

JIM CLARK
45   Handiwork
46   Loveless You Wander
47   Sunday Dinner
48   Black Dog Shadrick Mayhew

GERALDINE CONNOLLY
49   Blue Bridge
49   Quilting
50   Mendon
50   Lightning
51   Regrets

JOHN CRUTCHFIELD
52   Ox Creek Road
52   Wild Leeks
53   Trout Lake
54   Meteor Shower

DONNA DOYLE
55   Sunbathing with Elvis
56   One by One, the Animals

CASIE FEDUKOVICH
57   Sinners Gather at Paint Lake
58   Pocahontas Seam via Norfolk and Western

HARRY GIEG
59   Rubato

DIANE GILLIAM
61   Where I'm From
62   Pearlie Tells What Happened at School

NIKKI GIOVANNI
63   Knoxville, Tennessee
64   Nikki-Rosa

JESSE GRAVES
65   Tennessee Landscape with Blighted Pine
67   Johnson's Ground
68   Elegy for a Hay Rake

CHRIS GREEN
69   A Tree for Everything
70   Playhouse

CONNIE JORDAN GREEN
71   Coal Mining Camp, Kentucky, 1935
71   Late January Letter to a Retired Friend in Florida
72   Of the Wild
73   Boss

LARRY GRIMES
74   Get you up to the high mountain

KARI GUNTER-SEYMOUR
75   To the Woman in Walmart Who Was Dancing to Shakira in the Pots and Pans Aisle
76   Someone Needs to Bake a Pie

RICHARD HAGUE
77   Time Lapse Photography: A Mouse Corpse Devoured by Maggots
78   Talking Together

CATHRYN HANKLA
80   Brush Fires
80   Taking Pictures
81   Bee Tree
82   Ghost Horses and the Morning Sky

PAULETTA HANSEL
83   The Road
83   Facts About Grandmothers

WILLIAM HARMON
85   Versicles

MARC HARSHMAN
86   Small Town, West Virginia
87   Not All That Much

MELISSA HELTON
88   I Wouldn't Think Any Less of You
89   Upon Driving Away from Your Hometown

RAYE HENDRIX
90   Any Coyote

JANE HICKS
92   A Poet's Work
93   Deep Winter
93   Dust
94   Felix culpa

THOMAS ALAN HOLMES
95   Awning
96   Remember Roni Stoneman

RON HOUCHIN
97   Belief in Soap
97   Camping at Greenup Locks and Dam
98   If the World Were a Coalmine
98   Singing to the Fan
99   The First Christmas I Remember

SILAS HOUSE
100 Double Creek Girl
101 At the Opening of Coal Miner's Daughter,
         Corbin, Kentucky, March 27, 1980

REBECCA GAYLE HOWELL
102 No One Was Born Here
102 Every Job Has a First Day
103 What Goes Around

DAVID HUDDLE
104   *Religious Life*
108   *Not True*
109   *Hilltop Sonnet*

CHARLIE G. HUGHES
110   *Where I'm From*
111   *Lament for Mountains*

JANNETTE HYPES
112   *Raking*
113   *Late June*

EDISON JENNINGS
114   *Rainstorm*
114   *Spontaneous Combustion*
115   *Appalachian Gothic*
115   *Apple Economics*

DON JOHNSON
116   *Grabbling*
117   *Scatology*
118   *Almanac*
119   *Going to Chatham*
120   *Isinglass*

JUDY JORDAN
121   *In the 25th Year of My Mother's Death*
122   *Sandbar at Moore's Creek*
122   *Those First Mornings Living in the Greenhouse*
123   *Waking in Winter*
124   *The Greenhouse, Late September*

MARILYN KALLET
125   *Global*
126   *Brushing Aside a Layer of Dust*
127   *At the Beauty Salon*

LEATHA KENDRICK
128   *Tonight Weaving*
129   *Brought-On Bride*
129   *Morning of the Heart Test*
130   *A Lesson in Love Unleashed*

LISA KWONG
131   *Tai Shan, Canton Came to Radford, Virginia*
132   *Portrait of Appalachian Chinese Girls in Their Grandmother's Garden*
133   *Childhood Fade in Litany*

JEANNE LARSEN
134   *Ardent Things*
135   *Flowering Judases*
136   *Scar Garden*
137   *Wrong All These Years—It Isn't*

JUDY LOEST
138   *Sequence in Memory of George Addison Scarbrough, 1915-2008*

DONNA J. LONG
140   *Sago Mine Explosion*
141   *Hanging Audubon's Flamingo. . .*

DENTON LOVING
143   Under the Chestnut Tree
143   Feller

ROBERT WOOD LYNN
144   Not Hell
145   The River New

GEORGE ELLA LYON
146   Where I'm From
147   How Sunday Went
148   Report Card
148   Vocation

JEFF MANN
149   Mountain Fireflies
150   Creecy Greens
151   Digging Potatoes
152   Maple Syrup
153   Goldenrod Seeds
155   Homecoming
156   Locrian

MAURICE MANNING
158   The Yonder Side of Sourwood
160   A Reaching Thing

JEFF DANIEL MARION
163   The Unexpected Guests
164   Short Wave
165   Ebbing & Flowing Spring
166   By the Banks of the Holston
166   The Lost Nickel
167   The Dying Art
168   The Man Who Loved Hummingbirds

MICHAEL MCFEE
169   For My Sister, Dead at 54
169   Robert's Lake
170   Arcadia Dairy Bar
171   Sorry
172   Bear Jam, 1951
173   Saint Lucy

ROSE MCLARNEY
174   Realizing
175   Remains

KELLY MCQUAIN
176   Dolly

JIM MINICK
177   Clear Blue Spring
178   Her Secret Song
178   Waspy Apples
179   Ghost Stump, Sun Music

THORPE MOECKEL
180   Bartram's Trail
181   The August Listener

JANICE TOWNLEY MOORE
184   Windows Filled with Gifts

ROBERT MORGAN
185   Prophet
185   Horse Fiddle
186   Burning Spring
186   Apple Howling
186   Translation
187   November Light
187   The Years Ahead

RICK MULKEY
189   High Lonesome
189   Hunger Ghazal
190   Toward Any Darkness
191   Homecoming
192   Devolution Theory

TED OLSON
193   Baptism
193   The Short Leash
194   Displacement
195   Swallows

LISA J. PARKER
196   Return
197   I Mark This Gone Place with Foxfire

LINDA PARSONS
198   Driftwood Found on the Greenbrier Trail
198   I Dream You Speak the River
199   Rosemary, for Remembrance
199   Hands
200   Repossessed
200   Jarflies

CHARLOTTE PENCE
202   At Opry-Mills Mall with God
203   After Two Weeks Without Rain

EDWINA PENDARVIS
204   Melee
205   Scarab
205   While We Sleep

PATRICK PHILLIPS
206   The Rules

LYNN POWELL
207   Fragments of a Lost Gospel
208   Indian Summer
210   Kind of Blue
211   April & Ecclesiastes
211   Revival
212   Etudes, for Unaccompanied Voice

RITA SIMS QUILLEN
215   Sunday School Lesson
216   My Mother, She Was Very Old-Fashioned
217   Passing Suite

MELISSA RANGE
220   New Heavens, New Earth
221   Bloodroot

RON RASH
222   Three A.M. and the Stars Were Out
223   The Corpse Bird
224   Watauga County: 1803
224   In Dismal Gorge
225   Good Friday, 1995, Driving Westward
225   Speckled Trout
225   A Preacher Who Takes Up Serpents...

MARK A. ROBERTS
227   Of Local Habitation

JANE SASSER
228   Scavenging
228   Second Shift
229   A Catalog of Lost Things

ELIZABETH SAVAGE
230   Forgiveness, West Virginia
231   January

GEORGE SCARBROUGH
232   Singularity
232   Drouth
233   Monday
233   Monday II
234   Ancientry
234   Dragonfly
235   Roots

VIVIAN SHIPLEY
236   Alice Todd, Outside Cecelia, Kentucky

SAVANNAH SIPPLE
237   Get Out While You Can
237   Triptych of a Drowning

ARTHUR SMITH
238   Easter
238   More Lines on a Shield Abandoned During Battle
239   Kudzu in Winter

JAMES MALONE SMITH
240   First Freeze
241   Harm's Way
242   Hen

NOEL SMITH
243   Ada's Poem

R.T. SMITH
245   Mockingbird
246   Mallard

STEVE SPARKS
247   Vespers at the Bishop

HENRY SPOTTSWOOD
250   Fall Cleanup
250   Life in the Mountains

DARIUS STEWART
251   My Mother's Hands
253   Self-Portrait as Future Third Person
254   Statues in the Park
255   The Ghost the Night Becomes

A. E. STRINGER
256   April Snow
256   My Father Asleep

DAN STRYK
257   Hawk in the Kudzu
258   The Mountains Change Aspect Like Our Moods
259   The Smell of Wild Onions, Mowing
260   Red-Eyed Cicada

LARRY D. THACKER
261   Called
262   The Rune of Out-longing: Wanderlust

ERIC TRETHEWEY
263   Frost on the Fields
263   Things
264   Sign

LINDSAY TURNER
265   Dogwood
266   Tennessee Quatrains

SUSAN O'DELL UNDERWOOD
267   Commencement
268   Specter

DOUG VAN GUNDY
269   A People's History of Randolph Co., WV
269   Hymn for Coal Smoke

FRANK X WALKER
270   Nyctophobia II
270   Juvenile Delinquents
271   Poem as Prayer
271   Urban Lullabies
272   One at a Time

WILLIAM WALSH
273   Ode to the Andersonville Dead

ROBERT WEST
274   Presto
274   Lullaby
275   Still
275   Oasis

JACKSON WHEELER
276   Ars Poetica
277   Backhome Story
278   The TVA Built a Dam

DANA WILDSMITH
280   Bones
281   Speed

MATTHEW WIMBERLEY
282   Materials for a Gravestone Rubbing
283   Potato Digging at Trosly Farm

ANNIE WOODFORD
284   The Four Hundred Angels of Henry County
285   A Long Line of Hard and Angry Women

SYLVIA WOODS
286   Wearing My Grammar Girdle
287   What We Take With Us

MARIANNE WORTHINGTON
288   The Girl Singer
289   The Unclouded Day
289   Love in the Cold War

AMY WRIGHT
290   Part, Mudlick
291   Part, the walking men

CHARLES WRIGHT
292   "Well, Get Up, Rounder, Let a Working Man Lay Down"
292   The Light at the Root of All Things
292   The Song from the Other Side of the World
293   Celestial Waters
293   Anniversary II
293   Outscape

JAKE ADAM YORK
294   Knoxville Girl
295   From A Field Guide to Etowah County
296   At Cornwall Furnace
297   Letter to Be Wrapped Around a Bottle of Whiskey

JOHN THOMAS YORK
300   Brains
300   June
301   Puzzle
303   Egret

305   The Poets
319   Acknowledgments

Series Editor's Preface

In an interview I conducted years ago with Jesse Graves, my friend and a co-editor for this volume, I asked whether he felt his poems, and the poems of his Appalachian forebears and contemporaries, were in an unspoken aesthetic war with recent "disjunctive" and "compositional" poets, the likes of John Ashbery and Jorie Graham. I should have expected Jesse's rare mixture of openheartedness and acuity:

> I tend to have a big-tent, utilitarian view of poetry, in that there ought to be room for as many approaches as poets are inclined toward. Obviously, I don't value them all equally, and though I might prefer the emotional openness and authenticity of Jane Hirschfield, I can still appreciate the sardonic wit of Charles Simic, or the crystalline economy of Michael Palmer. . . but a commitment to the poem of Meaningless Meanings seems as limiting to me as committing to writing nothing but straight English sonnets from here on out.

Jesse goes on to say that, conversely, when poems become transparently prosaic, stories without sculpture or syntactical risks, they "suffer" and "give away too much of their mystery, a problem with lots of narrative poetry. The best narrative poets . . . are still writing with lyric concision and an openness that permits surprise and mystery into their work, and their poems feel neither boxed-in nor mundane. . . ."

The poems in this volume of contemporary Appalachian poetry are clear-eyed renderings of the Appalachian South and its many narratives, yet their mystery is undeniably present, nestled just beneath the images, a lifeblood humming the words to life. On a general level, this pulse in the poems derives from their largely shared tendency to engage with the grand motifs: Time with a capital T, the natural world, family, history, identity, love, and death. Sound reinforces this mystery, the poems' rhythms mostly sculpted from the Anglo-Saxon, adopting the aural essences of the actions they describe: Michael Chitwood's hatchet "chops" and with the "blunt side" "knocks," while Thorpe Moeckel's narrator tells us that to follow Bartram's trail "is to crawl, is to hopscotch / between the doghobble and the yellowroot." Yet even the longer, less onomatopoetic Greek and Latinate words brim with sonic lushness, as with Lynn Powell's "glossolalia" and "delphinium," words that embroider vividly into "Fragments of a Lost Gospel" and "Kind of Blue." Whatever the etymologies of their words, the poems in this volume flare bright and gemlike, shimmering and chiseled like sapphires among lesser stones. All the while, they preserve their mysteries in the best ways, like Joseph Cornell shadowboxes, and in their vibrancy balance sound and sense admirably—often, as Richard Wilbur has written, "blurring to sheer verb."

Most of all, the poems of this collection ring *true*. I first discovered some of these poets in my early teens, when I decided to write seriously. Because of this exposure, I became aware blessedly early that poems were not necessarily puzzles to decode: Instead, they could be radiant songs. Thus, I feel most indebted to the poets of the Appalachian South. As a Southerner but not an Appalachian, I still feel drawn north to the highlands from my native Piedmont South Carolina, haunted by these old words and ways—walking near creeks flanked by bloodroot and rhododendron. I want to stay here, deep in this timeless, vital music.

William Wright
Marietta, GA

Preface to the Second Edition

Welcome to the second edition of the *Southern Poetry Anthology, Volume III: Contemporary Appalachia*, a remix more than fifteen years in the making. So much has happened in Appalachia since 2008 when William Wright and I first began dreaming of an anthology of the region's finest poetry, and since 2010 when the first edition appeared in print. We were driven by our realization of just how vastly under-represented Appalachian poetry was in the mainstream of American literary conversation. We wanted to make our own small stand against the imbalance between the excellence of the work and the sparse recognition it had received outside the region. Since that time, the great Robert Morgan and Rose McLarney have published books in the Penguin Poets series, Maurice Manning's work has appeared in the *New Yorker*, and Melissa Range received selection in the National Poetry Series, to mention just a few accomplishments. Two of our novelists, Barbara Kingsolver and Jayne Anne Phillips, have won Pulitzer Prizes in fiction. We have much to celebrate in Appalachia.

And yet, I am writing these words under great sorrow in the immediate aftermath of Hurricane Helene, with the devastation to our region still unfolding. Helene has left such destruction in its wake that fully taking stock of the damage, and of our new environmental reality, feels both overwhelming and probably impossible to comprehend so soon. Perhaps, for now, we can take some needed respite and recuperation from the good words of our poets.

The editors expected difficulties would come with trying to craft a new work of art while preserving as much of the original as we could. We knew that space would be intensely limited for adding new voices to the anthology. New folks in the book are represented by only one or two poems, while some earlier contributors have many more than that. We tried to preserve as much of what made the first edition so special to us as possible, while still allowing room for as many new voices to the collection as we could. This imbalance is not a reflection of anyone's preferences or evaluations of merit, just a natural consequence of trying to make something new while respecting the old. Poets new to this edition include legends like Nikki Giovanni, George Ella Lyon, and Crystal Wilkinson, alongside emerging poets with only one or two books published so far, such as Matthew Wimberley and Annie Woodford. I can think of many writers whom I wish were in this volume, young poets who will soon publish their first full-length books, and there may yet be established poets whose work has eluded us.

Despite those challenges, we felt much joy in bringing these poets together here, but there was profound sadness as well. We have had to say goodbye to many of our friends and mentors who appeared in the first edition. We honor, In Memoriam: Kathryn Stripling Byer, Fred Chappell, Harry Gieg, Ron Houchin, Charlie Hughes, Jeff Daniel Marion, Arthur Smith, Steve Sparks, George Scarbrough, Eric Tretheway, and Jake Adam York. We also lost an original editor for this volume and the long-time director of Texas Review Press, Dr. Paul Ruffin. It was Ruffin who gave the initial green light to the vision of a precocious graduate student, William Wright, for a multi-volume series that would help expand the scope of Southern poetry.

Many special thanks are due to the folks who helped bring this second edition together. My graduate research assistant at ETSU, Erika Perez Cortazar, did invaluable work helping me reach out to poets and to keep track of files, documents, and correspondences. It is with real pride that I thank my graduate assistant on the first edition of this volume, Catherine Pritchard Childress, who is now an essential contributor to this second edition. Thanks to my old friend, Chad M. Pelton, who designed this and many other volumes of The Southern Poetry Anthology, and who took the photograph on the book cover. Chad visited me in Sharps Chapel, TN, many years ago and made this picture in the hallway of the house I grew up in, showing generations of my own Appalachian ancestors. Invaluable contributors Pauletta Hansel, Linda Parsons, and Marianne Worthington each assisted in making important connections with poets. For the first edition, Will and I worked under the benevolent guidance of Paul Ruffin, with ongoing good-humored assistance from Claude Wooley and Kim Davis, and for this new edition we have been so fortunate to work with our new co-editor, J. Bruce Fuller, and his amazing crew at TRP, including Charlie Tobin, Christina Ellison, Elijah Keith, Miranda Ramírez, and Bonny Tunnell. We are especially grateful to the teachers and librarians who brought the first edition to their classrooms and bookshelves, without whom no second edition would have happened. Thank you most of all to the poets included here, who so generously shared their work with us and whose words continue to inspire.

Jesse Graves
Johnson City, TN

Introduction

Every place has its own poetry. "The music of what happens," as the great Irish poet Seamus Heaney has called it. For some places, the poetry appears in the tones of voice between neighbors in the grocery store, or in the spirit people share when a high school football team brings them out of their houses on Friday evenings, or even through the sounds engines make as they idle in traffic on the road out of the city after a workday. The poetry of Appalachia sings in all those familiar ways, but also in the music of the particular poems collected in *Southern Appalachian Poetry, Volume III: Contemporary Appalachia*. This anthology of contemporary poetry arrives from one of America's most vibrant literary communities, an area with a rich storytelling history and beautiful natural landscape, the often-misunderstood Appalachian South. Readers familiar with writing from Appalachia will be pleased to see work from such favorites as Charles Wright, Robert Morgan, and Fred Chappell, yet will be intrigued by the already distinctive voices of emerging talents like Melissa Range and Darius Antwan Stewart. This collection of poems is the only one of its kind, a snapshot album of a timeless place, as it is represented at the present moment.

In the middle and late 1960s, a number of events converged to shape the current Appalachian poetry. The most important of these occurrences was the publication of first books by a group of young writers, including Charles Wright, Fred Chappell, and Robert Morgan, who wrote about life in the region in a style that was unmarked by sentimentality and provincialism. This time period has been called the "Appalachian Renaissance," because it brought a renewed sense of identification with a distinct literary culture, and it held out a promising future. A second important event was the 1967 publication in *The Yale Review* of Dean Cadle's essay "Man on Troublesome," a brief exploration of Appalachian author James Still's work and life. Although the essay now seems somewhat basic in its analysis, it played a significant role in exposing James Still's thematic concerns and his eastern Kentucky way of life to a new generation of both regional and national readers. To that time, Still, despite such notable works as *River of Earth* (1940) and *Hounds on the Mountain* (1937) and inclusion in the Lincoln Memorial University group of Appalachian writers (James Still, Don West, and Jesse Stuart all studied at the small mountain school in northeastern Tennessee in the late 1920s), was largely unknown. The appearance of Cadle's essay helped establish a tradition for Appalachian literature, ushering in James Still as one of its major authors. A third important event is more of a cultural context. In the wake of Theodore Roethke's final collection of poems, *The Far Field* (1964), American poetry moved away from the urbane (and mostly urban) poetry of the 1950s, and back toward a vision that celebrated the natural world. Poets as different as A.R. Ammons, Gary Snyder, and James Dickey privileged the imagery and mythos of nature in their work, as did the place-based Ohio poems of James Wright and the Kentucky poems of Wendell Berry. A space was now cleared on the national poetry terrain for the kind of writing that would emerge from Appalachia over the coming decades.

A number of themes develop throughout this book, such as the importance of family relationships, particularly across generations, and the need to keep alive a conscientious link with the past. Perhaps no single concern emerges so strongly from these poems as the importance of landscape in preserving a way of life from the past, in the present, and for the future. The two generations of poets represented in *Contemporary Appalachia* have witnessed transformational changes in both the economy and the environment of the region. Many poems address the impact of coal mining, particularly the stripping away of our mountaintops, as well as the disappearance of family farms as a means of sustenance. If an elegiac note is struck for all we have lost from the past, it is counter-balanced by many joyous sounds of celebration for a rich and expanding culture, still deeply in touch with its natural environment. Note the predominance of landscape in the titles of Appalachian books, both poetry and fiction: *River of Earth* by James Still; *The Trail of the Lonesome Pine* by John Fox, Jr.; *The Landbreakers* by John Ehle; *The Unvanquished Earth* by Wilma Dykeman; *Green River* and *At the Edge of the Orchard Country* by Robert Morgan; *The Mountains Have Come Closer* by Jim Wayne Miller; *Ebbing & Flowing Springs* by Jeff Daniel Marion; Maggie Anderson's *Windfall*, and Kathryn Stripling Byer's *Wildwood Flower*. This continues among emerging Appalachian writers with Silas House's 2002 novel *A Parchment of Leaves* and Maurice Manning's 2007 book *Bucolics*, a term which refers to an ancient shepherd's song of the land. Landscape in a general way is central to Appalachian writing, but particular places are just as important, as a quick scan of our table of contents demonstrates. Robert Morgan has talked about the way literature creates "a community across time," the idea that reading allows us to take part in the lives of another place and time. That phrase articulates as well as any what a close look at the poetry of contemporary Appalachia might accomplish, a demonstration of both the continuity and change reflected in a region's way of life in our cultural moment.

Since this collection of poems belongs within the *Southern Poetry Anthology* series, the poets included have a relationship with mostly Southern Appalachia. We did not take a "Natives only" approach in our selection process, and did not wish to see the birth certificates of the contributing poets. So while we were not "birthers" of any sort, we also did not want tourist poems from afar, so it seemed appropriate to send out a call for submissions that gave poets the opportunity to self-identify with the region. In the editorial process, we wrestled with the boundaries of Appalachia. Questions led to other questions: Is Pittsburgh an Appalachian city? Yes, we agreed. Gertrude Stein was born in Pittsburgh. Is Gertrude Stein an Appalachian poet? That's more complicated. We had already decided to include living poets only, because the picture we wanted to frame with our book is like a large family portrait of writers now at work. We hope that in reading these poems you will feel the spirits of Jim Wayne Miller, Louise McNeill, and Jonathan Williams presiding, not to mention Jesse Stuart, Byron Herbert Reese, and Emma Bell Miles. Those poets, however, belong in a different anthology, a still much-needed comprehensive collection of poems from the region that starts at the beginning, with the myths and songs of the Cherokee, and which ends with poets as recent as Maurice Manning and Frank X Walker. Our classrooms and libraries need that book, and so do our aspiring poets. Snapshot anthologies serve a vital purpose when the material covered changes quickly or exists in a state of flux. The individual volumes in the *Southern Poetry Anthology* resemble time capsules, or documentaries, in that they present a lasting image, for the public record, of a particular place over a particular period of time.

    The voices of the poems represented in this anthology are diverse and multi-layered. The editors hope that you, the reader, will feel as we do: that they belong together. If they are not all blood-kin, they nevertheless form a family through the marriage of a particular place and the inspiration it produces. Poetry remains an essentially solitary engagement, both in the writing and the reading of it, and the strongest poems always emanate from a distinctive individual perspective. Nevertheless, poets and their poems thrive in community with others: Conversations flourish, ideas circulate, arguments occur—this was true of the expatriate American Modernists, the British Romantics, and the Greek lyric poets, and we believe it is equally true of the poets collected here. All kinds of life happens in contemporary Appalachia, and we hope you enjoy the music that rises in the air above so much living, music that our poets have translated into the words that fill these pages.

Jesse Graves
Johnson City, TN

Gilbert Allen

Stairways to Nowhere

for Bernard, Bennie Lee, Rudy, Jim,
Louise, Cecilia, Linda, and the rest

Once you live here long enough, you see
them everywhere. Today, for instance, driving
to the washerette (doing what's become
a weekly chore while we're remodeling
our laundry room), I passed the concrete steps
rising from a cracked sidewalk to only
a weedy field—a vacant lot between
the new library and the county park.
Within my memory, those steps led to
an elementary school my wife almost
taught in, job-hungry, in the 70s.
Before that? To the high school that preceded
the one now being torn down, across town,
for the new one—roughly halfway between.
More empty steps there soon. Which *there*, you ask?
Take your pick. It's only, as they say,
a matter of time. What every stairway says,
despite its length, or angle of ascent.

I load the washers, get back in the car
to take it for its weekly cleaning, too.
Air-drying, I'll recycle plastic bags,
aluminum, clear glass, and Styrofoam
my nagging conscience shoved into the trunk.

Why am I so compelled to rid myself
of almost everything? As if my life
itself were dirt, to wash into the void
from which the latest earth will soon return.
A cartoon from an old *New Yorker* pops
into my head: *Only what I need, O Lord,
but make sure it's the highest quality.*
You could do worse for articles of faith.
The washers stop when my (clean) car returns.

I've always been a sucker, I suppose,
for staircases. Our first remodeling
involved replacing a straight wooden one
with a black metal spiral—clockwise down.

Precisely the opposite, I learned, of Yeats's
tower, of the medieval preference—
counterclockwise, to let right-handed lords
use their dominant arms against intruders.
In nearly thirty years, we've never had
a break-in. Officially, the mountain ends
across the street, so we're the outliers.
Our terraced yard must be a burglar's nightmare—
pretty as hell, but even harder to
negotiate, especially in the dark.

But now is bright November sunshine, so
I'm hanging sheets and towels out on the line
in the backyard. Returning to the car
for the delicates, I'm struck by our front
entrance—with its landings, planters, leading
to the foyer, all redone ten years ago—
a young architect's *tour de force*. And I
recall the old brick stairs, marching straight up
the broiling western side of the house. The plan
was elegant, as mathematicians put it—
no steps had to be torn away. The old
served as substructure to the new. And as
I zigzag up, landing to landing, holding
empty laundry baskets, I remember
buried friends who walked those buried stairs.
Above, around, about, my dirty sneakers
hover. *We love, and love what vanishes.*
That's Yeats (misquoted). But for now, my feet
have the last word, for nowhere, and for once.

Some Week

One plane streaks the clearcut sky.
From up there, we must be dazzling—
December's body ice-rigored into
incredulous attitudes, limbs askew
with questions. Big oaks?
Smitten by their own thunder.
Cedars? Splayed. Pines? Down
and out, uprooted. Only the understory
intact—white tongues lolling, every dogwood
rabid in the returning sun.

Three days ago, power poles snapped
like wishbones on every
right of way—short ends strewn
across pavement. Black arteries clog
black arteries. Beetles slowly
Volkswagen over the carcass.

A once-in-a-lifetime event
but we're still here, trying
to drive into town.

Under the unbroken roofs?
Old couples, curled up
with unvented kerosene heaters.
Pipes weeping before they burst
into bad fountains. Whole freezers
spoiling, while whole families shiver
beside them.

An auxiliary generator brightens
one diner. We park

and walk inside. Women
with name tags monitor flat lines
of feet against counters, register
station, vestibule. Open spaces only
on the coat racks. At the corner booth
a family of parkas
is saying grace. From the rafters
the radio swears we'll all be up
and running by Tuesday. *Some week*
DEBBIE whispers, double-shifted
into dementia, hoping somebody tips
for an act of God.

Late Garden

Long since cleared
and mulched with leaves
from Bradford pears,
the garden still grieves—

or seems to grieve
from our upstairs window
this Christmas Eve.
Why should sorrow

fill this fallow,
rain-soaked place
and time, to harrow
mere empty space?

Only to trace
right there, below,
on barren grace,
imagined snow.

Maggie Anderson

Long Story

> To speak in a flat voice
> Is all that I can do.
>   –James Wright, "Speak"

I need to tell you that I live in a small town
in West Virginia you would not know about.
It is one of the places I think of as home.
When I go for a walk, I take my basset hound
whose sad eyes and ungainliness always draw
a crowd of children. She tolerates anything
that seems to be affection, so she lets the kids
put scarves and ski caps on her head
until she starts to resemble the women who have to dress
from rummage sales in poverty's mismatched polyester.

The dog and I trail the creek bank with the kids,
past clapboard row houses with Christmas seals
pasted to the windows as a decoration.
Inside, television glows around the vinyl chairs
and curled linoleum, and we watch someone old
perambulating to the kitchen on a shiny walker.
Up the hill in town, two stores have been
boarded up beside the youth center and miners
with amputated limbs are loitering outside
the Heart and Hand. They wear Cat diesel caps
and spit into the street. The wind
carries on, whining through the alleys,
rustling down the sidewalks, agitating
leaves, and circling the courthouse steps
past the toothless Field sisters who lean
against the flagpole holding paper bags
of chestnuts they bring to town to sell.

History is one long story of what happened to us,
and its rhythms are local dialect and anecdote.
In West Virginia a good story takes awhile,
and if it has people in it, you have to swear
that it is true. I tell the kids the one about
my Uncle Craig who saw the mountain move
so quickly and so certainly it made the sun
stand in a different aspect to his little town

until it rearranged itself and settled down again.
This was his favorite story. When he got old,
he mixed it up with baseball games, his shift boss
pushing scabs through a picket line, the Masons
in white aprons at a funeral, but he remembered
everything that ever happened, and he knew how far
he lived from anywhere you would have heard of.

Anything that happens here has a lot of versions,
how to get from here to Logan twenty different ways.
The kids tell me convoluted country stories
full of snuff and bracken, about how long
they sat quiet in the deer blind with their fathers
waiting for the ten-point buck that got away.
They like to talk about the weather,
how the wind we're walking in means rain,
how the flood pushed cattle fifteen miles downriver.

These kids know mines like they know hound dogs
and how the sirens blow when something's wrong.
They know the blast, and the stories, how
the grown-ups drop whatever they are doing
to get out there. Story is shaped
by sound, and it structures what we know.
They told me this, and three of them
swore it was true, so I'll tell you
even though I know you do not know
this place, or how tight and dark the hills
pull in around the river and the railroad.

I'll say it as the children spoke it,
in the flat voice of my people:
down in Boone County, they sealed up
forty miners in a fire. The men who had come
to help tried and tried to get down to them,
but it was a big fire and there was danger,
so they had to turn around
and shovel them back in. All night long
they stood outside with useless picks and axes
in their hands, just staring at the drift mouth.
Here's the thing: what the sound must have been,
all those fire trucks and ambulances, the sirens,
and the women crying and screaming out
the names of their buried ones, who must have
called back up to them from deep inside
the burning mountain, right up to the end.

House and Graveyard, Rowlesburg, West Virginia, 1935

I can't look long at this picture, a Walker Evans photograph
of a West Virginia graveyard in the Great Depression,
interesting for the sharp light it throws
on poverty, intimate for me because it focuses
on my private and familial dead. This is where

my grandparents, my Uncle Adrian and my Aunt Margaret
I am named for are buried. Adrian died at seven, long
before I was born. Margaret died in childbirth in 1929.
The morning sun falls flat against the tombstones
then spreads across Cannon Hill behind them. I see

how beautiful this is even though everyone was poor,
but in Rowlesburg nothing's changed. Everything
is still the same, just grayer. Beside the graveyard
is Fike's house with the rusty bucket, the tattered
trellis and the same rocker Evans liked. Miss Funk,

the school teacher, now retired, and her widowed sister
still live down the road out of the camera's range.
I remember how my Aunt Nita loved that mountain,
how my father told of swinging from the railroad
bridge down into the Cheat. Nita worked

for the Farm Security Administration too, as Evans did.
She checked people's houses for canned goods, to see
how many they had stored, and she walked the road
by here, every day. I can't look long at this picture.
It warps my history into politics, makes art

of my biography through someone else's eyes.
It's a good photograph, but Walker Evans
didn't know my family, nor the distance
his careful composition makes me feel now
from my silent people in their graves.

Mining Camp Residents, West Virginia, 1935

They had to seize something in the face of the camera.
The woman's hand touches her throat as if feeling
for a necklace that isn't there. The man buries one hand
in his overall pocket, loops the other through a strap,
and the child twirls a strand of her hair as she hunkers
in the dirt at their feet. Maybe Evans asked them to stand
in that little group in the doorway, a perfect triangle
of people in the morning sun. Perhaps he asked them
to hold their arms that way, or bend their heads. It was
his composition after all. And they did what he said.

Spitting in the Leaves

In Spanishburg there are boys in tight jeans,
mud on their cowboy boots and they wear huge hats
with feathers, skunk feathers they tell me.
They do not want to be in school, but are.
Some teacher cared enough to hold them. Unlike
their thin disheveled cousins, the boys on Matoaka's
Main Street in October who loll against parking meters
and spit into the leaves. Because of them, someone
will think we need a war, will think the best solution
would be for them to take their hats and feathers,
their good country manners and drag them off somewhere,
to Vietnam, to El Salvador. And they'll go.
They'll go from West Virginia, from hills and back roads
that twist like politics through trees, and they'll fight,
not because they know what for but because what they know
is how to fight. What they know is feathers,
their strong skinny arms, their spitting
in the leaves.

Street Scene, Morgantown, West Virginia, 1935

Neither of the black women behind the table
confronts the camera. I know this street,
High Street in Morgantown, where Walker Evans
documents the resourcefulness of poverty,
its make-do and carry-on by calculating
what to sell, or raise to sell, or what
to barter when all the cash is gone.
The women's dark faces are exhausted
from such improvisation. They look away,
will not look a white man,
even with a camera, in the eyes.

They have to think of everything: how long
before food spoils in the heat, how much money
a cake's worth, how cautious their conversation
has to be with customers. My mother might have
bought from them. I wish I knew if she was polite,
if she could afford to be. I wonder how aware
she might have been of the men, who loiter
across the street in straw hats, smoking cigars,
reflected in the plate glass window above
the table so they rise like ghosts of abstract
thought behind the women's turned heads.

Darnell Arnoult

Medicinal

I might as well kill that aloe plant and take it with me, you said. You will just kill it
after I die, you said. And, I did. Almost. We moved and I set it next to a flower bed,

under the edge of the roof with a debris-filled gutter. Might have known debris
would be the culprit. Water spilled over the edge in a big rain that lasted days and it drown

the aloe. Almost. Then I prayed for the aloe. And I prayed for you. And I prayed for us.
With our son's help, I pulled the rotten blades away. Together, we peeled it down

to its hearts. We replanted them with more love than we knew we could hold.
Each cluster of arms, frail and fragile, floundered. But miracles happen. I've seen

them unfurl. Eventually, dying arms reach for the sun. The aloe lived. I don't think
my thumb, brown as a grocery bag, could've pulled that off. Yours could. The boy's

maybe. Maybe you reached through the boy's heart, so then we could heal
from your leaving. Salve that brief moment I stepped away, and you left, the drowning burn of it

Lake Michael

The water is low
for some reason, and there are no ducks to feed the old dry bread to.
So we settle to search for fish you say you recognize. You call out names

you've heard while fishing with men. Bluegill. Bass. Trout. Crappy.
The small fish and minnows scrap and scramble for a nibble of bright white

enriched grain, cheapest on the shelf. One piece you throw in
with your little hand is too big. It scares the fish away as it undulates

like a live thing on the brackish water, swelling thicker with dark watery grass and silt.
Then you try again. This time the fish scramble fearless for a smaller tuft

and devour it, destroy it. Joy floods your face as the fish dart back
into the shadows, the mossy shallows crowded with what we never see
when the water is high.

Joseph Bathanti

House-Hunting at Four Thousand Feet

The road's not but a ledge,
near straight up, shale
and millstone. Mud.
Good God, come winter.
Three slough-bellied brown
and white bangtail paints cleat
to a shelf in the mist,
then a bouquet of pink plastic roses
stabbed in the scarp ahead of the fall-off.
By the time we find the house,
fog's set in and we can't see to turn around.
Shear on both sides.
The children wear those silent worried looks.
They don't want to live in the sky
where a thing mishandled plummets
the better part of a mile;
and all there is for it is to cock an ear
and reckon altitude by the *whump*.
Pray each time your foot touches earth.
Hold on like Hades.
Folks up here are born cloven and slouch.
Purchase is bred well-deep into them.
The house is slant, lank,
with enough give to weather gravity,
and thus plumb.
Appalachian physics.
We creep up and beam the brights on it.
It eyes right back, querulous
like a bedridden crone, but old man too,
finicky, the tin roof
a rusted skullcap.
Thick watery glass windows,
cataracted with silica,
yellow dauber nests
like sleep mortised into the panes.
Up here is odd enough to make a house
not just thingful, but a someone
with blood and breath. Secrets.
Voices. Some say
you get used to it:
catamounts, fog, rime-ice,
the wind like Deuteronomy

when it gets het up,
snow beading down,
shrinking everything in its alabaster clout.
We venture no farther than the spinney
gnarling the busted porch,
demur like the beholden Israelites
and wait for a sign, our eyes
discomfited by everlasting up.

Wall at Second Manassas

It attends the moon in secret lean.
Creviced in limestone and granite,

agate and mountain quartz gleam,
a regiment of stone

bordered in buckthorn,
locked against another morning of battle.

Stones not sanctified by whim,
but borne uphill

by patient raging hands.
This need for a wall

comes late in life, vaguely,
with a sense of fear riding night –

much like idolatry,
all in all, a trick

in no way connected to soldiering.
One hundred years

will call its craft contemplation.
Its places will fill with bone.

The Vilas Flood

From the outset, the wind
signals the water's rise,
its sudden inflorescence
stitched across the meadow,

trout heaving on the swill, speckled,
mortis-eyed. Crows: black
ingots on the green-gray gout.
Goldfinches drown in mid-flight.

Swallowtails sucked off in the spindrift.
Look out and it's a downpour.
Glance again and it's a river licking
at the porch, Crawfords' house

about took, Jacky's trailer under,
sun burning up there in the calamity
bright yellow–some diluvial hex.
What rolls out of the gap cross-lashes

the bridge spanning the gorged stream–
fenders of water, six, eight feet high–
detonating it. A red geyser spouts
from the plank flinders and sprung sandbags

as though the cork capping Purgatory
has gassed out. Linville Creek,
a dark glistening documentary
of outlandish migration flashes

through the flume, on its back
the archaeology of Vilas.
Isaac's bawling calf, split tether snaked
in the roil, rushes by.

As if spirited out of the tallow,
coyotes, smoky whisps of bony pelt,
mince on the oozing bank,
paw and snap, weep and coo

as the baby angus disappears.
Then an entire apple tree
loaded with red winesaps.
Buckeyes still ivory asleep

in their green sarcophagi.
A pumphouse. A gazebo
and a wagon tongue.
Cord upon cord of split wood.

Then the coolers and tools and baby dolls.
Kayak paddles. A Lousiville Slugger
signed by Rocky Colavito.
A white leatherbound Bible,

its writ in Spanish. Whatever
might dislodge from largesse
and parsimony. The grand.
The infinitesimal. All left to rot

and propagate, finally forgotten,
as far downstream as Zionville.
Even the wedding gown draped
like a jilted bride over a haybale.

Running

for Leon

I recite the rosary
Hail Mary when I run,
a wooden bead *full of grace*
per so many meters: for the winter wheat,
coy *blessed* barely green beneath
the purple *art thou* Lenten crown vetch;
the sun that rations color *among women and blessed*
sitting in its cupboard ripening
like a pomegranate *is the fruit*;
the frayed, porous moon *of thy womb*
dissolving on the tongue
of blue morning *Jesus*;
cows, musk of their bowels
scenting the fog, still as tintypes;
deer *Holy Mary* gazing skyward in wonder
at the cry of Canada geese;
papery corn shucks whispering at my feet;
strips of loose tin from an infolded barn
thundering in the wind-lash;
my print *Mother of God*
alongside the raccoon's and skunk's
as I leap the creek bed

and cross Stikeleather land,
posted black letters on yellow handbills
tacked to the shaven thighs of Sycamores;
chicken houses a mile off
on Midway Road whitening in the now-
lightening horizon *pray*;
and far beyond in Alexander County,
on looming Fox Mountain, nectarines
that will hold migrants hostage
all spring flower.
I gulp another quart of ether,
dig *for us sinners*
up the steep farm road to intercept
the risen sun, sprint the crest,
my chest filled with pink shrapnel,
and fall into it,
a stretched and sweating shadowgraph.
For this searing instant
one chases *now and at the hour*
in the darkness every morning
the improbability *of our death*
that legs with hearts to prompt them
may keep lurching, decade upon decade,
chaplet upon chaplet, toward salvation *Amen*.

Laura Treacy Bentley

Closet Appalachians

> *Oh, can't you hear that pretty little bird singing with all his heart and soul.*
> *He's got a blood-red spot on his wing, but all the rest of him's black as coal.*
> —Billy Edd Wheeler

He spends a lifetime losing his accent,
living abroad, wearing Versace,
and alligator shoes.
The consummate cosmopolitan—
organic food and bottled water,
Ballets Russes and The Met,
sushi bars and chardonnay.

She never tells where she's really from
until a corporate boss from West Virginia
calls her bluff.
Turns up her nose at bluegrass and Billy Edd,
but alone in her Lamborghini,
she tunes in *Mountain Stage* and cranks up the volume
when Kathy Mattea sings *Red-Winged Blackbird*.

Their high-rise ways are grounded
in shadowed valleys and windy ridges,
soaring eagles above Cheat Mountain,
quivering trout below icy shallows,
and mornings so country quiet,
they've cut a seam deep inside them.
Her roots nor his

may never be revealed unless late at night
after downing one last glass of champagne,
they confess to a sleepy bartender
that she may look like a city girl,
that he may look like a city boy,
but *all the rest*
is black as coal.

Gas Station

I'm pumping gas at 7th & 9th.
It's a real gas station
with rubber ropes that ding
when you run over them
and RC cola in glass bottles.
The sun is out, and I lean
against the rear bumper,
watching the numbers
spin to $10.00 even.

When I walk in,
a respectful silence falls
over the station regulars.
I tell the man behind the counter
how much I owe.
He believes me
and takes my crisp, ten dollar bill
in a blackened palm.
His passive blue eyes seem bluer
against a miner's face,
dark from rotating tires
and checking brake fluid.

He *chings* one key on an old cash register
and the drawer opens.
My money is placed under a metal spring.
His fingernails are seamy,
and the air smells like cigarettes
put out in cold coffee,
motion sickness,
and Teaberry gum.

I turn to leave and talk resumes
in starts and stops
about sputtering manifolds
and gaskets blown.

A car burning clouds of oil
pulls in behind me.
The men study the newcomer
like tobacco-chewing surgeons
behind plate glass.
Their minds spinning
with possibilities.

Nickole Brown

Self-Portrait as Eastern Wood Rat

Let us begin with my hair—
that frizzy, god-forsaken mess sprung

like Velcro from my head at thirteen, that hormone-
fed explosion of caustic fuzz that laughed in the face
of any hair goop or oil or spritz we could find
at the dollar store. It was a middle-school tease, a homeroom
landing pad for paper planes and spit wads, half-chewed
gum and gummy bears, a regular sport at my school

with one goal in mind: to make the redneck girl
in her high-water jeans cry. My hair, not just
unmanageable or *unruly* or *going through a phase but
a real fuckin rat's nest*—and that's just what my mama said,
brush in hand. This, friends, is where the learning begins,

because what I didn't know was only one rat
builds that kind of miracle nest—only one rat's a genuine
pack rat—and that rat's made for the land that gave
it a name. You see, I was wrong: I thought
a rat was a rat was a rat, but I should've known better

than to call similar beings all by one name, to hate them all
the same. This rat's not the undifferentiated mass gnawing
wires of downtown neighborhoods and subway lines,
not those garbage-lickers that once I squeezed my way
to the city squeezed me, making me feel dirty no matter
how much I scrubbed. No, this rat's a real forest nibbler,
wearing its ever-growing teeth down on ground-fall pecans, happy
for just what the seasons bring. And here's what I can't let go:

Despite the talk of rats taking over what we call
our world, this rat—forgive us—is nearly
extinct. It's our fault, working hard as we have to
pave ourselves over, our best tracts strip-mined or stripmalled,
our mountaintops literally *removed* for a vein
of coal, because like a mistreated girl whoring in the back
of her daddy's Chevy, it's as if we want to throw away what
we were given because we were once made to feel
it wasn't worth a damn anyway. This might be about

shame, like how I worked so hard to scrub
my tongue of the talk that, like me, came up
from this mud—
or how when I told mama what happened at school,
she put down the brush and quit her fussing, said, *baby,
they're pea-green with envy is all, don't you give a rat's ass.*
What I mean to say is I grew up

and figured how to shellac my hair into something
nearly presentable, to trick it into looking like something
it's not, but still, when I look in the mirror, it's
that little girl from Kentucky staring back. No. What I mean is

there's this kind of rat who works on a single nest all its life
and lives in that one place til it dies, just as I can't seem to quit
and leave this place behind.

No, that's not quite right.
Let me say this plain: What I mean is
I once thought myself white trash—that rat
of all rats. But now I know I was only listening to the trash
I was told. Because a close look at the eastern wood rat reveals
a creature maybe destructive and more than a little
hungry but meant to be here and still
holding on, making a high holy mess
of sticks and branches, broken glass and dried shit,
crow feathers and rusted cans, wood screws and napkins
and candy wrappers, forgotten flannels and cassettes,
Barbie limbs and lost gloves, shreds of anything, just
anything it can find to
survive, all things sacred and profane to keep
safe and warm in a place it can call home.

Parable

Let us not with one stone kill one bird,
much less two. Let us never put a cat
in a bag nor skin them, regardless
of how many ways there are to do it.
And let us never take the bull, especially
by his gorgeous horns. What I mean is

we could watch our tongues or keep
silent. What I mean is we could scrub
the violence from our speech. And if we find
truth in a horse's mouth, let's look

her in the mouth and bless her
ground-down molars, no matter how old she is,
especially if she was given as a gift. Again, let's open
her mouth—that of the horse, I mean—

let us touch that interdental space
where no teeth grow from her gums,
where the cold bit was made to grip.
Let us touch her there, gently. Don't worry:
again, she's old now; she's what we call
broken; she won't bite. She's lived through
two fourteen-year emergences of cicadas

and thought their rising a god infestation,
thought each insect roiling up an iteration
of the many names of god, because god to her is
the grasses so what comes up from grass is
god. She would not say it that way. Nor would she

say the word *cicada*—words are hindrances
to what can be spoken through the body, are
only what she hears when
straddled, one leg *giddy-up* on one side and other
whoa on the other. After, it's all
good girl, Mable, good girl
before the saddle sweat is rinsed
with cool water from the hose and a carrot
is offered from the palm. Yes, words being

generally useless she listens instead
to the confused rooster stuttering when the sun
burns overhead, when there is also the sound of insects
yet to sing just now filling their wings to make them
stiff and capable of flight. To her, it is the sound

of winter-coming in her mane or the sound of winter-leaving
in her mane—yes, that sound—a shushing made liquid
like the blood-fill of stallion desire she knew
once but crisper, a dry crinkle of fall
leaves. Yes, that sound as they fill their wings
then lumber to the canopy to demand
come here, come here, come here,
oh, please come.

If this is a parable you don't understand,
then, dear human, stop listening for words.
Listen instead for *mane, wind, wings*.
The lesson here is that of the mare and the insects,
even of the rooster puffed and strutting past.
Are the two words worth knowing,
the plea of every living being
in this field we call ours:
let live, let live. Oh, please,
let us live.

Kathryn Stripling Byer

Drought Days

for my grandmother, Carrie Mae Campbell

1.

Rain, because prayed for,
was always called God's answer,
God being what gave
or withheld whatever we needed.

A merciful god, and we'd smell dirt beginning
to dampen. But judgment? That He in the sky
would become in my nostrils the odor
of earth at its most unforgiving.

God stank like a singed field.
His taste in my mouth like a rusty nail.

I wanted him kept well away
from the places I loved,
his narrowed eyes raking the world.

2.

The sky must have shone back a message
on drought days, the way
she'd look into it over and over

to see if a cloud might be forming,
and inside that cloud a small storm seed
of hope from the heavenside.

*Let's pretend we could walk through
the mirror. What would we find on the other
side?* She never liked that game,

it went against God's design,
and too much like walking into her own dark
as if through the eye of a hurricane.

To enter the kingdom,
she'd stand in the kitchen and look
out the window at what He

had wrought, corn that sang when
the wind came, a husband who shoveled hay
into the cow pen, the empty yard waiting

for the child growing inside her: her life
seeming suddenly all mass,
and her knees almost too weak to bear it.

3.

Every shining surface seemed mirror.
The shaft of a carving knife.
Kettle-shank polished to clarity.
Windows that framed her by day
and at night by the oil lamp
revealed her as lost in a ghost forest.
Suddenly she'd set to work
righting lopsided hair ribbons.
A lapsed curl.

Even the yard that she walked upon
served as a backdrop for shadow
while she flounced her skirt like a jonquil.

Or playing at age,
humped her back like a guinea hen,
clucking her way toward the garden,
grown old in a trice.

Was this vanity?
To look on what she had been given
and see herself everywhere in it?

4.

After supper she roamed to the highway
to watch how the sun swelled,
a hot-air balloon,
or else threatened to melt like a butter-pat
after which heat began loosening its tourniquet.

Then came the jays back, the grass-singers
piping up. Then came the moon over pitch pines.
Came wind and the screech owl.

She ducked into woods
where the sun seen through
pine needles wavered
like wild fire when she winced.

Just one spark.
That's all she ever wanted.

5.

At the moment of death he'd hear
rain, he joked.
Drought over. The pond
rising. Flint River cresting to record
heights. Heat lightning

banging its anvil. Sparks
flying. Rain thumping tin
like the school marm's rebuke
she knew he'd not forgotten.
Nor had she.
The ruler's pop. Three times.

Swarmed by the dust he stirred,
she knew how he clenched his fists
round the tractor's wheel.
She knew how he'd ground
his teeth on the grit of his field.

6.

Now take this, she'd say, her mouth
full of pins—a bird's tail
of fastenings held tight
against revelation. What now?
And where? I was lost
till she lifted the limp tape

and held my hand hard on
the selvage while she reckoned
grain-line and measurement.
Taking the straight of it
so that the garment would fall
clean to plumb. What she called a good
finish. A clean sweep to hem-level,
a dress in which she could walk out the front door
or be laid down at last like the lady she knew she was.

7.

To measure the cloth needed,
she'd hold each bolt against our flesh,

folding the crisp panels over
by arm's length till she had her estimate.

She could spend hours stroking broadcloth
and dimity, mulling the question of how much

of what and for whom while we watched
our identity come down to color and texture.

Which of us orange flowered broadcloth
that shone like her kitchen linoleum,

which the cerulean blue dotted swiss
(marked to half-price) that tickled her palm

or the lavender crepe de chine
sliding through fingers that soothed it?

8.

With feathers she had plucked herself,
she stuffed two pillows
for my marriage. Crocheted

With silver hook a chain of white lace,
Stitched it round the edges of two pillowcases.
Soon her fingers could not thread

A needle, nor hold fork or spoon.
By then her man was gone,
Wrapped tight inside a dream of trees

that leafed out every spring: time
to plow, time to seed, time to bury
yet again what he had sown.

(I wonder, do the trees commiserate
about the leaves they let go,
all the loosenings they must live with?)

If I could, I'd stitch a Double Wedding Ring
Against the morning when they woke to sun
Stuck, days on end, to every window pane.

9.

When the pond dried up,
My cousins and I filled oil drums
With my grandfather's hoses

and pulled on our bathing suits,
climbed in like daughters of lawyers
or bankers and stood there pretending

we dawdled at Myrtle Beach
or Sanibel Island. The clouds passing over
might that very morning

have darkened the boardwalk
in Panama City. Her white leghorns scratched
in the sand. His pigs wallowed.

The water began to smell
rusty, more tractor oil to it
than tropical coconut. We hauled

ourselves out, feeling
silly and shriveled, our skin flecked
with rust, knowing we were still stuck

on the farm. We would always be
hicks. Pink and flabby like pickled
pig flesh in our grandmother's jars.

Soul food, I grew up to hear it called,
as if the collards and side meat
we set on our table had been sanctified

but by stories we knew were not ours,
in which we were no more than
bystanders, and not always innocent ones.

Wayne Caldwell

Fence Posts

You can't get warm at all with central heat.
Can't get but one side warm with a fireplace.
But a big cookstove and air-tight heater put out heat
To make sawing and busting and stacking and toting worth it.
I mind Papa talking about how cold it was in ninety-three.
That's 1893, when he was first married
And the weather was so bad by February he'd burned
All his firewood and ever fence post on the place
And was fixing to dismantle the barn when here come a warm snap.
Don't get that cold anymore, least not for as long at a time.
Don't snow as much, either, heck, I remember a stretch
In the '60s, that's 1960s,
When school was out two-three weeks at a time
And if you went anywhere it was by foot or muleback.
I miss that like you miss a month of in-laws.
I would miss wood heat, though. If I had to go
To one of them homes, perish the thought,
I'd die from cold—
And florescent light—
And disinfectant.
Lord, If it's all the same to you
Let me die right here where I'm warm.

Peeper Frogs

In just-spring me and Tomcat like to sit

On the old front porch at dusky dark

To hear the peeper frogs a-singing

Their filthy-minded little heads off.

It's a natural music that makes Pole Creek smile.

Whole world needs a lot more of that.

Bird Tree

You know spring or fall's a-coming when you see a bird tree.
Least that's what I call it when them no-tailed
Blackbirds take to skreaking together. Might be
Two dozen in a walnut talking about joining up with a bigger bunch.
Or might be hunderds of the varmints in a tall poplar,
Yammering like rusty gates, without regard to manners or respect.

Go south no go north no George yonder's got a map
No he don't if we fly east we can roost at Martha's mother's folks
They got a tree over a clothesline and Lord's plenty of skeeters
Phooey head toward yonder black gum with the mistletoe up top
Just past it a branch goes into a creek then flows into the big river
Into Tennessee that's north rivers don't flow north this one does birdbrain
Didn't they learn you that in school you can rely on old Fred
He's got a compass well, shoot, what good's that to a bird?
I say we find a peach orchard and get drunk where you gonna
Find one this time of year hot-toe-mighty there's a redtail

And they lift as one from the big old tree
And head east then north quick, like an oiled hinge
And turn west almost to blot the setting yellow ball
As they speed their way to where God's finger points.

Shuly Xóchitl Cawood

Inheritance

My great aunt was not the type of lady to smoke
out on the porch. No, she lit up in her living room, and up
and down the stairs, and in her bedroom on hot
Mississippi nights with the windows thrown open.

My great aunt read faster than other women cooked, cleaned,
baked cookies. One night she read *Gone with the Wind* cover to cover
while sitting on the toilet. She didn't have much use
for clocks or schedules: if she wanted to sleep, she slept.
She didn't have much use either for men who wanted to court her,
even if the man was her ex-husband, a Navy sailor who wanted her back,
a man she once loved. What did she need him for? She had her own money
from her government job after the war, and then from when she started
collecting vintage furniture. She opened

an antiques store on the first floor of her Vicksburg hilltop house
and sold enough not to have to bother with customers
who rang her doorbell when the day called for a nap instead
or when she had not yet drunk a cold bottle of Coke
or smoked her first cigarette of the day

or her last.

High cheekbones, big, almond-shaped blue eyes—
my great aunt was the best kind of beauty: the kind who didn't care.

Her cantankerous calico cat, Miss Molly, slunk from me and my sister.
We were gentle girls and desperate to pet her. The cat let no one near
except my great aunt, who bought Miss Molly cans of wet food
and let her claw at whatever antique chairs she pleased to scratch.
My great aunt made my father promise that when she died,
he would put down Miss Molly, too.

No one's going to take care of her the way I do.

My great aunt was long on conversation: sometimes,
during our visits, we'd find our father in her kitchen
and hear her chattering in the living room. We would ask him,
Who's she talking to? and he would answer:
Me.

But she was never short on opinions. If we went out to eat

her steak was always undercooked or overcooked, or the soup
too salty or too cold. She never hesitated
to send anything back. I was a young girl then.
I should have paid attention

for one day I would be given a thing or two
and not have the courage to send them back.

I was only seventeen when my great aunt Eloise
died. My father flew down to Mississippi and took Miss Molly
to the vet, and into the casket the cat went.
                              I wonder about all
the other things my great aunt took with her, things I'll never
get back, answers to questions I should have asked. I inherited
the almond shape of her eyes, though mine are brown,
and an opal ring she had crafted in Europe, a ring whose stone
eyes me with its bright specks and dazzle
and dares me to stand up straight
and have a damn opinion.

Another Poem for Donna on a Crowded Saturday Afternoon in Kroger

She's there again—she's always there—at the customer service counter
as I and everyone else wheel our steely carts from aisle to aisle in search of
meaning in a bag of potato chips or a can of cream of chicken soup.
She is solving problems, taking back people's discards, all the things
gone wrong in their life, all the ways they have changed their mind
about what they don't want anymore. She could stand there and give
a bunch of men money for the wives they have tired of, tell them,
"Sure, we can take her back. Do you have a receipt?" Or the children
we wish we hadn't had after all, or the jobs we have all been stuck in
for a time or two, or maybe just the boss we put up with who can't stop
brushing by us. Can we get a refund here? A do-over? If anyone can
grant us that, it's Donna, there ringing up the day's bad choices, or last
month's or last year's, all our regrets. She takes the receipt from our
eager hands and does magic with the cash register or gives us in-store
credit that most of us forget to use, but still she makes us feel like we are
time travelers, able to undo all our mistakes, able to soothe all of our hurts,
able to get everything we want—instead of everything we ever had.

Fred Chappell

Stopping by the Old Homestead

The Interstate is audible from here.
Five miles east, its low, autonomous hum
disturbs *the stillness that then stood*, the calm
you found *when you came here last time*, eight years
ago, *climbing the same hard road* you toiled
in youth *that slants a steeper grade* today,
this path *by the twisted apple tree* whose shadow
tensely *holds a darker tone*. You breathe
harder *than when you stopped to see* this farm
back then, where *claims your life had made* against
the future *and never paid to own* decayed.
Old times *shriveled and largely gone*, you think,
and trudge all down the hill to find your Chevy
rust-eaten, blind, jacked up on cinder blocks.

All the Good Times Are Past and Gone

More idle than curious, she plunders through
A junky corner of the cramped garage.
Cardboard boxes piled nearly to
The rafters sag and stink and bulge.

Here a spattered tarpaulin
Shrouds the dented, heroic frame
Of a Harley Davidson
That scoured this county like a flame

Back in the time when Dad and Mom
Pursued with streaming locks the strip
Of bright horizon where would loom
That blithe utopia they would shape

According to a visionary blueprint
For a California dream that soon
Would stand irrefutable as the shoeprint
Of Neil Armstrong upon the moon.

Zoom, says the Harley in her mind.
Vroom zoom. She pictures them free and wild,
Mingled with song and speed and wind,
Unburdened by Selena the child,

Because, age twelve, she wasn't yet born.
A threadbare fate her stars have woven...
What bliss to have lived in that great morn
When to be young was very heaven!

From a side-split box she brings to light
The ancient vesture and dons it at once:
Her mother's leather with eagle in flight,
Her father's helmet with skull and bones.

Vroom zoom. She hears America call
And tries to muscle the Harley free
Where it is wedged between the wall
And the impassive SUV.

A Glimpse of the Traveler

With each step, divergent pathways open to the girl
Who strides emphatically, attempting to outpace
The empery of moonlight. One way wends
To the snow-dapple mountain, one way to the river
Where the moon stretches longwise on the water.

Where, girl, do you fare as night extends?
I go to every place my journey conceives.
Why do you travel so, knowing not where?
I go to leave behind the things that I must leave;
I go to seek what yet has been unsought.

There is a grove ahead wherein the shadows
Clutch and hold the wanderer with fretful doubt;
Ravines on either side yawn so vast and black
Moon cannot fetch their depths with her long spear.
So I have heard and do in part believe:

Yet if I stood just here and walked no farther
All my destinies would wither, shrivel and decay,
And I would have no part in them, not even
As witness. I would give over to what is already over.
We shall not go your roads. We wish you well.

I think you do not. I think you are eager to forget
The very sight of me in my silk dress, with my bright hair
Unbound upon my shoulder and all my happiness
Shining in my face.
                    Do not say so, for you cannot know
Our hearts so small and mute and craven.

Halloween Moon over Huddle Knob Graveyard

Skinny McCaudle is called forth on Huddle
And in his bone hand his skeedaddle fiddle
That used to put cloggers on their sweaty mettle
                Cries out again

> *While the moon swoops out of the wind*
> *And the wind swoons into the moon*

Over Huddle Knob the Great Hunter straddles
And down the long westward a meteor hurtles
With a sound like red pokers plunged in a kettle
                Of blackberry wine

> *While the moon floats royal alone*
> *And the wind divides into forty minds*

In our hamlet below we sleepers fuddle
And wallow in dreams of passionate riddle
As McCaudle's hilltop diddle tweedle diddle
                Thrills over the land

> *Deep in the moon thin wind*
> *Skirls like a twisted violin*

And calls to us sleepers to scurry to the saddle
Of moon-fingered wind-worried Huddle
And dance till bony Skinny's swift fiddle
                Reenters the ground

Till the beech leaves all heap in a restless mottle
And their bare branches thrash with a skeletal rattle
And we all stretch our limbs and yawn and settle
                To sleep again

O yes there's something beyond all this fiddle
That Time inches onward with its steady treadle
O lady there's Something beyond all this fiddle—
                We've seen its sign

> *Over Huddle the moony wind*
> *Shivers the silver Halloween*

Catherine Pritchard Childress

Polysemy

My mother is a two-story Victorian
restored to original, then rented
to a family of five.

                A concrete goose,
dressed in seasonal sweaters,
waving from the front porch,

store signs that read
God Don't Like Ugly.
Bait. Knives. Jesus Is Coming.

Sometimes my mother is a cloistering maple
hiding heaping hulls of pop-up campers
and littered yards just beyond the bridge.

Sometimes Tootsie Rolls or gospel tracts
thrown from beds of pick-ups, tractors,
vintage convertibles, and from horseback.

Tent Revivals. Youth Revivals.
The full bloom of Rhododendron
and Decoration Day graves in June.

She's the web of ridges that thread
every holler to every creek—
Dark, Sugar, Sinking, Roaring . . .

A five-a.m. mountaintop sunrise
heaping the sky with dish, dish, dish
of banana pudding, peach cobbler, creamsicle fudge.

Mostly, she's a roadside field burned
to dry dust with a promise
that Echinacea, asters, and yarrow will thrive.

Portrait

I bathed and lotioned you to a pink sheen,
sponged away milk curdled in your folds,
dressed you in starched linen and leather
lace-ups—shoes mailed with coupons clipped
from a Gerber cereal box—to be bronzed
so they could flank the photo your father
waited in the side-yard to capture.

He chose the cushioned rocker to prop you in,
dragged it out beside the fading Shrub Rose—
its blooms so much like my nipples, cracked
as your smacking lips drained my breasts
in twenty-minute intervals. Lullabies, rocking,
each day's routine subject to your rhythm.

He snapped three shots to wind the film.
I posed you in the chair's corner—certain
cherry arms and spindles could not keep you
from toppling heavy-headfirst into overgrown grass—
backed away from his composition, away from you.

Your constant hunger hanging heavy;
his, looming over a four-poster bed.
Your soured spit-up on my shoulder;
his musk between my thighs. Your weight
stretched like every month's last paycheck
across my hips; his, thrust against them.

I didn't tell you I needed my body back
from you—from him, didn't tell you
lullabies are lies (pictures too),
that diamond rings turn brass; glass
breaks; babies fall; bronzed shoes tarnish:
and mothers disappear

                                      just outside the frame.

Michael Chitwood

Those Dying Generations

I. The End of the World, at Least for Today

That would have been in March
of the year Elaine was born in January
was how she remembered
and created my past's past,
begetting me, all of us, out of the daily,
as though every event was a tit for tat,
this happened because of that
which is how I might remember a happiness
in the year that blank space
that's unbalanced my grandfather's stone,
he for years with two dates, her with one,
is filled in
as the earth will be beside him.
What will be forgotten I hope
are these afternoons, these long evenings,
unable to remember the names
of children, no one answering the bell,
not this for not that,
the nothing that happens
for so long each night.

II. Attendant

This is the past's warehouse.
The past gags youngsters
coming into its fumes of urine
and regurgitated saltless meals.
You get used to it if you work here.
You hardly hear the moans and shouts,
those calls for husbands, mothers, fathers,
thirty years dead but again alive
and leaving the ones who shout alone
where they can't get out of bed
and they are being robbed of money,
dresses, the bread we baked for the preacher,
the preacher who married our daughter
and took her off to Iowa one winter
where she froze, oh he killed her,
as they are killing us with rays
from the TV, with what they put in the food,

with those blue booties cutting off
our circulation, our feet, our breath.
Us. Them. Our. Are they here yet?
The dead make regular visits.
You get used to it if you work here.
These are the ones who churned butter,
and primed tobacco and made dresses
out of feed sacks and killed hogs,
ah God I hate when they kill hogs,
the smack of the flat side of the ax,
the scalding, the scraping,
working the meat, shoulders, hams,
liver and lights, the brains, cleaning
the intestines, the intestines!
And they complain about what
we bring them to eat.
We killed day after Thanksgiving.
We killed first full moon after the frost.
We killed when the persimmons ripened.
Damn that past with its happy butchers.

But this is the last of them,
last of those ones who did without,
last of the ones who hate having
anything done for them.
This is the last of the ones
that knife you with their eyes
when you help them, clean them,
keep them alive another day.
Bed-bound, burning with memory,
they know you as sister, brother,
son, daughter, one of them.
They think I should know better
than to help them, feed them.
They hate the living I earn
at their living's expense
and you can't get used to that.

III. The Cure

It's taken eighty-eight years to get her body
so that it will lie here
beneath this blanket while a story spills out
in whispers or maybe just sighs,
the stitchery of her thousand veins visible,
the workmanship showing
in her cheeks, her arms, even her fingers,
every visible piece of skin.
No grease; no fatback; no salt here,

the bendable straw cocked to her mouth
like a microphone, the oxygen snout above her head ready,
the call button on its cord dangling within reach.
"They don't come when I call"
and we come when we can, called by eighty-eight years of her,
the one famous to us for our lives,
and the stories of our lives,
draining out of her tethered to the IV,
to the medication, to the physical therapist, the psychotherapist,
the dietitian, the physician, the x-ray technician,
it was Uncle Jim Bennett was called
because I had gotten the erysipelas
from a bob wire scratch
and Dr. Gale had come with some black grease
but my leg still burned
and Uncle Jim Bennett says there could be nobody in the house,
save us, and I could not look
but what I felt was him breathing on the leg,
it could have been some words he said.
He came back every hour for three hours
and I walked the next day therapist, the dietitian, the
psychotherapist, the physical therapist, the
chaplain, the social worker, the radiologist *one of them,*
it might have been Nancy, had the thrush,
broke out all around her mouth and could barely eat.
Somebody, it might have been Papa ET,
sent for Sis Angle
and she cupped her hand around the baby's mouth
and blew out the thrush.
Say what you will
a baby don't know to get better but did.
This spook talk amuses, puzzles,
is a manifestation, a symptom, a way of self-grieving,
nonsense mumbling to the physician, nurse, psychotherapist,
physical therapist, chaplain.
It's ignorant or at best unlearned,
accented, these days unheard of,
though never actually heard but felt in the saying.
It has lived this long
and still there are whispers.
Here, right now. Whatever these sighs mean.
They might be words,
the cure in them.

Heat

A Coke bottle stopped
with a sprinkle head
sat at one end of the board.
She'd swap iron for bottle,
splash the cloth,
then go at it with the iron.
The crooked was made straight,
the wrinkled smooth,
and she'd lecture from that altar
where rumpled sheets went crisp.
"If Old Scratch gets his claws
in your thigh or neck,
you burn a thousand years
and that is the first day."
Our clothes got rigid,
seam matched seam.
Our bodies would ruin her work.

The Great Wagon Road, or How History Knocked the Professor Cold, or A Storyteller's Story, or Why Appalachians Are Mountains and a People

Scottish, by way of Ulster, Philadelphia,
the Valley of the Shenandoah,

generous, clannish, violent, kind-hearted,
they walked in (the Germans rode)

and stayed mostly out of county records
and the backs of Bibles, unlettered.

Their only correspondence with me,
son of their children's children's great grandchildren,

is this ditch, these nearly healed wheel cuts,
the line they traced in the earth.

*

Locally, it took its name from where it was going,
the potent away-from-here, the better place,

the how-it-could-be, not wintering on beans,
the infant not dead with the flux,

the ground not snagged with roots

that sang from the plow's cut and welted the shins.

Yonder. Chewed with scratch biscuits,
smoked in the porch shade,

something to be believed
when believing was the only solace.

*

"Fortunately, only Single Brothers
made this trip. This trail

at times is impassable and these folk
are wild, unpredictable.

Unlike our brethren,
they came not seeking but fleeing,

the almshouse, the sheriff,
a shamed woman or her brothers.

We sought the freedom to worship.
They worshipped freedom from seeking."

*

"I don't know now, though I knew. . . ."
Her palsied hand goes to her forehead

as if to draw memory with a touch.
My past grows dim,

illiterate, abandoned,
free for the taking.

*

A boy of four, he killed
one of the King's overlords

for casting a desirous eye on his mother,
and stowed away to sail the whale road.

Saving the crew and cargo from storm,
he was rewarded in Philadelphia

with a seventeen-hand stallion
and rode out of the city stench

to the Blue Ridge which reminded him of home.
There he killed and married Cherokee,

fathered seven sons and seven daughters,
coaxed Highland pipes from fiddle's catgut,

distilled moonlight, slaughtered hogs,
lost fingers in sawmills,

hoed, suckered, topped and primed tobacco,
discarded washing machines in creekbeds,

learned to read the Bible, believe obituaries
and recite where he was and what he was doing

when the first Ford, radio, television
and news of JFK's death arrived.

He put on a tie, conditioned the air
and forgot the song of the whippoorwill.

*

"There is no history, but histories."
His shoes aren't right for this rough ground.

The sapling branches whip his back
as he backs into where we're going.

Educated, tenured, he hopes to publish
a study of The Great Wagon Road.

"Until documented the facts are in flux."
He is lecturing backward into the understory

where a honeysuckle vine catches his heel.
He barks his bald spot on a sweet gum

and is silenced into the fact of himself.
Out cold, he's received his dissertation's introduction.

*

Count Casimir Pulaski, Bishop
Francis Asbury, Lorenzo Dow,

the Moravian Single Brother who wrote
"We had to watch our horses closely...."

They crossed Maggodee, Blackwater,
and Pigg, scribbled down some thoughts

that I'm stealing outright,
keeping an eye on their horses, too.

Warrior's Trace, gospel road, going now
into sumac, scrub pine and books.

I take your dirt in my hand.
I take your dirt in my hand and move on.

Transport in Early Spring

Twin-engine prop jet, Morgantown terminal.
One runway. During rev-up I notice

the dandelions, yellow buttons in spring's
new green. They'll launch later.

Up, we wheel toward Pittsburgh
and buck on the invisible shocks

of carnival air. It's a county fair
ride up here—knocks,

dips and whoop-de-doos. I use
my ticket for a bookmark,

close the box of words
and watch West Virginia slide.

Down there a train makes its way
like a sentence, cars distinct as parts of speech.

It works along a river,
supple for an archaic mode.

Coal, stone, grains and lumber.
Those antique loads could not be lifted.

Locality pulls back on being pulled.
Language only half releases. Its drag is true.

Woodpile

A cure for suburbia,
this short stack of Vs, As and Os.
At least that's the way I read
the butt ends of the logs
snug between two living trees.
It's playing at work,
not like the head high, quartered wedges,
four deep in four racks,
they had to make and hope
a log or two would be left come spring.
They, unread, strong-handed, strong-headed.
Me, one callus on the second finger
where the pen rides, making
my alphabet burn for them.

Black Locust

The mocking crown of thorns
I figured to be black locust,
some young limbs wreathed.
Did the weaver's hands bleed?
You needed a local tree
to hitch myth and truth together.

Margin lover, bent and gnarled
as if with the misery
of Old Arthur, the elders'
name for arthritis' grip,
it had a way of getting
around, filling in, coming back.

Kids used the leaves for money,
valuable as Confederate script:
it came in fronds, enough
on each one to buy a baby
doll or a cavalry mount,
whatever we could imagine.

You could barely chop it.
It would gnaw a saw
as much as the saw gnawed it.
Yellow, mean wood with its own
teeth that bit through gloves.
Its brush clung and scarred.
Things happened when men

went out to cut it. Some were
pinned or slapped flat
when a pinched trunk kicked,
some were sliced by a bucking blade,
some were knocked cold, some died.

But if you needed to separate,
keep something out or in,
it made the best fence post.
It would hold a nail
tighter each passing year
and the buried part

stayed trig, nearly lived.

Hatchet

What a gift, a dangerous baby
in size, handle like a spine,
a sleek, flattened S
that fit the hand and remained
perpetually cocked, ready.
I could chop. Or knock
with the blunt side.
And I could take fingers
and toes I was warned,
delicious risk and heft.

I blazed trails from the backyard
into our patch of woods,
notching the way I'd gone
belt-high on big trunks.
Like a witcher's wand
it led me to the creek
and the quiet big stone beside
that once or twice as I rode it
through a summer afternoon
swayed, I swear, like a pachyderm.

It took me by the hand.
Little primate, I evolved
into Cortes, Crockett, Clark,
seeker, mapper, destroyer.
Back home, I'd swaddle it
in a lightly oiled cloth
for the sheen it gave the handle
and the gleam it gave the head.
Full of ideas and new territories,
I could hear its hum under my bed.

Jim Clark

Handiwork

for Jane Taylor

The figure of the woman in the garden,
the brightly colored fruit poised at her lips,
is not archetypal—she is a friend of mine.
Granted, she has known some good, some evil,
but she has come by such knowledge honestly.

She has met me here to help
build a barn. All morning
we have been raising beams, supports,
until now, near noon, we lie
in the long grass looking
at the wood skeleton, all done
but for a couple of ribs.

We drowse for a spell
and after awhile begin again.
It's hard work—sweat
sheets our foreheads, arms.
We move surely, methodically, knowing
what comes next. Across the river
our echoing hammers build nothing.
Hours pass.

Suddenly, from deep in the canebrake,
something thrashes, cries,
struggles into the air,
then falls, breaking
into our rhythm of work.

It is a young quail, not able
to fly. My friend puts down her hammer
and gathers the bird into her hands.
Quietly, evening rises about us,
breathing out from plants,
from soil and water.
Now and again the quail peeps.
From the slick leaf mold at our feet
a cricket rasps
its dark counterpoint.

Loveless You Wander

Places chip away at you,
the only
figure in the landscape.

You travel through lives
easy as a salesman
through towns, states.

Chameleonlike you offer
the perfect pitch:

In Boise they loved
the Horatio Alger number—
"Scarcely modified," you said.

In Bayonne, it was
early Brando, updated.

And how they roared, the good
citizens of Duluth,
at your tales
of the pathetic rubes in Boise:
The undertaker
who could recite "Thanatopsis"
but always broke down in tears
at all those who *shall leave
their mirth and their employments,
and shall come
and make their bed with thee.*

Loveless you wander
the riotous world,
God's plenty
strewn in your wake,
the road you will take
straight and clear before you
as far as it goes.

Sunday Dinner

"Go and bring a hen to the smokehouse door,"
My grandmother said when I was eight years old.
Dust motes swam in sunlit shafts, as four
Birds roosting eyed me, venomous and bold.

The one on the right, a fat, querulous thing,
Cocked her sequined eye as under her I slid
A trembling hand. I blinked, she struck, my ring
Finger oozed red, jumped in my pocket and hid.

"Now go and get Betty," my grandmother said.
"Tell her to bring water, a knife and some salt."
I looked and I looked, but Betty had fled;
I ran to the smokehouse and ground to a halt.

A shower of red rained down on my head;
My hurt finger quickened, and my heart raced.
My grandmother's apron from her lap bled
Scarlet drops onto her dusty shoes unlaced,

As round my legs a small white fury danced,
A feathery balloon someone let go.
At its head, or where its head should be, I glanced,
Recoiling in terror at its dumb show.

And that was Saturday noon. Sabbath morn,
We arose and to the meetinghouse went.
And when the preacher said "Ye must be reborn—"
"Washed in the blood—" I knew what he meant.

When the song of invitation sprang
From lips in dark faces I thought I knew,
I made my way down the aisle as they sang
And faced the preacher, and tried to answer true.

I stood in water, the back of my head
Cupped in his right hand. I answered again
The questions he posed, and afterwards fed
On the grape and the bread, though my mind in circles ran.

So home we went, and, famished, awaited word
Of blessing—the Sunday table, steaming, spread
With the bounty of earth, the crisp, golden bird.
We ate the blood and the body. We resurrected the dead.

Black Dog Shadrick Mayhew

I'm the one they won't tell about,
barn burner, horse thief, cheat.
In the hills of Corbin County, near
the Kentucky line, in the curve
of Horseshoe Bend, I carried
fifty-pound bags of sugar and corn
to my daddy's still when I was ten.
I stirred the mash and kept cold
the water that cooled the worm,
and clapped my hands at the first
clear drop that clung from copper,
then fell into the waiting jug.
Underneath the chestnut tree
my daddy snored, drunk on profit.

When I was seventeen I asked
Abigail Simpson to be my wife.
Yes, she said, but hadn't reckoned
on her Pa's tight-lipped No, sudden
and final as a shotgun blast. That night
I sloshed kerosene on stable floor hay
of his new barn, struck the match
and held it, eye level, till the flame
licked my fingers, then dropped it.

I lit out for Tompkinsville, and there
lived for five loose and lawless years,
vowing never to ask another man
permission of what I wanted.
And what I wanted I took and people
all along those Cumberland ridges
gave me wide berth, and a name—
Black Dog Shadrick Mayhew.

Then war came, and fire and death
and thievery marched the valleys,
a smoky cloak of pestilence hugging
the ridges I rode. Under cover
of a uniform, gray, with a little box
of a hat, I robbed and killed and burned
my way back to Corbin County.

When they slapped the horse's rump,
and I felt the stiff hemp bite
into my neck, I danced above the earth
and watched the smoke plait and curl
from the ashes of Jess Simpson's barn.

Geraldine Connolly

Blue Bridge

Praise the good-tempered summer
and the red cardinal that jumps
like a hot coal off the track.
Praise the heavy leaves,
heroines of green, frosted
with silver. Praise the litter
of torn paper, mulch and sticks,
the spiny holly,
its scarlet land mines.

Praise the black snake that whips
and shudders its way across my path
and the lane where grandmother
and grandfather walked, arms
around each other's waists
next to such a river, below
a blue bridge about to be
crossed by a train.

In the last gasp
of August, they erase the time
it might be now, whispering
into the darkness that passed,
blue plumes of smoke and cicada,
eager and doomed.

Quilting

February. Hanging
icicles, music
of passage as they break.
Toward the light
that frames her we look
at sorrow, at the little coffins
of pattern that engage her,
sheltered by stitching.

Her needle, her weapon
would like to break
into blossoms of smoke,

of leaf, transparent grace,
the true wildness
within her.

Mendon

Beets sweetened in the straw basket
and rains poured
from the downturned lake of sky.

Each wet morning her hands kneaded
dough and pulled, sliced the rye loaf
on the pine cutting board,
pinched white geraniums to send

ghost blossoms up the windowpane.
Her reflections spun like a lightning wheel.
Then she rolled rice and meat
into pockets of cabbage, counted them,
smothered them in sauce.

When she sat down to sew,
bad ankle stiffening,
she placed the patch of silk
next to a square of tweed
then plucked one silver button
from the jar of dark ones,
resolved to make something new.

Gleaming thread drifted
like a thought
through the needle's eye.
She knotted it
and pierced the cloth.

Lightning

Fish bones rise
in the black trees.

For a moment, distance
does not exist.

The world cracks open
into the past.

I had imagined
her death

like this,
a white rage,

a bridge suspended
over narrows,

then the bridge
falling.

Regrets

Out of their secret places
in autumn, from under

dark logs and smooth gravestones
they come, black snakes,
stripped, floating free

in the golden September sunlight
which drifts as they try
to hold onto it.

They lay their bodies
across our warm paths,
branches of misspent hours,

limbs from low gullies.
Past school children and old men
they wind, making no sound,

sliding the earth in silence,
riding a world that seems dull
and hazy, half-spent,

beautiful errors
that rise up as we gasp.

John Crutchfield

Ox Creek Road

Waking to snowlight, stillness in the woods,
& at the feeders wrens & juncos frantic,
scattering husks on silence lying thick
& crystalline, a coast no tide abrades:

the lone flare of a cardinal in branches
intricate as syntax etched, a word
of blood in bone-dry stanzas disinterred
by prophesies of wind: as if to choose

to speak into this simple light were nothing
more: the kettle's quiet knock, a whiff
of tea, the nut-brown scent of toast: as if
our bodies' shape beneath the blankets' breathing

warmth could be inhabited again
once shed, left crumpled, cooling in the room
this light finds last of all, finds just in time
to catch its gold reflection in the pane.

Wild Leeks

You'll walk right by it in the highland woods
not knowing what to look for: *ramps* the locals
call it—first fresh vegetable of spring,
a modest harbinger of winter's hold
relenting in lost coves & sheltered gaps,
a loosening of ice-locked sap & silt
on frozen tufts along the dead-leaf trail:
a spurtle of green then, clusters of it, low
to the ground, the bladed fronds conferring
softly in a breeze still tinct with snow;
but it's the hidden bulb you want, a knob
the bluish pale of April flesh exposed
to sudden sunlight, tipped with groping roots
& self-sheathed like an onion—good, they say,
to cleanse the blood of winter sediments
& quicken eye & ear; & once a year
in Cosby, Tennessee, where Caney Creek
spills down from Cherokee National Forest,

they've held a festival since '54,
& even crown a local beauty "Maid
of Ramps." A word of warning, though: the taste
is mild as scallions, but the feral smell
that taints both skin & breath for days: garlic.

Trout Lake

Out Winklers Creek from Boone the corn-stitched valley
crimps to bramble gulch & palisades
of cattail, tufted thicks where copperheads
hunt mice & muskrats use, dead branches lie

flood-stacked & silt-encrusted, & the stream
comes purling black & cold from laurel hells
impervious to day, & farther, shoals
of rhododendron churning the balsam gloom

where chestnut stumps subside beneath the slow
green tide of moss, the current quickens, pures
on rocks that home to red-lipped salamanders,
sullen crawfish, trout & schooling minnow,

back through beech-lit glades & boulder-spills
till sparks fly from the water & above
a glimpse of blue the parting branches give,
& now the lake, the wind-appointed aisles

of light across the surface, where many years
ago my friends & I would sneak to dip
on autumn dusks, our molted clothes adrape
& glowing in the dark branches as the stars

clicked on above us, strange & glittering
& framed by ridges black as beetles' wings.

Meteor Shower

Way back in the mountains, up beyond
old barbwire snags & warnings, laurel hells
so thick & gnarled intruding flesh goes blind,
a wounded groping over frost-locked spills

of boulder, rotted lichens slick as ice
on crags where Ox Creek springs fully formed
& lucid from the mountain's skull to fleece
the stones with moss: there, whiskey-warmed

I make my bed of leaves as darkness drips
from twig-tips, flows on quartz-veined rock
to sluice among the moon-inflected shapes
of trees, & swelling, whelms the measured wake

I drift, past archipelagoes of dream
& stormclouds gathering black sheaves of air
tobacco-sweet & burning to relume
a piedmont town, a girl left years ago,

an arc of light translating time's dark ore
to fluent tongues, pale leaves to psalms of snow.

Donna Doyle

Sunbathing with Elvis

Sometimes he wrapped my hair
around his hand like kite string,
lifted it off my sweaty neck,
let me do most all the talking, until
he got tired of hearing me complain about the heat.
Not that we argued.
He rolled over onto his stomach,
watched me walk toward the house,
I know because I kept looking back
over my shoulder, perfecting the move
I learned from Lot's wife.

When I found my mother and told her:
Elvis wants me to cut my hair,
she did not ask questions
or make me change out of my swimsuit.
She waited for me to put on sneakers,
held my hand while we walked
around the curve in the subdivision,
down to Bea Russell's basement beauty parlor.
Sitting on a stack of *Vogue, Butterick,*
McCall's and *Simplicity* pattern books,
eyes closed, chunks of hair fell,
landed on the vinyl cape like quiet leaves,
new words, *pixie...babyfine...cowlick...*
snipped in my ears.

Bea's hand pressed faith healer flat on my forehead;
she cursed the damage done by cows caressing.
That is when I pulled back, opened my eyes,
opened my mouth to claim what was mine,
my mark in life, to be cow licked, licked by cows,
see that girl goin' there?...she has been licked by cows.

Walking home the long way, we saw them,
spotted like spilled milk, living in green,
giving more than I knew,
words I would not learn for years,
comrade, pastoral, vegetarian.
Quiet giants, they must have gathered
around my bed while I was sleeping,

cud breath lowing over their new savior.
At home, Elvis waited,
sunburned, happy to see me,
loving me tender with his bovine eyes.
We had a lot to talk about.
If he had not told me to cut my hair,
none of this would have happened.

One by One, the Animals

Not long after he died,
the animals we lived with,
one by one, disappeared,
lost in humid hollows
beyond calling, beyond searching.
Our eyes strained to see through
summer thick haze.
Our parched throats ached,
called out name after precious name
we had named them
so they would always return.

Without their instincts,
we grew apart in grief.

Separately in sleep each night
we called out, "Father,"
woke restless in a quiet house,
another day of looking
for what we had lost stretched out
like a heat hallucinatory highway.

Summers he haunts me most.
Days of longer light promise more,
cloud over with dying.
Red cemetery dirt shoveled over him
echoes the garden he left behind.
Every loose running dog, every darting cat
opens my mouth to call out.
My hand slaps hard the mosquitoes
taking away even more blood.

Casie Fedukovich

Sinners Gather at Paint Lake

Praying Indian friends tug at heavy
        denim, hands soundtracked by noseeum
hum, mosquito whirl. Sharp slaps against stoic
        faces punctuate splashes against mountain rock.

Thirty men and women, up to knees
        in snow runoff, rope the new bride
and groom, twining verses circle young
        heads like garlands. Sister Bertha's

best dress gathers silt in lace. Body long
        against six pairs of outstretched hands, she
relaxes into water, white dress reflected in the Reverend's
        pupils. Holy coal-stained fingers pinch too hard her small nostrils.

His palm slaps belly too big for fresh marriage,
        tongue lolling, tasting metallic lake
pooling in Sister Bertha's temples. Brother Dennis
        follows her interrupted swirls, small German teeth grind,

heavy boots stir hellgrammites from mud.
        Mine soot behind ears exchanges with lake
bed sediment, lungs pull Holy Ghost water, bumps breath
        from lungs, same smother of coal caves, low ceilings,

skin dark with rock. Brother Dennis drinks God, gathers
        elements with blurred eyes that flash once, sublime
heat gathering under still-lake mirror, before congregation hands
        lift gaping fish-mouth to air.

Pocahontas Seam via Norfolk and Western

Vance Family Album

Oren first, hot German blood splashed on rock
as pick slips, chews into thick upper thigh.
A bit of index finger in a cart packed
for Scranton. His lungs stay in West Virginia where
they shrivel with dust, lush flowers planted in sand.
Tall Paul next. The foreman sings his reach to other mines,
"Feller don't need no ladder, born with a ladder of bones."
One leg to Hershey in Load 96. His son, Dennis, cauterizes
the artery with a blowtorch, digs his father's room until
two moons spiral overhead, a silver fall rinsing
mountains with light, shadowboxing the trees
as Dennis slouches home, elbows to knees, spine of tender glass,
finds his father freebleeding in the narrow bed.
Dennis undercuts a face thirty years later, twitches under
half a ton of rock for three days, body shrinks enough
to slide away,
half an ear sandwiched between anthracite humps.
The only part of Dennis to leave the mountains.

Harry Gieg

Rubato

A skinny white guy, maybe in his early thirties—

in faded jeans and a faded short-sleeve shirt

(everything about the guy
                       kind of faded and white)

and carrying what looks like
a folded umbrella maybe two-feet long, green
and white and tucked under his left arm

—stands by himself
                      at a bus stop waiting

his hands and legs drawn up hitched, somehow

his head lolling
   like he's palsied.

                     Facing oncoming traffic, he doesn't seem to see the
older man—
                isn't aware of
   or doesn't care about him passing by

on the other side of the street.

                    And suddenly, the younger man
draws out the umbrella with his right hand

                    and twirls it once, twice, a fifth and sixth time—
awkward
   but boldly assertive martial—

                  and he never drops it, not once. And the umbrella
is not an umbrella nor a baton

but a six-gun

    the storied equalizer. And the man
isn't
physically
challenged
    nor a drum major

but a shootist defending what's right.

                  And when their eyes meet, the older man—
looking back in passing—calls to the younger man
from across the street "Mornin'."

                  And the younger man nods, smiling—
chin drawn up and back—

and answers, "Mornin,'" a smell of sulphur in the air,

the umbrella smoking.

Diane Gilliam

Where I'm From

> *after George Ella Lyon*

I am from Hopie and Odell, from Rumi's anteroom
    of souls—some kind of late night wedding chapel
    where, as my parents married, my soul stood up
    at the sweetness of their faces. *Yes,* I said.
    I will. I do.

I am from Sweet Jesus glowing honey brown
    on the back wall of the church, and my mother's cousin
    Darlene leading song service up front, her arms
    waving like a drum major's—
    I'm redeemed   by love divine
        I'm redeemed   by love divine
    Glory, Glory, Christ is mine, Christ is mine
    —the men singing the echo part and the sun
    pouring in all wild.

I am from the uncool table of girls who polished rocks,
    made up songs in little notebooks and spoke in the language
    of the Once and Future King. From learning to say *Grandma*
    instead of *Mamaw*, and to not tell about the poke
    Daddy pulled from the side of the road for supper. I am from
    the time I asked Laura Grinstead of the smooth hair
    and matching clothes a question about English class,
    and Nancy Grimm informed me: *Were <u>you</u> talking to <u>her</u>?*
    I am from watching my sister-in-law to learn what to wear.

I am from ten years of graduate school and always only one
    right answer for every twenty-five students, from the full professor
    who said to me, as I sat in his office eight months gone—shame
    I was having babies instead of books.

I am from my girls who birth me every day into this world.

I am from heart attacks and strokes, from Daddy playing his guitar
    and whispering hope to Uncle Ted at three a.m.
    in the Morrow County hospital, and from my cousin Debby
    who punched out the nurse that tried to stop him.
    I am from the man who took off his hat when I cried
    in the elevator in Saint Joe's and from the woman
    who prayed with my mother in the bathroom at Walmart
    the fourth day after chemo.

I am from the same waiting room
    as you-the one where God said *Who will go*
    to this world I made only out of things that die
    and find out for us how much sweetness that adds?
    And we all of us raised our hands.

Pearlie Tells What Happened at School

Miss Terry has figured since we are living
in a coal camp, we ought to know geology,
which is learning about rocks. Every day
we got to bring in a different rock
and say what it is. Even our spelling words
is rock words, like *sediment* and *petrified*.
Yesterday, Miss Terry says, *Who can use*
"petrified" in a sentence? and Walter Coyle
raises his hand, which, he don't never
ever since his uncle Joe—he was the laughingest,
sparkliest-eyed man you ever seen, ever since Joe
got sealed in at Layland and they ain't never
gonna know if he got burnt up or gassed
or just plain buried. So Walter says,
and he don't never look up from his desk,
he says, *Miss Terry, can a person get petrified?*

Miss Terry thinks he is sassing her, 'cause she
don't know about Joe Coyle, and about
how Walter don't never sleep no more
nor hardly eat enough to keep
a bird alive, as his mama says.
Miss Terry sends him to the cloak room
that was the last we'd see of Walter.
He come back this morning, though, pockets
filled with rocks, and with a poke full of rocks.
Spreads them all out on Miss Terry's desk
'fore she even asks. *Well, alright,* she says,
suppose you tell us what these are.

Walter stirs the rocks around a bit, so gentle,
picks up a flat, roundish one and lays it
agin his cheek. *This here,* he says,
is the hand.

Nikki Giovanni

Knoxville, Tennessee

I always like summer
best
you can eat fresh corn
from daddy's garden
and okra
and greens
and cabbage
and lots of
barbecue
and buttermilk
and homemade ice-cream
at the church picnic

and listen to
gospel music
outside
at the church
homecoming
and you go to the mountains with
your grandmother
and go barefooted
and be warm
all the time
not only when you go to bed
and sleep

Nikki-Rosa

childhood remembrances are always a drag
if you're Black
you always remember things like living in Woodlawn
with no inside toilet
and if you become famous or something
they never talk about how happy you were to have
your mother
all to yourself and
how good the water felt when you got your bath
from one of those
big tubs that folk in chicago barbecue in
and somehow when you talk about home
it never gets across how much you
understood their feelings
as the whole family attended meetings about Hollydale
and even though you remember
your biographers never understand
your father's pain as he sells his stock
and another dream goes
And though you're poor it isn't poverty that
concerns you
and though they fought a lot
it isn't your father's drinking that makes any difference
but only that everybody is together and you
and your sister have happy birthdays and very good
Christmases
and I really hope no white person ever has cause
to write about me
because they never understand
Black love is Black wealth and they'll
probably talk about my hard childhood
and never understand that
all the while I was quite happy

Jesse Graves

Tennessee Landscape with Blighted Pine

Dry summer and the upper field quiet at noon.
Spring's green pirouette tangled in barbed wire,
Its promise snapped like matchsticks, burnt-orange
Pine needles cracking loose from stiff joints,
                                      Silence dropped so low
It rings like a bell's soft echo.

Here once was a boy running with a black and white half shepherd dog,
Hair summer-blonde, hands darkened to rust by wet clay
                                      Rummaged for arrowheads.

No fear then but the darting tongues of timber snakes:

That certainty lost to whatever passes for time,
                              The ground skipped beneath his feet.

              *   *   *

Once I stood here through a mid-day snowfall, sky staring and nearly dark,
        Watching my shoes sink in the white sheets,
Petals of frozen clouds feathering down through my eyelashes.
        Home from college, free of Introduction to Business
And Media Arts, endless boredoms that passed for a life of the mind.

Not a sound that whole afternoon, nothing more alive than my breath,
        Silence in the snowy field, the heavy trees,
Known in sense but not by name, nothing really known by name.

              *   *   *

No one came here to build the perfect city.
They came out of Philadelphia and before that New York,
                        Before that Baden-Baden and the Palatinate.

A narrow river unspooled out of the mountains, Alamance County,
                                  Western Carolina, and washed them up
Before what must have seemed God's own promise:
                Tall fescue and cleft hoofprints of deer on the muddy banks.

Here they could harvest what grew, tear life out of the ground.

They started with trees, built a lumber-mill and floated log-rafts downriver

To settlements in Rockwood, Oliver Springs, and Chattanooga—

1792.

Already the name had been lightened to Graves, and only old Johannes,
Born 1703 in the Rhineland, still kept himself Graff.

* * *

Left alone, indoors, I tend toward sounds not found
In the open field, *Sotto voce* of Mahler's *Misterioso Symphony*,
      Surge and retreat of John Coltrane's *Crescent*.

No analogue in nature, no precedent in the high branches.

One night in Faubourg Marigny I heard Kidd Jordan ignite the air
With a tenor saxophone.
      It sounded like ashes falling, each speck a thousand pounds.

* * *

Life abounds on the perimeter, overflushes the fencerows
      Most years, honeysuckle lacing the cedar posts,
But now the heat beats its odd rhythms and the billion tiny teeth
      Of the blight work through this zone and the next,
Leaving orange skeletons standing over variegated shadows.

Chestnuts once shouldered this ridgeline, owned the horizons
From Sharps Chapel to Jellico Mountain, on past the blue smudge
      Of Clinch Mountain to the east.

Impossible to picture it today, three generations after aphids cut through them—
      Floorboards and ceiling joists, finely-grained paneling
In the old houses the only proof that an existence once so sturdy could vanish
      Like clouds into clouds.

* * *

So many years ago a man toiled here, clearing and reaping the barest life.
    How many years?
        The years themselves do not know, do not count turns
            In their circle.

Before Lincoln, before Darwin, before Marx.
      One of his sons killed in the field by a Cherokee.

An X by "His Mark" on the deed. An X by "His Wife's Mark."

The words Jesse Graves quilled below it in the practiced hand of a magistrate.

                        *   *   *

The dead move through us at their will, their voices chime
        Just beyond our hearing.
How else do we feel our names when no one speaks them?
How else catch the echo of footprints two decades
        After running through the grass?

Alone in the field, and never alone. Quiet and not quiet.
                                            Home and away.

Johnson's Ground

We sit under the awning and watch them descend in unison.
A flock of thirty or more down through the heavy rain
we weren't supposed to get, pecking where grass is thin
for what the moisture turns up.
                              They look like the sound of the word
grackle, scavengers with wings muted black as painted iron rails,
as wet tar, their empty beaks flashing a bright citrus smear.
Memorial Day weekend and the weather drives us for cover,
beating down plastic flowers and darkening family gravestones.

Each year we arrive, distant relations, to admire new babies
and find out who has changed jobs or gotten married.
I come to see who's left to sit in the shaded chairs
where my grandmother sat with her oldest sister Minnie
for the last time, neither of them able to name the other,
but both staring as if into a clouded mirror.
                                    In the memory of their faces
I see pillars of stone, pillars of stippled salt,
where the hammer of time drives the chisel of living,
the opaque blue of their eyes, each pair reflecting the other,
sky blue buttons threaded through a dark blue dress.

Homecoming at the cemetery: they never let us go, even the ones
laid under before our births continue to make their claims,
to draw the interest on their spent lives.
                                  My grandfather waits here,
Houston buried in Johnson ground—such is the appointment
he made with them. He was dead two years before
I was born, but of whom do I remind the old people?

Whose picture did I stare into above the living room fireplace?

My great-uncle Gene tells my father and me about the base
he served in Korea, how bombs sounded hitting the village,
while a hundred feet away from us is my cousin Garry,
killed in Vietnam, telling his story into our other ears,
into the soles of our shoes.
      The foraging birds drag worms
out of the ground; we pull dark meat from the bones
of chicken thighs and split boiled potatoes with plastic forks.

Damp air hums in our lungs and old people begin
covering dishes—the rain always seeps in,
even under shelter.
     I offer my hands one more time,
to the company who packs their leftovers and drives away,
and to the company who stays behind, under the tall grass,
left in the restless turning of what we remember of them.

Elegy for a Hay Rake

To every thing its season, and to every tool
its final turn; to the Farmhand rake my father
bought hard-used in 1976, rust has eaten away
all your labels, all your sheen and simple function;
to what I hope is my last sight of you, unhitched
and standing in the field like a photograph
from the Great Depression;
      farewell to the cut hay left
scattered on the ground to rot, nothing ate you
but the soil that birthed you; to the tractor tire
those long grappling points missed by inches
on every sharp turn, you survived without puncture;
to the long afternoon hours spent digging clumps
out of the balers' clenched teeth, good money
cannot buy you back;
    so long to the lucky machine,
lucky I won't sell you as an antique, that no one will
paint you red, white, and blue and plant you in a garden,
or hang you on a restaurant wall; goodbye to the five
leaning wheels, their crooked tines turning, reaching up
like broken fingers to wave hello, hello, goodbye.

Chris Green

A Tree for Everything

The sky burns blue over the spoked
remains of spruce firs atop
Mount Mitchell. Valleys stretch out
like arms veined with a single road,
but green green green. Descending
the mountain, off the Blue Ridge
Park Way, pines cycle to autumn maples,
punctuated at each turn by low stands
of pines, even rowed sprouts and saplings
replanted to fill the hill's emptied quiver.

Before the fire that night, you follow
the flare of embers shooting into the sky,
trace their tails until they fade.
Now the pyre blows high, and sparks flock
toward stars, pour like migrating monarchs
from trees and disappear, forsaking
your heart. So long cleared, so long contained,
now it lays bare to all that lands
and departs, rogue gambit of belonging.
How lucky they were to find rest
amid core-struck fields and forests,
for recall when you tried to stock this worn
spot rooted deep within. Like an aviary,
you clasped and housed all that alighted,
until your cage collapsed, packed
and overflowing. You loosed the lock,
numbered, and tagged them, hoping to track
their routes. You cried after all that left.

In your nights on the clear-cut mountain,
open the shaking barn of your breast.
Let each ember alphabet that longs to ride
deep into the wind settle in its hollows
and squat on the slats of your ribs.
Yes, what rises from roost seeks only
a silent span, and without regret
spreads rumor of shelter and eventual return.

Playhouse

> *"Each life is dirt and time and rhyme and stone."*
> *–Jesse Stuart #678* Man with a Bull-Tongue Plow

Rain pummels the playhouse we've set up for Eleanor.
It pours and sings hisses and puddles on our back porch.
Eleanor wails about the thunder and hides in hugs
against the downpour that threatens to push away
her new tower in which she desires to play queen
and castle, swing rope and air trip, kitchen and treasure.
She's deaf to reassurances that lightening won't strike
her here inside or raze her newly risen wood house.
"I'm scared!" she cries, burying her face in the couch.
What do I tell her? That she is right? That we all go?
That each of us faces silence and wind at the end—
we hope as our families gather around in song?
"I know," I say, "it'll be okay." Tomorrow she'll run
around our cats' graves (their stones effaced with flowers)
and alone she'll climb up the ladder into her home,
sailing the ship of dolls and rhymes into that day's bend.

Connie Jordan Green

Coal Mining Camp, Kentucky, 1935

We were there, my sisters and I,
hidden in their cells, unseen, unfelt,
waiting for the two of them to look up,
see one another, waiting for recognition
to leap the charged arc between them,
my father glancing at Mother
as she shrugged out of her coat, as she
reached to hang it on a peg, the jersey
of her dress stretched across her breasts.
Later she would tell us what he said,
"Hot damn, I gotta get out of here,"
how he grabbed his hat and sprinted
from the room. She had laughed, thought him
the sissy college boy come to run
the company store, couldn't know years later
he would load more coal than her father
or brothers, would carry his daughters
on his shoulders, would dig and plant,
hammer and paint, would build their world
with his sturdy hands. At that first meeting
we were unjoined, half a chain of DNA
powerless to set off the spark that would
fuse us into being—chance its own windstorm
fanning the fire in my father's eyes,
Mother never guessing how eagerly
she would step into the flames.

Late January Letter to a Retired Friend in Florida

Here in East Tennessee crocuses
think green while mountains wear white.
Robins flirt with spring among
yellow stalks of dry grass,
juncoes and titmice refuse
to relinquish winter's gray.
I grow weary of woodpile,
woolen socks, cows
huddled facing into the wind.
Mudtracks mar our floors,

windows fog, frost over.

Newspapers offer the usual:
Snow-women sculpted
like Renoir's females.
Children sledding on a hill,
eyes shut, hair flying.
A pair of ducks
immobilized in a pond's ice.

The neighbors' forgotten
Christmas lights wink
through fifteen-degree nights.
Last evening, in winter's clear air,
the maple near my back door
cradled Orion among her bare limbs.
I send him to you in his icy clarity,
reminder of your friend
enduring late winter's elements,
fixed in earth's sure revolutions.

Of the Wild

> *There will be*
> *A resurrection of the wild.*
> *Already it stands in wait*
> *At the pasture fences.*
>   —Wendell Berry

On the hillside beneath the power lines,
honeysuckle, blackberry, locust seedlings
have entered the third day. Not all the mowers
in God's kingdom nor all the spray in the devil's
workshop will convince them life is futile.
Again and again they bow down, become dirt and dust.
Dead, the government agents proclaim, climb
into their pickups, ride away, gasoline cans
clanking in the beds. There is a spirit
in seed, spore, and root that man's vision cannot
comprehend. A few days of rain, a sunny
spell, jubilation breaks forth again, vine,
sprout, and seedling in a riot of life
that will not put period to man's sentence.

Boss

My dead grandfather roams the farmhouse rooms,
peeks into an upstairs chamber
where his own father's handmade cherry casket
sat twenty-four years awaiting the old man's death,
pauses at the door to the front bedroom
he and my grandmother shared.
He wanders into the kitchen,
looks out at the chicken yard,
notes grape vines on the porch posts
grown large as his forearm.
He remembers breakfasts after milking,
cream from his cows, eggs and ham—
food he grew with the strength
of his body. He remembers, too, an old man
sitting at the table, jar of peanut butter
for dinner, his own ghostly presence
after my grandmother's death.
He smells wooden furniture rubbed with beeswax,
linens fresh from the clothesline,
the scent of lilac—early May's gift to the hall table.
He will not go to the barn, will not toss down
from the loft forkfuls of hay that lured
cows to the milking stanchions,
will not go to the garage,
crank his old truck, odor of oil and gasoline
embedded in floor boards.
He roams the house of his parents,
his children, his grandchildren,
visits them all where in life
he had no time to linger.

Larry Grimes

Get you up to the high mountain

> Isaiah 40:9

We were climbing slowly out of the deep
valley under heavy canopy. It was dark there
beneath the trees. We could feel the valley rise
step by step. Our thighs loosened. The pain left.
The trail flattened and ran straight along a ridge.
Then, to our right, we saw it. Where trees had been
the full sky was alive with light. Stars. Galaxies of stars.
We walked out onto solid rock, stood, stared
into the bright. The moon hung in cresent,
the love star reached down beneath it.
We put our packs down on the rocks
pulled out a loaf of flat bread, broke it and ate.
Then we slept in the soft glow, waking
In crisp dawn looking down into a meadow
where a young boy carried a lamb in his arms.
Behind him the ewe followed toward the open
door of a barn.

Kari Gunter-Seymour

To the Woman in Walmart Who Was Dancing to Shakira in the Pots and Pans Aisle

I'd had a shit day when I stumbled
into the whole bo-bop,
your back to me, all *hips don't lie*,
hands flinging corporate America's
flimsiest filtered warehouse air,
my own feet beginning to slide
and shuck, drawn into that vortex,
adding my own brand
of *Arriba, Arriba* to the mix,

our cha-cha-swoops
reminiscent of broom swipes
laid down by my Great Grandmother,
who I was told swept daily
across a series of rich men's floors,
to keep her children fed.

What a sight, both of us raggedy
as a couple of used books,
plainly living lives we did not choose
or didn't choose wisely—
life, a holier-than-thou hand of cards
dealt by a duplicitous deity.

Who can remember which of us
was first to grab a long-handled pan,
a wooden spoon, our need
for percussion fierce, our efforts
quickly evolving into a cautionary tale.
For the record, I don't give a hot damn
about what the manager said.
I was planning to buy a saucepan anyway.

Someone Needs to Bake a Pie

Grandmother, you would be juddered
by the utter lack of charity,
self-interest, reptilian behavior
of way too many in today's
one Nation under God.

I know you would be confused,
no matter how slowly I might unreel the facts,
the fields and forests once cherished
devoured by bodies, so many
insatiable bodies scrambling for a foothold—
the greedy so calculating.

My pale lips press desperate
against the ghostly velvet of your name,
my sleep pleached with heredity
and sanctity of the covenants,
wisps of apple and cinnamon,
the flake of a lard-made crust
tendering my tongue.

Too many have forgotten the old ways,
the smell of fertile soil,
a coyote barking its wild.
Do unto others, you would say.
Thank God you are not here.
This world would break all your blessings.

Richard Hague

Time Lapse Photography: A Mouse Corpse Devoured by Maggots

At first, the grave familiar scene:
a mouse lies among stones and weeds
like a painter's subject
in a tiny landscape of ruin.
This, we say, this is what
we know of death:
arrest of motion, frigidity,
bleak consummation
of life's fling and jig.
Death, we know, holds still.

But then the mouse's body
swells, flexes, rolls,
seems almost to dance in place.
Supermouse muscles bunch
beneath its coat,
rippling its flanks
like the waves of an earthquake
approaching and departing:
maggots, en masse, migrating
from organ to organ,
feed to feed.
Meanwhile
its claws tap rhythm on the ground.
It even shakes its mousy booty—

Then, as if spent
in convulsions
of laughter or grief,
collapsing, matted fur
parting, small bones erupting
from the carrion,
it implodes at last,
flat smear of darkness
in the stricken field,

While its soul, transformed,
now voiced and winged,
ascends, a cloud of thick black flies
that sport and hiss
on the stinking air
and innocent as fresh angels
carry the dance away.

Talking Together

Annual meeting of the Southern Appalachian Writers Cooperative,
Highlander Center, Tennessee, 1982

Lord, how our voices often mingle,
creeks rounding down from a thousand miles
to wed the same bright river

And how we mouth our favorite names:
say *poplar, sycamore, broom sedge*
like prayers

And how we have seen the same birds
flock among the white pine groves
of the oldground we've helped heal,

And how we seem to have heard the same stories,
seen the same men on street corners
of small towns so barren
they have no football team

And how we have loved women who look and speak like sisters
and how we have hunted the same deer
on stands decades apart,
and how we have found the same stones in creeks

And how we have seen the same wonders at night
in places hundreds of miles distant
(wild cherry branches shuttling in the breeze,
Arcturus living like an eye above the oak)

And how we have failed the same jobs,
workers slumped over Chevys and Fords,
machinists hurt in our hearts by slivers of steel,
hunters limping upridge with bloodied feet

And how, when we find ourselves together,
standing around gas pumps or stoves in old stores,
waiting for tires to be changed,
for children to be drilled by the clinic dentist in town,
for fathers to die in the hospitals of county seats

We find something to say that means us,
that names us neighbors and kin,
that finds within us words to connect:
coon hounds loved in common,
a relative with the same name,
a character true to type in all our places:

Lord, how our lives often mingle,
how we mouth our favorite names,
how we sing in voices old, flat, or sweet:

How we know we know one another,
how we love even what we hate
for how it brings us together.

Cathryn Hankla

Brush Fires

I sit in trees, a place foresters call "fuel."
The understory becomes me, grouse and turkeys
Know my sour moods, my sounds as I move
Around shuffling papers, searching pens.

A neighbor starts his clearing ritual, stippling
His arms with brambles. A thorn rips a zipper
Across his crown. His wife daubs
The seeping blood then offers a match.

The whole stack crackles at nightfall.
It burns bright, rekindled. Anxious, I watch
The creek as it turns, the fire as it burns
On the other side: flame morphed to embers.

Taking Pictures

The scent of death turns up a deer,
Neither mature nor spotted, rolled
To the roadside below the weathered
Tombstones. Disturbed by late sun—
If they were bright leaves this light
Would shine right through, but as it is
White stones reflect the years.

Two men stride out of the woods
In orange hats and vests,
Dump rabbits by the ears
Into the long bed of their royal blue
Truck. A lone duck flaps
South over my head. Too late,

I train my camera on the blazing reds,
The orange and yellow dancers
Down hillsides in warm spills
Of wind. In the back of my mind
The raccoon mother lies still,
On the one-lane bridge,
With one of her young too near.

Bee Tree

A bee colony,
black hole
in a split juniper trunk.
Gnarled, rough mounds of bark
guard a slash of buzzing dark.

Wild bees delight,
work and hover—
dive into an artificial night.
They pass each other
to cover cones with stolen nectar.

This could be the last bee tree
in a food chain of cultivated
colonies. Bee homebodies
thrive—imports mingle
without improvement,

and migrants sicken, shipped
on flatbeds cross country.
No swarm, only purposeful acts
in a daylong dance to and fro.
The gash of hive is low

on the trunk, the whole
secret two feet high.
This fir bearing cones
like shrunken blueberries,
with bark striations of whitish grey,

resembles a faded fence post
more than a living tree.
Inside there is a kingdom
waiting to collapse
on a queen so plump with life

she cannot see the danger
of such sweetness. Expanding
honey cores the juniper,
as sinkholes honeycomb the comet's
nucleus until it cries out,

its coma burning bigger than Jupiter.
17P/Holmes explodes gas
and dust as sun strikes it.
To the eye, a fuzzy spot enlivens
Perseus. To the lazy

bees, tucked into a moon-lit tree
it is nothing. Soon, it is nothing.

Ghost Horses and the Morning Sky

Bright planets in the east, the north, the northeast,
Splitting the difference. One doesn't find skies

Like this. Cassiopeia, Thuban in Draco, Ursa Minor
Visible, along with Orion's belt and bow,

Bent by an arrow, notched forever.
And when it flings will this sky be unhinged?

Andromeda our terra firma?
I have fewer and fewer names for what I can see.

On the earth, in the nearby field
I think I hear horses stirring the limbs

Of October's bearing Osage Orange, of Walnut,
Of scrubby Virginia pines, of Juniper.

The horses' ridged backs, knobs of spine
Buried between fat flanks, find planet light, and shine.

My eyes transfixed, my feet shuffle pebbles,
And the sun is not far behind my journey.

I can see my hands and my feet when white
Laces blink. Keeping to the path, I skirt the dew.

Above me, this sky opens in the moment, an immense
Thought still caught in creation's throat.

May a poet still use words like these? I know
The answer is no.

Pauletta Hansel

The Road

Where I'm from, everybody had a flower garden,
and I'm not talking about landscaping—
those variegated grasses poking up between
the yellow daylilies that bloom more than once.
Even the rusted-out trailer down in the green bottoms
had snowball bushes that outlived the floods.
Even the bootlegger's wife grew roses up the porch pillar
still flecked with a little paint, and in the spring
her purple irises rickracked the rutted gravel drive.
Even the grannies changed out of their housedresses
to thin the sprouts of zinnias so come summer
they'd bloom into muumuus of scarlet and coral
down by the road.

Now driving that road that used to take me home,
I think how maybe it's still true.
Everybody says down here it's nothing
but burnt-out shake and bakes and skinny girls
looking for a vein, but everywhere I look
there's mallows and glads, begonias in rubber tire
planters painted to match, cannies red
as the powder my mother would pat high
on her cheekbones when she wanted to be noticed
for more than her cobblers and beans.
Everywhere there's some sort of beautiful
somebody worked hard at, no matter
how many times they were told
nobody from here even tries.

Facts About Grandmothers

>   *(Margaret to Etta, 1596-1991)*

One granny was a granny woman
along the York River
tending after birth in 1646,
one whose *water scalded her*.
One granny came unbidden
to my birth in 1959,

to tend her daughter
at the breaking of her water,
only to see her swept away
behind cold metal doors.
Most grannies raised the next of them
along the banks of hungry rivers.
They died of cancer, consumption, paralysis,
causes unknown.
They outlived husbands, children,
died before they were grannies at all.
They died with nothing,
died with livestock, jewelry, servants,
slaves. One granny
willed to her grandchildren
another child's granny,
another granny's child.
Three grannies left me photographs,
each with sunken cheeks and unreadable eyes.
I have no words
writ with a granny's hand.
A mark upon the page—ix ye sign.
One granny snored beside me
in her featherbed, her Indian hair
unleashed from its Pentecostal coil.
One granny shot an Indian with his own gun.
Four pairs of grannies shared each other's names.
One granny gave me hers,
and combed her fingers through my feathery curls.
I have laid my hands on stones above four grannies' bones.
Three grannies—more—
lie beneath salt water's rising tide.
Two grannies—mother, daughter—
lay beneath the same man's—husband, father—
grunt and thrust,
pushed from their bodies
that same man's sons.
Some grannies I don't know,
I don't know,
I don't know.
Not even a name.

William Harmon

Versicles

Somebody's old glove
Much run over in the road
Giving the finger—

. . . . .

What keeps me humble?
That crablouse attached to my scalp
When I was born.

Marc Harshman

Small Town, West Virginia

after Tomas Tranströmer

Town is closed today.
Smokeless chimneys, rain-slicked and empty streets.
I don't know why.
It hasn't asked much of me lately.
Like a fever, perhaps, it will pass, open again tomorrow.
The sun glints on the damp pavements
        and a few windows shine
            in the dark face of the warehouse.

I haul myself up the ridge
        to where my words race, then tumble, soundlessly
            over the cliff.
I hold myself close, and listen,
        and with my back to the wind,
            lift my arms, and try again, say
                the word *feather*, say the word *soar*.
The quiet answers with its own names.

I should do this more often,
        and whether or not the peopled world below
        goes on or not,
        this older world remains
        as these sun-drenched warblers testify
        with their reedy whistling.
I should more often do, at least, this much.
I should this much do, as if even the least of us mattered.
I lift up a stone and watch it soar.
I can almost see where its feathers begin . . .

Not All That Much

It wasn't all that much, you might say, nothing
        to write home about, just
        a heavy green floor of ground cedar and springy peat
        littered with reindeer moss and lichened stones,
        here and there evidence of flying squirrels,
        muddy punctures in the cloth of the moss,
        and coyotes, their ropey, black scat,
        and overhead a canopy of
        birch, beech, and red spruce,
        the latter the local's yew pine whose pointed, black lances
        bristle along the ridgeline.
Not that much, perhaps, and our only companion,
        a still and remembered, peculiar silence,
        a silence with weight,
        and the kind of karma you can't get
        from books, or gurus, or poets.
I lean against the gray birch,
        or sit on the white sandstone,
        or kneel in the faded leaf litter, and pray
        without thinking God or prayer,
        pray by simply staying put, letting
        time fall away from me, letting
        thought fall away from me
        until it's just me, and this, these
        things that don't seem all that much
        but are.

Melissa Helton

I Wouldn't Think Any Less of You

if you admitted that actually,
some babies *are* ugly, if you admitted
you once called in sick at work saying
your dog had broke its leg when it hadn't,
or that you secretly wished for a disorder
so you'd have an excuse for the way you act.

I wouldn't think any less of you
if you told me you were growing a little
pretentious about butter after watching
a *Youtube* video of this old French
place and its old French butter-making ways
which seemed mesmerizing and romantic.

I wouldn't think any less of you
if you said you couldn't respect your alcoholic
cousin, or if you said you don't think
you loved her anymore but you visit anyway
to spend time with her arthritic border collie
and to make your uncle happy.

I wouldn't think any less of you
if you stole from Walmart and refused
to use their self-checkout because
you're not going to provide free labor
to increase their profits when they
won't pay their employees a living wage.

I wouldn't think any less of you
if you wished you were queer because men
can be so scary, that you're tired
of calculating which seem to be humans,
and which monsters, while you're out
looking for someone to love.

I wouldn't think any less of you
if you were near phobic of herringbone,
or that when that certain country song
comes on over the ceiling speakers,
you walk out of the restaurant or hardware
store to wait until it's over.

I wouldn't think any less of you
if you said you weren't afraid to die,
that the idea of quietly sleeping in the dirt
wrapped in a quilt your momma made
is an alright end to your story, that you don't really
expect you'll miss anyone, not even me.

Upon Driving Away from Your Hometown

This sadness is a shark,
   ancient and without bone,
   cartilage allowing it to squeeze
   into small spaces.
This sadness is a shark.
   It has to keep moving to stay
   alive. It never sleeps.
This sadness is a shark.
   It sprouts extra rows of teeth
   year after year.

This sadness is a blackberry thicket.
   It grows unpampered
   and is near impossible to eradicate
   once it has set root.
This sadness is a blackberry thicket.
   A random burst of spike
   and thorn, little dark jewels
   hidden in underbrush.
This sadness is a blackberry thicket,
   always tart enough to draw
   your mouth, made palatable
   by deliberate silver-lining sweetening.

This sadness is a zoo,
   expensive and gaudy, leaving
   feet aching and shoulders sunburned.
This sadness is a zoo,
   the wild recreated in pretend
   containable habitats. Even the animals
   can tell the difference.
This sadness is a zoo,
   open 9-5 today, free parking
   with your membership. Stand outside
   the glass and gape. Point your finger
   when you spot a living body.

Raye Hendrix

Any Coyote

Like tongues of fire on the mountain
the red tails of fox squirrels flicker

as they run from our presence—
the crunch of my boots, chaotic joy

of my large yellow dog who follows
them like smoke. This morning

my father sent me out with a rifle.
We're meant to be searching

for something but I can't remember
what. The woods are like that. Dark

spokes of evergreen wheel overhead
to obscure all that lives beneath

and above—their needles sew away
the sky. Behind us an owl

questions everything, and in the clear
cold air the boulders—without

their spring muffle of moss—repeat
the inquiry. Today even the wind

won't whisper its guesses through
the bare branches of trees less fortunate

than pine. The long ghost of its body
quick and gray, a coyote wisps

through the brush. My dog
pursues it out of sight, returns

with one of our missing chickens hanging
broken from his jaw. Yes, that's right:

my father sent us after the coyote—
my dog to find and I to shoot it—

while he repairs the plundered coop.
The coyote, he said. By which he means:

any coyote. My dog leads me back
to the coyote's den: a hole full of red

feathers, gnawed bone, the old blue collar
of someone's missing cat. No—I mean

anyone's cat. The mountain
doesn't know any of our names.

Jane Hicks

A Poet's Work

> "The aim of the poet and the poetry is finally to be of service,
> to ply the effort of the individual work in to the larger work
> of the community as a whole."
> —Seamus Heaney

For Jeremy Davidson
2001-2004

Spare me the post-modern pout
about dog piss in the gray snow
near the subway entrance,

Or the academic angst over a shaft
of light like the one in a scriptorium
of an obscure Tuscan monastery.

Witness meth labs that spring up in our rural
gardens, a quick pay out or fuel for three
piddly jobs, two to live, one to pay daycare.

Recount farm foreclosure, our food modified,
altered atrocities, the domain of agribusiness
conglomerates, the family farm a curiosity.

Clutch the child who sobs silently,
her mama a nurse in the Guard, called up,
goodnights from a webcam image from Basra.

Behold mountaintops removed, laid low by greed,
hollows filled, wells poisoned, God's majesty
flattened, fit only for Wal-Mart, the new Ground Zero.

Support the woman who tosses in fitful sleep as a dozer
strips her mountains under cover of dark, who wakes
to thunder, boulders tumbled upon her baby in his bed.

Revile the judgment of life's worth in coal country,
a fine levied at fifteen thousand, less than the price
of a good pickup truck, how the law measures a baby's life.

Spare me the post-modern pout, the academic angst.
Travel ruined roads, moonscape mountains, failed farms
and ponder judicial disregard, mindful
of a poet's work, the naming of what matters.

Deep Winter

for Silas House

The dark solstice sleet stings,
December sketches glittering glyphs
on a slate sky. Silence falls easy, settles
at snow start. Snow has a sound,
I know this. It begins as quick spiders
on fallen leaves, starched curtains stirring.
Then snow becomes soft wings,
moth applause, blossom-rain
on orchard grass. Heavy feathers
of stern snow pile in resolute rows
by fence rail and frosty road. Bare limbs
shake loose their covers as sibilant evening
stirs, stretches, and sighs, the sound
of snow lost to the wind.

Dust

I am teary this morning, not with longing
but with the dust of dying summer, whirled up in the wake
of county machines trying to tame the yellow ditch rows,
trailed by tractors as farmers glean the last scant hay
as a wrinkled veil reddens the ridge top, a perjury of promised rain.
My ridge life perched near woods, rusty dogwoods, and fox bark
is my grandfather's life far from paved road bustle,
my road is paved, but my well tastes of limestone
crisp and cold, like his well where we drew
long plungers to swirl in galvanized buckets.
In dad's house on the raw edge of suburbia, town water
smelled of bleach and hot tar, not bedrock.
Past our house at the end of the street, town dropped off
to deep hollows and steep fields, a bridge to where night
dripped like fire when the rains still came.

Felix culpa

Too wet to plow, we climbed
the ridge where Jack-in-the-pulpit
and Fire pinks fringed woods' edge.

Spent of love, he lay crucified
across my Garden Path quilt, hat low
on his brow to shade the sun.

Stretched beside him, I thought his feet
the prettiest I ever saw on a man. Upright,
they framed the wet bottomland below.

Blue veins traced a mystery map
to his toes. I wiped them with the long towel
of my hair, woke him to adoration.

A cast of hawks rose on a draft
towing spring in their talons,
snaring us in a greening spiral.

I think of those elegant feet,
boot-shod, mud-logged, entrenched
below shell-plowed, fallow fields.

Summer fades, no word comes, I soon
harvest what he sowed before following war.
Tiny feet beat sad tattoos under my heart.

Preacher calls me Magdalene. I refute
him, knowing her wiser in her choosing,
blessed by loving, not damned.

Thomas Alan Holmes

Awning

Beneath a beauty parlor,
Cullman Awning Company,
My dad's own self-employment,
Lay only small town blocks away
From our home, just far enough
To warm up his truck's engine.

A younger man, most evenings,
On worknights, after supper,
He parched peanuts, filling home
With rich smells of toasted shells;
Earthy, red-skinned roasted peanuts
Tasted good when dropped in Coke.

From corrugated metal
And aluminum square tubing,
He built made-to-order awnings
Bearing fifty years of weather
All across north Alabama.
That bandsaw hurt his hearing
After years; after years
My teeth clamp on edge
As I think of shrieking metal
And imagine pampered
Ladies seated under
Space Age plastic dryer
Domes in preparation
For their Pentecostal
Towering hair. AquaNet
Never filtered down enough
To contend with musty
Metallic tang and sawdust
I swept up those special days
That I could go with Dad to work.

When his time comes, and by God
I am not prepared for it,
I would shell him like peanuts
And strip his old man hull
To free his blond-haired, red-armed
Self whose blue eyes wink at me
Beneath angel floss white brows.

Remember Roni Stoneman

Do you remember Roni Stoneman
On our old black-and-white Zenith,
Picking banjo every Saturday
Just after Dad got home from work
And you were broiling club steaks
That our butcher, Mr. Dutton,
Sawed from short loin just that morning?
In the kitchen, dicing peppers,
Some Vidalias, some tomatoes
For a salad, Old Dutch dressing
Sweetly mixed up with my ketchup
On fake Dresden-themed blue dishes
That we bought from Sears and Roebuck
That first summer we cleared money,
That first summer I was mowing
So that Dad no longer had to,
Before dates took weekend evenings,
Graduation took me further,
Then my job so many miles away
From syndicated bluegrass
And fresh-showered weekend evenings
When a day of rest starts early
And a blessing is a table
With someone at every chair?

Oh, Mama, Roni Stoneman,
Wearing pigtails, a grown woman,
Slightly wall-eyed, slightly buck-toothed,
And buckdancing between breakdowns—
Was it meant to be a costume,
Was it Sadie Hawkins cuteness,
Like some Minnie Pearl theatrics
Before *Hee Haw* turned her ugly,
And she put her banjo down?

I remember Roni Stoneman,
Motor oil and sweat-through workshirts,
Porter Wagoner and Dolly
Hawking dishcloths in detergent,
Sharp-scent dandelion, horsenettle,
Martha White self-rising flour,
Flatt and Scruggs, and Wally Fowler,
Prell and Go-Jo, Zest and Lifebuoy,
Pressure cookers, canned tomatoes,
Gasoline and garden hoses,
Six-day workweeks as we knew them,
Spending Saturdays in summer
Finding rest about sundown.

Ron Houchin

Belief in Soap

At seven, I understood the power in those white bricks
that smelled like cleanness and death.
They kept me safe from the Devil, next to God.

Of course dirt was the world and soap invented by Jesus.
When I sat in the waters of Saturday nights watching
the Ivory float by like a small benevolent barge,

I understood the good Grandma had made me taste.
Truth was harsh and somehow the color of milk.
That which I brought to the rough cloth

was anti-soap. I touched the bar like a base.
Each drop hanging from the faucet showed the world
dangling like fruit no one picked, that dropped into dirt.

Camping at Greenup Locks and Dam

This river has only a throat.
It practices Germanic vowels through
the concrete fluting of the dam.
We think we are fishing in gray-green water
at evening, Zebco lines pissing from our hands
past the swollen torsos of locust and cottonwood
frozen there like last month's murdered.

The wind tries to unturban the towel from
your washed hair and nothing
wants to be where it is.
God forbid either of us catch a fish
and try to reckon its origin.
As it grows late for a Sunday, I question
our Mondays and the machine that brought us here.

And I have no patience
for these boulders thrown about
like pocket change from the moon. I watch you
crouching at the end of the dock trying to think
through a confusion of filament and I want to lick
the sand from that biggest rock
for its understanding of time.

If the World Were a Coalmine

We would be blackness of air and night,
our lives playing out like that of mine ponies
in a Balzac novel, living, dying without a moment
of ease or free breath—our folk music, timbers
creaking; and our art, a guileless dream of light.

Our living, our work, and our walks,
like long trips through the house when the power's out.
Our sleep, like waiting for a cave in.

If the world were a coalmine, we would be the coal,
our fate in the black tunnels surrounding,
bituminous souls that coalesce with smoke
and sleep in the same poor bed with our cousin earth.

Singing to the Fan

Though we left the big window fan
on, slicing the air thin, all night,
mornings were still thick and stirless.

I'd hum "Wildwood Flower" into
it's thrumming heart—green
harmony from unruffled trees.

Close enough to conspire,
the way singers breathe as one,
we wove our song.

A warm world fluttered in my face.
I had no love with so sweet a breath
or way of repeating my name.

I close my eyes, now as then,
and there's a dark whirring, a whiff
of mint and mountain laurel,

distant coal smoke, laughter
from the kitchen. I hear
another chorus before it begins.

The First Christmas I Remember

Huntington, WV, 1956

had nothing to do with bicycles or Lone Ranger gun sets.
It had little to do with anticipating surly uncles
and quarrelsome aunts or a happy little bearded man.

Looking out our front windows, I watched the street
and houses disappear under snow. At one point,
I couldn't see beyond the porch, and the ice

on the windows threatened to do more than frame
the world. That's the way it was in that house.
Any distance from the stoves in December was chilling.

I was forced to go to the Nazarene church and watch the singing
about the appearance of a star. It happened every
year. It was no longer news. I couldn't see the good.

Mostly, I remember waking one night near the 25th
when the wind stopped and I could almost hear
the clouds evaporate. I scuffed to the big window

in the freezing front room and rubbed the curtain on the glass.
It was clear. My feet were stinging, but I had to open the front door
and tiptoe onto the porch. The air was whiskey, and the sky

had turned to black glass. Even the three ruts of ice in the road
were lost in the anonymity of more snow. But my memory flashes
on the fox that stood bewildered among blanketed

houses. I've longed to know what he thought he saw
standing there trying to find his forest, his red fur brighter
than snow, like blood on the throat of a lamb.

Silas House

Double Creek Girl

for Sylvia Woods

They don't expect much out of girls
raised on Double Creek.
Up where the pines hang low
over the road like a tunnel
and the sun doesn't rise
until the rest of the world
has had its coffee and forgotten
the magic of morning already,

up where evening mist breathes
over the clean graveyard
and gardens with their straight rows.
They don't think girls from a place
like Double Creek will amount

to anything at all.
Especially when you were little
and they had pictures of girls
like you in all the magazines.
Life and *Look* and *Time*. Once
a man from *National Geographic*

came and took pictures up there.
Girls in dresses their mothers made
them and stringy hair, hollow-
eyed, hungry-eyed, sad-eyed.
But you defied them, Double Creek girl.
You showed them. Every time
you opened a book and drank it up
like spring water. Each time you read

a poem and closed your eyes at the end,
savoring it like a good hunk
of cornbread, seeing it
like an azure sky, tasting
the words like the wet in a bloom
of honeysuckle. You showed them
when you listened to every word
the teacher said and walked
that commencement line and took
your degree from the hand

of the professor who was
secretly one of them. He never
thought you could do it. But you did.

See here, our Appalachia, our
bone and blood. Listen, our
Double Creek girl: you are
what happens when we know
that God lives in between
the pages of books and at the tips
of pencils and on the sharp
edges of notebook paper.

That's something they'll never know.

At the Opening of *Coal Miner's Daughter*, Corbin, Kentucky, March 27, 1980

The line snaked down the sidewalk
all the way to the Piggly Wiggly.
People stomped their feet to stay
warm and plumes of white puffed
out of their mouths. When snow started
falling, a little murmur of joy
escaped the crowd. My aunt, Sis,
was not fazed by the cold.

She drew hard on her Winston and eyed
me, leaning down. Blue eye shadow,
chipped fingernail polish, hands worn
by waitressing and too much loving
and factory work. "Are you froze
to death, baby?" Yes, I was. I didn't care
if it *was* Loretta Lynn. Why

did we have to wait so long anyway?
Sis plucked the cigarette from her lips
and looked me right in the eye.
"Because," she said. "She's one of *us*."
Before that I had never known there was an us,
but ever since the world has been divided in two.

Rebecca Gayle Howell

No One Was Born Here

Across the white highway, dogs drift unmoored
Silver-tipped seagrass, but no cactus. An offing
of shopping plazas, their harsh light and low roofs.
That's the way with drought; first dissent,
a worm belief that one place could be another.
I bet it feels good to twist a head of cotton
clean from the stem's fat and browning boll.
I bet it feels good to stand in irrigated rows.
Most people smile around town. Big, too.
We're so pleased to meet you. But we met last week.
Days, gone with a handshake. The thing about dogs is
they actually need us. Otherwise they're half animals,
scabbed raw with mange, scared of the noonday sun.
As for me, I came here to keep my mouth shut.
Did I mention the dust?

Every Job Has a First Day

Slade was pulling minnows out of the dry river
the day we met. Puddles, more or less, was what
was left. But what could live wanted to and tried,
treading narrow circles, a glide of brittle fins.
He wore those rubber boots, though the sun was
an anvil, and very little wet; he smiled, I remember
that, his nickel smile right at me, his fingers
letting fall the small fish muscles into a bag filled
with yellow tap. I didn't ask his name, or what
it was he thought he was doing, but we talked,
I listened as he taught me to relax the hand just enough.
They can smell, he said, the oils our pores release
when we tense to catch. You have to believe it,
he said. You don't mean any harm.

What Goes Around

Not all wells are tapped. Some draw sufficient
to run a hose to a house, the low sulfur cloud
a mark of the wet-mouth advantaged. As if that's
not enough, they buy the sprays in shades
like police-tape yellow or this-is-not-yours red,
so I can't believe The Kid who, in broad Tuesday light,
slinks under sills to unscrew nozzles and tug
the umbilical weight of rushing water all the way
to his mother's corroded truck bed, where they go
to work. She, bent over like she's burying a sin;
The Kid with arms raised revival, pouring whatever
don't spill at the air into their drought tank.
My mother, hairnet tied fist-tight at the back,
was made to cook; she left early, returned late,
and dark raced dark in her shift. That was the days
of commissaries, when sharing was plenty. The Kid
don't know those days. Love is funny, in that it's dead
but not dead.

David Huddle

Religious Life

Was a church in Glory River—
    nobody'd go
        except for those not thought
            to be of this place
                mostly because they went to this church—
            chapel they called it,
    plain old building
      needed paint,
needed steps fixed,
    boards replaced,
        weeds pulled, grass mowed, etc.
            & you'd think somebody'd
                bust out window panes
                    or maybe go contribute
            turds to the interior
              or get serious
                  & burn the place down
            we do that in Glory river—
    let the fire make a statement,
        & some of us thought
            a statement needed to be made
because a church says
    one thing & we say another
        & Charlie Dunford said he'd oblige
            the place with some destruction
                if we'd buy him a six-pack—
        which of course we did
           & helped him drink it, too,
before he went in—
      we didn't know what Charlie
          had in mind, we just shoved him
              out of the car & said
          Go do some harm, Charlie,
& he was good at that, Charlie was,
    a kind of harm-specialist,
        & so we waited out in the car to see
            the place go up in flames
                or Charlie come running out
            & snickering into his hand
        to tell us he'd be-turded the altar
or pissed on the kneeling cushion

or bashed up the pews
  or just toppled over
    the old pump organ they said
      was in there that an old lady played
        whenever they had their church in there
    which was about once a month
& then it was only like two families
Heldriths & Daltons
 & old lady Heldrith was the one played the organ
   & wasn't anybody in Glory River
     could stand that old bat
       but Ann Dalton rode the school bus
     over to Wytheville High School
  & she was pretty
& Mr. Bill Heldrith was a boss
at the powder plant in Radford
 & by God we wanted Charlie to do
   just the kind of mischief that would tell them
    they were dirt like us, we knew
      they threw their trash out like we did
    we knew they drank till they puked
   we knew they diddled & cheated
& stole in their own ways & still they thought
they could go to that church
 & think they were so much better
  than we could ever dream of being
    & so by God we wanted Charlie to turd
     their church or smash it up bad
       or burn it like an old truck
      with gasoline poured all over it
   we wanted to see those flames rise
   & whiten the sky over Glory River
 but what we saw
was a shadow trickle down the steps
  of the place & slow as an old turtle
    on the river bottom
      weave its way toward Joe Lee's car
     where we waited
       & then it was Charlie & he was
   standing by the car not saying
   anything
     & finally I said, What
did you do, Charlie?
 & he said, Nothing.
& we all said What?
  & he was quiet for a while,
& then he sighed & said,
  You all go ahead in there
    & do what you want,

                    I'm going home
                              & he headed up the road,
                                    which wasn't like Charlie,
          who always wanted a ride,
                    but we didn't come out that night
                              for nothing to happen,
                                    so we go in, almost running
                                              we're so crazy to rip that place up
                                    & we slide in the front door & in
                              another door & all of a sudden
                    we're just standing in the aisle,
          like we'd come to church
                    on Sunday morning
                              except it's dark with a spooky light
                                        beaming in through the windows from the stars
                                              or the moon, someplace I can't say
                              & I can't even tell you why we shut up
          right then, the four of us
                    & Hal pulls out his pecker—
                              we hear the zipper & we know to stand away
                                        & Joe Lee strikes a match
                                              & Gilmer does, too, & I pick up
                                                        a stack of hymn books from a pew
                                              to throw them through the windows
                              just before we run
                    & we wait to hear Hal's piss
                hit the floor
& it doesn't
          & Joe Lee's match burns his fingers
                    & Gilmer shakes his out
                              & I set the hymn books back where they were
                                        & we don't say anything
                              we just turn around & walk out of there,
                    almost tiptoe
          don't even slam the door
or stomp down the steps
          & we get back in Joe Lee's car,
                    quiet, closing the door soft
                              & Joe Lee drives us straight up
                                        to the school house where we all four
                                                  had to go through seventh grade
                                                        because they made us—
                                        & even here, in this hateful place
                                   it's not necessary
                    for us to talk,
          we know what we want
& we do it
we burn that hell-hole school house
          right flat down

                        to the ground—
                                it's two days before it stops sending up
                                        little flames & another week before you don't see
                                                smoke coming up—
                                field of stinking black ashes is what it is
                                        which is just what we want
                & some will tell you doing a thing like that
will make you feel bad,
        but that's not so—
                        we feel fine, Joe Lee & Gilmer & Hal & I—
                                we'd by God do it again
                                        if it was another school house
                                                around here & the other thing about it
                                                we know is that leaving that church
                                        standing & unharmed
                        was what we had to do—
                no choice about it
because Hal says God came right up beside him
                & whispered, Hal Jones,
        don't you piss on my church!
                                & Joe Lee says God told him not to drop the match
                                & Gilmer says him, too, word straight
                                        from God into his ear
                                                & I don't say any of that
                                        I just shake my head
                                                don't say anything,
                                because I don't want to tell you—
                how scared I was, I was
old man scared & little girl scared
I was animal scared
                I felt like I'd set one foot
                        through the front door of Hell
                                & something had a hold
                                        & was tugging me
                                                further inside
                                        but when I set those hymn books down
                        I knew I was right back here
                in Glory River
        and I'd be all right
I'd be just fine.

Not True

is high praise
in Glory River
because everything's
pretty much true

here in the Valley,
boys bashing their
skulls in falling
off tool sheds,

suicides rising
from the dead,
houses unpainting
themselves, car

wrecks of every
variety, decapitations,
drownings, fights
with rocks, knives,

baseball bats, kitchen
utensils, & most
especially stories
about the unlikely

& comical & often
unappealing antics
of the love-struck.
It's all true,

says Jeep Alley,
spitting a stream
of brown juice
just to the left

of your shoe-tops.
*Tell me something
that ain't & I'll
fucking marry you.*

Hilltop Sonnet

Who visits this high meadow, lawn of the dead,
   to see blue and bluer mountains that rise
      out of the west; to converse with the crows,
         great-winged turkey buzzards, black kites riding
            thermals in seamless silence; to greet deer
               here at twilight grazing near the wood's edge;
                  to scare the huge groundhog that lives inside
                     the brick-walled graveyard: Who moves through this space?

        A yellow dog leading a deaf old man
     who likes to talk, a girl and her boyfriend
    who sit atop her car's roof murmuring
   quietly, two off-leash labs ignoring
  their shouting owner, a policeman who
parks up here to feel lonely, guarding the wind.

Charlie G. Hughes

Where I'm From

after George Ella Lyon

I'm from the muddy swirl of Cecil's Creek,
the polluted currents of Salt River
where bare-assed boys swam beneath
dead hogs, flood-beached and bloated
on the limestone shelf of the river bend.
I'm from the aroma of new-mown hay,
tobacco hanging in the barn, manure
spread on the spring fields, earth freshly turned
by the John Deere plow.
I'm from Joseph's Chapel Methodist Church, sunlight
through its bare windows on Sunday morning,
the drone of Brother Ed Delaney's sermons,
those revivals on summer evenings,
all the things I never believed.
I come from Farmall tractors, New Idea mowers,
International Harvester hay balers, sweat
and chaff, straw and hay.
I'm from alfalfa and livestock,
my Jersey cow, the black lamb rejected by the ewe,
and white leghorn fryers, necks wrung on Saturday,
fried on Sunday, the milking parlor and hay loft,
pastures and the shade of maples in the yard.
I come from the Warm Morning stove, darkness
beneath piles of quilts, a gas heater
in the bathroom, ice in the bathtub.
I'm from poison ivy and Calamine lotion,
Luden's Wild Cherry cough drops, castor oil
in the Frigidaire, and my mother's hand
on my forehead.

Lament for Mountains

Look, the night
is upon us.
The mountains have come

to darkness
and the last deer has given
itself to the hunter.

The trees are dissolving
into their own shadows.
The trumpet vine

has sounded its final call,
and the tap root
of the honeysuckle is pulling

its last breath of fragrance
from the earth.
The fox has no truck

with the rabbit
and the squirrel in its nest
dozes and twitches

while the bobcat
sharpens its perfect claws.
To have learned anything

in this life is to listen.
Still, no one hears
the blacksnake swallow

the robin's blue egg.
The cricket has ceased
its raspy saw

and there is no whisper
of water
from ephemeral streams,

nor any owl
or whippoorwill calling
in this dark.

Jannette Hypes

Raking

for Stephen L. Gardner

To clear this land could take months.
Readying for winter, so leaves won't freeze
then mold in the thaw of spring, I row
through this backyard pushing piles
large as my car street-side. Red-browns
on top, wet-black underneath, heavier
than they ought to be. Trees are empty,

even of birds. Shoulders tighten, burn;
palms tingle in spots sure to whiten, peel,
leave skin rich-pink and ripe to air like grass
paled beneath leaves: newborn and dying

together. In this place, this half-worked
yard of bare oak and splaying dogwood,
everything speaks your distant and holy
language: glass chimes clink, catch sun,
dazzle bark with bending light. A ribbon
of blackbirds finds wind, glides away.

Late June

for Stephen L. Gardner

More than seven months since I lifted your hand
from the hospital bed, my thumb petting its warm
dry back, rougher than imagined, trying to coax
out the coma through the pores, summer arrived:
heat, before the Solstice, pouring in on the ferns,
exploding the lilies, open-mouths of spotted petals,
stamen reddish brown as the psoriasis on your skin.

Because there is no gravesite to visit, headstone
to trace with fingers pressed in to carved out words,
I memorialize you often and in strange places: once
my tires crunched an ice cream cone, sweet and brittle
on asphalt: I imagined ashes stuck in tire tread, traveling.

At night, curled in the hospital recliner, your breath
too rhythmic to be natural, I searched for the silence
I could sleep in. Some moments you were present
as someone resting; in others, the room was empty
of you: I questioned your consciousness, how much
you were seeing, hearing of this room full of wife,
mother, friends, me—somewhere between student
and daughter, never one and not the other.

In your last days I wondered if I was doing it right,
questioned the proper vigils to take: hand holding,
consoling, praying, reading Roethke—sure familiar
vibrations of words would reach, maybe even wake,
you. When they didn't, I went back to rubbing, this time
the thumbs, letting gravity and the natural bend
of your fingers hold my hand in return.

Now, when June turns to July and fireflies are lazy,
dotting the shadowy undersides of maple leaves,
I return to writing poems. It is what you taught me.
It keeps you close. Syllables bloom into stanzas,
wrap the page in pigment and ash.

Edison Jennings

Rainstorm

> The Lord sits enthroned above the flood.
> —Psalm 29

Lost in rural Georgia, we did Jesus
one better and drove on water,
hydroplaning gully-washers
churned up by mid-summer heat.
The Caddy shimmied in the curves
and fish-tailed down the straights,
past red clay archipelagoes
of tenant shacks and trailer-parks
rinsed opal in the shifting squalls.

We lunched on RC's, Scooter Pies,
and watched the wipers skim
momentary half moon vistas
lush with peach and pecan groves
whipped by drenching scarves of wind
while gospel stations ghosted by
then crinkled into static shards
and billboards asked if we were saved,
promised Hell if we were not.

The front condensed a midday dark
above the hootchy-koo Savannah,
holy-roller serpent lady
spawning creeks like mud-brown snakelets
curling through her tangled banks.
Shimmy, dear old Caddy, daddy's car,
shake and roll, old rattling gospel—
the waters came, we leapt like calves
across the rich and sinful south.

Spontaneous Combustion

> The Meadows Farm, Abingdon, Virginia

Later, you insisted on calling it a bush, but it was more like a stump,
though sure enough burning where it had gone punky in the middle,
and when you came upon it, you knelt and asked its name,

then took a pull on the flask that maketh glad the heart of man.
The liquor hit and you hollered: "You *am*? You *am* what?"
It was May, lambs and ewes in one field, heavy with wool and milk,

rams sequestered in another, butting curled horns, the two of us,
working the meadows, drinking whiskey, mending fence,
sipping fire that maketh glad the heart of man.

Appalachian Gothic

Come fall, the walnut's canopy is dull.
when despite the season's fanfare it turns
brown, droops, and sheds. Within two weeks, the limbs
are bare, my sidewalk draped in drab confetti
children shuffle through on their way to school.
And all around, the yellow birch, and maple
festoon the hills with gaud and decoupage
the roads in rain-glazed scraps of gold and red
lapped in jigsaw patterns, while day by day,
the light distills a blue so bright it burns
my eyes and graphs the walnut's screen of stems
into a tracery that holds the sky
like bits of glass, no two alike, a globe
within a globe, both made from what we breathe.

Apple Economics

for A.B.F.

Though livid and salacious, supermarket Red Delicious
don't deserve the name. But after bagging two or three,
I think of old-stock Staymans that grew behind our house
in weather-beaten, bee-infested rows no one ever pruned,
and all we had to do was reach. I must have eaten bushels' worth
while balanced in the highest limbs. With one hand full of apple,
the other swatting bees, I watched swallows tip
and skim the tree-rimmed skies already hinting cold,
the windfall left ungathered, the fallow years that followed,
and now this bag of garish fruit my memory grafts to vintage
among the rows of grocery aisles that green to fields of praise.

Don Johnson

Grabbling

in memory of Bob Higgs

Longer than any of us in air
or common light could not breathe
he would stay down, fishing
by braille in pools darker
than the skins of old bibles.

On the green bank, closing
my eyes, I would dizzy myself
holding my breath, trying
to picture him blind and unhearing
while he probed under root knob

and rock. I would come back
always to the sheen of slow
current, an empty boat, birds
I made call, "rise up, rise up,"
till he boiled up sputtering

like a sinner the preacher
upstream had lost (it was always
Sunday). He would toss each
fish at his bucket, fling the occasional
snake at the bank without speaking,

then rest, wide-eyed, at the gunwale.
I could not know what he did
when he ducked under, but squinted
trying to learn each surface gesture,
back-lighted move. And once

I called out above the river's hum
to ask him, "How?" His answer,
"Get wet, boy." He didn't say
that each time down grows longer,
fish or no fish, that rivers

everywhere are one, never the same;
that when you finally let go
to float up clutching whatever
you can bring back, worldly light
explodes, barbed, uplifting, almost holy.

Scatology

in memory of John Maher

Circles of matted grass in the orchard
tell me nine deer slept last night beneath the brown husks
of cider apples, uncurled after the hoar frost fell,
and tip-toed uphill into the yellowed hickories.
In each bed, scat gleams like oiled buckshot.

"Scatological." The last time we talked, our first
conversation in thirty years, I said that word,
and you smiled, remarking how it came so naturally,
and how I'd changed since high school. You probably
knew what that word meant then. You, the most promising
of us all, eaten up with cancer at fifty-four.

Last night, watching the World Series, I thought
of our playing a whole seven games between
the Yankees and the Dodgers one night on your mother's
kitchen table. I won. Pitching Don Newcombe
in four games, my arm tired just throwing the dice.
Eighteen years later, in Honolulu, I read a small
notice in the sports pages listing Newcombe
as a patient in Kaiser Hospital. They thought
he might die from liver disease. I lived two miles
away and thought of visiting him, but didn't.

Two days after last Christmas, I'd packed the car,
and was ready to leave when my father called me
into the cold garage to help him free the rusted knuckle
on the tractor's stabilizer bar, confessing
as our hands curled around the pipe wrench
that in the last two years his body had turned to shit.

In the past two weeks, another friend, a colleague's wife,
and a student who had dropped my Keats course
died. Still another friend called from Boston
three nights ago to say he had disconnected
his father's life support after a heart attack and stroke.

I didn't visit you, either, John, didn't call or write,
though I knew you were dying in Atlanta. No words
seemed natural, and you were my age and promising.

Yesterday, the second morning in a row, while the deer
ghosted from the stiff grass in the orchard, I rolled over
in bed and awoke with the room turning around me,
not in dream, nor metaphor, but spinning, really spinning,
so that for the first five minutes after getting up I walked
around holding on to things. Holding on to things. Shit.

Almanac

Eastern phoebes nest
each spring beneath the eaves
of my riverside gazebo.
Beavers never leave,
working the slough
like an assembly line
the nightly heron
oversees. Skunks
(less like Lowells's
than Heaney's) embalm
the yard after dark
in every month
without an "r."

And every year when lilacs
flutter to the ground
"Slim," the black snake
reappears, slow and logy
from his knotted sleep,
easily caught,
cooperative when I
stretch him out
and measure him
by halves. He was,
finally, just my length
last May.

        I found
his sloughed-off skin
in August in the pool
at the foot of my waterfall,
the current making it
look alive.

        This spring
I'll change the game,
combing the weeds
at lawn's edge
with a stick, overturning
rocks and deadfall,
hoping to start him,
just after Easter.

I need to know
if that last growth
pushed him past me,

or if that wavering,
translucent shape
abandoned
in the pool's spill out
was all I had left
to measure.

Going to Chatham

My grandparents would take me to Chatham
each May, on treacherous Rt. 60 whose
hairpin turns, my grandfather said, made our
tailpipe visible through the rear window.
I looked. My Virginia cousins said "tote"
for "carry"; "carry" meant "transport,"
as in, "I'll carry you to Martinsville
directly." "Directly" meant "when I get
around to it." They toted water from
a well and lived in a cabin my great-
grandmother had built—kerosene and smoke,
tilted floors, and a dark stair where Myra,
an older cousin, kissed me.

                        Sunlight
probes every corner of that staircase like
a new cat, now that my brother and I
have lifted off the rusted metal roof
above the steps. Myra no longer lives
anywhere. The sadness of second-hand-
store mattresses and dust suffuses the air,
four decades of mice,
                    the fragrance
of honeysuckle that has carried me
so often to this bowed tread where we stood,
gone in mid-August heat and the thunder
of roof panels my brother shakes free
from the purlins like wet sheets. He needs help.
I'll climb on up and lend a hand—directly.

Isinglass

From the rubble that was my great-grandmother's
cabin I pull a four-paned metal window
smaller than the nine of hearts I turned up
stripping thick linoleum from the loft
where seven people slept. Lifted to light
it's like looking at the place through a thumbprint.
Age and layered swirls of mica blur the logs
we've tagged and stacked, the blackened chimney
stones, the ochre clay the road smears across
the hillside following this morning's rain.

Riding out from town men called on her
to read their futures, postponing trips
or planting early, their faith in her foretelling
measured by the single coin dropped in her palm.

Weary from three days of reclamation,
all I can foreknow is work, the ache
and strain of salvage: rebuilding on my land
the home my father and his father were
born in, striving with each log re-notched
and lifted into place to fathom how
that tired woman, late at night,
her children aloft, her dime or nickel banked
in a leather purse, alone and staring
at the tiny window in the stove,
could divine anything beyond the fire.

Judy Jordan

In the 25th Year of My Mother's Death

When the land shifts at day's end
and light sifts slow across field-fetch,
sun smoldering the tombstones cresting
the near hill in a small wind
ripe with weed and rot,

my mother, no longer caring
how day gathers into itself,
does not step from the back porch
to watch the blue heron
reel above the sedge, hover
then plunge into the rising mist.

Soon pines drop from the horizon;
lamplight doesn't seep across the lawn
through air no one breathes
which fills with the scent of apples
and the pitch of apples, snapped stem
and branch, to the root-buckled earth.

Bruised useless, they're not lugged out to the horses.
Geldings, sold to buy a casket,
don't stride shank-high through pond grass,
climb dripping from the banks
and shudder like a sleeper
shaking off dream.

In this ebb and sigh of dark easing all around,
no one searches the sky
for Antares burning the Scorpion's heart
or hears the bobcat's cry like a woman's scream,
exactly like a woman beyond any words.

Sandbar at Moore's Creek

Here where the creek culls sand and silt
and rises against itself

to become something else entire. . .
   here I bring my sorrows
like the delft-blue mussel shells,
fingertip tiny, most beautiful when strewn wide with loss.

If I ask anything of them, if I search for an opening
  as if they were stars in a sand-sky
that fade each night when the real stars
descend to drink the mirror of water,

what does the creek care?

It's day yet:
  light shaking down
through the hackberry branches,

sky colored raw bone,
  caught on the water's unbroken surface.

Those First Mornings Living in the Greenhouse

I'd wake with a fine snow of my own breath
laced across my face, ice half-inch thick on the plastic
I'd scratch a stranger's name in before pulling
myself from bed. Sun crawling over the pines
prismed through the interior frost and turned it to water
and fog—the greenhouse a phantom of itself. Mist rose,
ice melted, plants unfurled from their cold,
from their wet sleep, stretched and fingered steam
as the sun staggered higher and shafts of light
swelled and tumbled and skirred
through the drizzle. Then the plants blinked,
                                      fully awake,
their veined blood beat faster, and the greenhouse
in that slaked field
                  open like a bleached eye.

Waking in Winter

In the graying sky and the barn owl's rough-edged wing,
    in the field mouse's rising scream,
in one knuckled moment between sleep and waking,
    I slip from this cold bed to memory, to streets swabbed old pewter
and steam billowing from the oil-slick manhole covers.

    I'd go to those grates for their dank warmth
lowering myself one slippery ladder rung at a time
    into the breathing, clanking womb of the earth.
The tunnels stank of gas and old sweat and piss
but also, like in this torn and crumpled greenhouse,
    of water and moldy dirt.

Even so, why does my mind carry me there now
other than the burnt end of another year, a century stubbed out?
    Though I've risen from the steam tunnels
under the gray-hooded stare of a hungry day,
risen and can say puddles trap the moon in their icy mirrors
    and mackerel-dappled horses chew stalls to splinters
in the jewel boxes of their mouths
while luna moths wait cocoon-curled in broken branches and leaves,
    my body knows the true scope of winter.

Pain scurls up from my swollen ankles
    and lightning-blasts my scarred back,
the early soot-shot sky squeezes down
    over the stuttering pulse of the pond
where buried turtles, frogs, and snakes coil close against the cold.

So I'm homeless again though this time with an army cot
and a rope dangling from the greenhouse's steel rods.
    The rope I pull myself up with deliberate hand
over hand, as each spasmed pain scurries
the blue flutter of my soul to wait outside myself
and the sky empties and the billions of small lives wait
                          huddled in hunger's claw.

So much loss
        still the snow shudders and its heart beats once again.

The Greenhouse, Late September

Geese stir in their nests, guineas clatter toward sleep,
restless horses kick stalls already slumping
toward a crumbled groan back to root and loam.

This night without moon or stars, pond pale and gray
under the fog's frail hands,
                                land disappeared
so that whoever watches us from the far side of the sky wonders
  if we're still here.

Bats sweep the sky, lonely pond weeds shiver in the sloughs,
and fish float on the rocky bottom
                                             dreaming of spring.

In this approaching season, the second winter
in the greenhouse, I too dream of spring.

A cold-stunned leaf-hopper dangles
    from a blade of grass, silent leopard frogs
cling to cattails and a lost wasp swirls in the sugared rot-hollowed side of a pear.

Deer look up from the brush at the wood's edge
and coyotes,
                yellow eyes blinking on and off in their narrow faces,
disappear into the matted leaves and ferns
                                          dripping with today's rain.

The greenhouse is a dark mole on the skin of the night.

I crouch down on the mossy bank
breathing the wet air, the fish stink, the miasma of mud
while night folds my body into its arms
though there's nothing but dew and mist in the labyrinth of my veins,
                                          the catacombs of my lungs.
Then the moon breaks through clouds and fires a path
through the woods, crosses the trampled field to the sycamore's trunk

whose muscley ease of being in shafts of moonlight
reaches beyond anything a mere eye can see.

And the bloodied muzzle of the past
                                      and the sharp teeth of the future
  pad quietly
          toward the eerie glow of the distant city.

Marilyn Kallet

Global

Mother would have loved global warming.
A good Alabama girl, she resented
cold Long Island mornings
and my Brooklyn-born father,
who had dragged her North, toward snow.

She'd phone me long distance at college,
in those days a hefty bill, her voice
all tremolos: "The paper's calling for sleet
in Boston! Aren't you freezing?
Be careful!" October through April.

Even in her mink stole Cecelia grew cold,
colder, when Daddy's sister Marilyn
lay dying of cancer. Leaning
over her, Mother spat out,
"You brought this on yourself!"

"Now I have to drive all the way
from Long Island to Rockaway.
So much trouble because of you!"
Aunt Marilyn, thirty-three,
too sick to cry.

After Daddy died, Mother grabbed the urn,
headed south like a migratory bird,
rejoined her Montgomery girlfriends,
most of them widows by then.
She tended her roses and hibiscus.

But she couldn't escape having lived
in New York. No longer at ease
paying "the girl" eight bucks a day,
she upped the ante to thirteen, a scandal.
White-haired in the New South, was she warming?

When Mother grew tired of ashes,
she up and buried Dad, without the mourner's
Kaddish. She had loved him like fire.
Then she dumped him. Cold act,
something a poet or dictator might do.

Yet Mother was afraid of frost,
of losing her mother's lap,
her sunny toddler's lawn on Le Braun Avenue,
her native tongue of slow syllables.
There was a dry, icy spot

inside her, and if she wasn't careful
(she rarely was), it would burn
her stylized planet, freeze her motherhood
and Brownie Scouts, forty years of Sunday School,
teaching at the Home for the Blind,

ice down the tenderness my grandma had left her—
Grandma planted next to Daddy's urn
in Montgomery's Oakhurst, not far
from poor Hank Williams, so lonesome he could die,
over in the restricted Christian section.

Brushing Aside a Layer of Dust

Across the highway
    At Sweet Briar
They miss Eleanor,

Who walked into the James
    River
In February

 Unfound until March
    hanging
from an oak

Black hair streaming
Haven't we told
    This story?

Part of hell is
    The repeating,
Mud, stones, her face eaten—

"No one doubted
    it was
human"

Wayne
And Robert cleaned out

Her house   They are emissaries

From a world
   Of kindness
     Wayne frets about time

Not enough of it,
   He sighs.
I'm older than my friend,

My roots grey
   as stone.
Language looks up at me—

   Where are we going today, Marilyn?
Not to the river,

I say.

At the Beauty Salon

Suicide is not romantic, Wayne sighed, slumping in his chair.
She was hanging from a tree where the James River left her, he said.

Someone showed us the photo. Her hair was black and streaming,
Clothes ragged.

We had cancelled dinner that night.
We had told ourselves we needed to back up a little.

She was draining us.
She had mentioned killing herself the week before.

Now the guilt.
Could we have done more?

Something had eaten her face.
We'll get together soon for crabcakes, he says.

Leatha Kendrick

Tonight Weaving

Tonight, weaving in threads
I am far from the safe night
dark's held in the ridge's
halfway up the sky.
I don't find it here where light
steady hours blue and yellow.
its smell muddy. Cancer
part of my smell—absorbed
turns into just another way
I am diseased. Despair's alive:
stare down, if I have to.
even my own—an exercise
let fear get the better of me,
stench until it's dry
in the rose is only life
devouring the folded heart,
those toasts to more life!—
makes it clay, hard and yellow
for our demise. We are
weaves these threads?

on the afghan I've finished,
sounds of the creek, where
long embrace, the weight of earth
Whatever shape defines despair,
reaches, the sky breathing
Death's weight is earthen,
that keeps coming back,
in skin and hair, molecules—
of being. Healed,
anything alive I can leave behind,
I can contemplate a corpse—
worth imagining—if I don't
if I can sit through the sweet
bones, whitening. The worm
craving more of itself,
growing fat. And red wine—
takes the soft living organ,
at our center. O we are Passionate
as grass—who dies? I wonder. Who

Brought-On Bride

> *Perhaps you consider yourself an oracle,*
> *Mouthpiece of the dead, or of some god or other . . .*
> —Sylvia Plath, "The Colossus"

Land of the picturesque or cursed backwoods,
perhaps you are tired of being romanticized
or roughened, rising regular as furrows
on a brow, assuming the shape of a mind.

I've lived here twenty years now, ostracized
from level fields. I've labored to lay aside
the weight of you, to clear the woodbine,
sweetbriared rock consuming the horizon.

Caught in a leap against the light, your spine's
anarchy stockades the sky. Your twisting
fogs like blinders strap my sight. Burrow
for weightless morning, dark den to evening,

you've held me. The sun creeps arthritic
up your steeps to lay its warmth along the hip.

Morning of the Heart Test

Look, he says, and casts his arm
toward a fissure in the trees
where morning glazes the mown grass
of our side yard. And he means, See
how the sun gilds what is ours,
see how the grass I've mown receives it,
see how day keeps coming back
to this spot we claim.
                        And the green air
holds light, holds his delight in our life,
this place, the trees, sunlight-scissored
riven with it. What I see is something gray
caught in a branch—a plastic bag?
a tent of caterpillars?
                        What I see is
how the hills here squeeze
the sunlight to a narrow corridor.
What I see is his heart riven
by light, the possible blockages,

arteries shrunken as these shafts
of sun,
                      stopped as that stuck
plastic stops the sun. Is that gray bag
a sign? He stands at ease, glass of water
in his hand—for the time being
he's given up coffee. He's leaving for work.
At noon we'll drive out of this valley—
highways funneling toward the city's
heart, the tubes, IV's and pre-op,
the eyeless machines that will look to see
if his way is clear.

A Lesson in Love Unleashed

She's gone, he says. Our back yard no longer swollen
with that raspberry dog's freckled noise,
short barks and long wails—the chewed-on wood
of the leaning dog house bare of her clamor,
cedar chips cold inside. *It's Lucy*, he says. *She ran away*.

Spring floods cut and gully fields,
move debris—even a body, says the TV news—
150 miles downstream. Flood waters quench house fires.
Many waters cannot quench love, Solomon said,
my husband's voice funneled a hundred miles
through air and wire into the gray block
walls of my office, thirteen stories

above the flooded ground. He loved that dog.
Floating past my plate glass window,
bloated by time, every past love, lost dog—
yes, I think, even in their distorted flesh,
I still desire what's gone. What I'm leaving.

Lisa Kwong

Tai Shan, Canton Came to Radford, Virginia

At home, there was an ancestor altar in the back room:
framed red signs in Chinese and tarnished brass pots filled
with dirt and burnt incense, stick men in half-hearted prayer,
and a small black and white picture

of a young man who looked like my father.
Eight years old, I asked, *Is this my dad?*
Ngin Ngin stopped her sewing machine. She told me
it was my real Ye Ye, my father's blood father.

Her face sad and static-crackling like a grainy film reel,
she recounted how soldiers raided their house in Tai Shan,
how she clutched my father, only one year old,
how she saved the picture staring at me

by hiding it in the inner pocket of her pants.
This is all we have left of him.
Ngin Ngin gripped me by the shoulders.
Do not tell your Dad and Mom you know.

She lit a new incense stick in front
of his sole surviving image, made me stand
a few feet away, put my palms together,
then told me to bow three times and say,

Ye Ye, I have been a good girl.
Ye Ye, I have been a good girl.
Ye Ye, I have been a good girl.

Into a loop the incense curled,
unlike the limp, head-bent stick men
surrounding the freshly burned halo.
Ye Ye heard you. He is pleased.

Sundays I wore dresses sewn by Ngin Ngin
and went to Calvary Baptist with my American YiaYia.
There I learned: there is only one God, all others are idols.

Portrait of Appalachian Chinese Girls in Their Grandmother's Garden

Navigating Ngin Ngin's maze
of winter melon and zucchini,
my little sister and I simmered
under the late summer sun
where men zoomed by
in pick-up trucks,
hollering, *Chinese girls!*
like they were hurling
butter knives at our heads.

Ngin Ngin's neighbors,
college boys, liked to bake
themselves on their roof.
We hated college boys.
A swarm of them
worked at Dad's restaurant,
always reeking of sock sweat
and bourbon & coke.
They'd loll around while we ate
Chinese sausage rice, pointing
at us, their laughter, a chorus
of snot trumpets.

Inside the metal crisscross fence,
we meandered as two boys eyed us
from their shingled perch.
Standing up, they yanked
down their trunks, butts
facing us, yelled *Nyahhh!*
and out came their tongues.

The gourds I was lugging
dropped from my arms
onto concrete.
Sis, don't look!
Only four, my little sister stared.
She remembers now,
*I wondered what was hanging
between their legs.*
I remember the butts.

Childhood Fade in Litany

Behind the crisscross fence I thought home was a safe place.
The door's lock loosened. I questioned home as a safe place.
Ngin Ngin took insulin shots and I looked away.

Ngin Ngin had a stroke. Home was no longer a safe place.

Main Street emptied of traffic and home was a safe place.
Smashed beer bottles kept littering the driveway.
Desperate men played lottery at Pak-n-Sak.

I watched her bones become landscape.
Ngin Ngin had another stroke. Home was not a safe place.

Girls cried at the strangeness of incense.
Smoke tendrils crawled down our throats.
My sister and I secretly went to the graveyard.

I questioned God. I asked why home was not a safe place.
Lightning squeezed my hand and home became a safe place again.
I cried at Ngin Ngin's tomb and used to think home was a safe place.

My grief grew a noose. I touched the letters on the tomb.

Jeanne Larsen

Ardent Things

> *I plant the thorn and kiss the rose,*
> *But they will grow when I am dead.*
>   –Anne Spencer, "Any Wife to Any Husband"

To build a garden is to build
a life. A moonlit work that lives

when noisy days have ended. As this arbored,
weathered, well-pieced *Edankraal* remains.

Here, husband-friend-constructor found her always
reading, making notes that maybe made

her truest poem. Now brittle scraps.
Now ash. Martin came here, Langston, Thurgood,

to sit in day's cool by the lower-garden pond
where DuBois' gift, bronze Igbo head, keeps gazing

at flawless nymphea. Sterling, Georgia,
Marian. Mencken. Robeson. And Jim,

that bold ex-coloured man, releaser of her soul
for whom she wrote "amid these green

and wordless patterns." Then stood for justice.
For herself she chose *Aloha, Crimson Glory.*

Mothersday. American Pillar. Blaze.
Her plantings, this weedy summer, burgeon,

thick with thorns. She too so long
an *American Beauty* (rootstock Seminole, plantation

owner, this overcast Virginia, various
Africas) goes on. She too, again & still, within

her leafy half-world & a free far country's
eden-home, with words, in words, aflame.

Flowering Judases

In spring, they are manifold, self-sown

or planted: dispassionate pea-flower nubs,
plum-red buds like no human
blood. Rain-mercury branches

spindle toward heavenly brilliance,
a fiction refused them by dense pines,
towering sycamores crowding

creek's bank, north-facing road-cuts.
By the wages of sin against something
or someone said to be other than nature.

As if that could be. Their twigs
are called *spicewood*. Their inner skin
stains. The buds taste sharp, display soft

as peach-blow, as blossoms of apples
in songs about love or this season of kisses,
sacrifice, suppers with bitter herbs,

the palpable's small deaths. Its births.
Season of wrong-headed lusts
for transcendence. Then are earth's

woods a parable? Or a koan, twigs' tang,
the gold dye? And the crucial dear
friend, poor idealist—did he know

that oceans away, five-nerved hearts
would hang down & deciduous trees
would blush, boughs made weak

by his cast-off, lean, unseeded weight?

Scar Garden

Held back by cold, this spring's late.
Compressed between weathers

like flesh between flat
glassy plates for the x-ray, they speed:
cherry & crab-tree at once. Ghost-breaths

of pistils hold as small leaves move
forward into their world.

The Bradford's dull symmetry, limbs struck
by windstorm, ice, stands porous
in a new irregular beauty

& pain. Try to see

with the artist's eye how
last year's dry nest sits rough in the fork

& shows you *sleek bark*. See pollarded
trees' knots. See the hills' lesion
where among charred stumps,

houses arise like perennials.
See sinuous veins of freeway, its overpass,

cut through a valley once
roses & groves. As she sees it: the copious
shading, lithe lines

of those forms. And here, now,

her quarry. A keloid
on earth's chest—& alive.
Liquid blue.

Wrong All These Years—It Isn't

       soft April, but March, thin & particular,
that we require. Or dryly imagine we do. Also wrong

       (this is Daido roshi, though not his words) to believe
in the 1-way rapturous linear run after roll-out

       from gate, & that flight deck's sharp calibrations
tell truth. (They do, of course, as long as plane chooses

       to view these down-washing south Appalachians, splay
-fingered reservoirs, parking lots' black, impermeable

       lakes.) Wrong to clutch for what's bound
to be next: a lush month that scorns the unbinding

       way. Right now, it's Atlanta (where else) 5 parallel infinite
concourses serving as high-security hub of the 10

       -000 things. Serving well as any dimensionless point
on the star-strung mesh of hollow unfolding. The roshis

       say intimacy comes (not with sweet Zephirus, showers,
the woods' inspirations) with forgetting of rapture, that lie

       of an anxious serial liar, the self. With dissolution:
here/other, now/not. With just *this* as *yes* on the vergeland,

       a blink before touchdown, on March 9th when
there is no before, no day after, no spring—

       a white grove of Bradfords (up north at take-off,
only branches in 1st bud) laced with precision,

       past full bloom, pivots. Half petal, half green.
Uninvolved in *ekstasis* or motion.

Judy Loest

Sequence in Memory of George Addison Scarbrough, 1915-2008

Rooms

Your snug room in the nursing home
With one window and low ceiling
Will sometimes blur at night into one
Of the corn crib-sized shanty cubbyholes
Of your sharecropping childhood
Or the bartered dorm room at Sewanee,
Even, on good nights, your old bedroom
In the white cottage on Darwin Lane
Now locked like a closed museum,
A lifetime's artifacts moldering
But rocked in the creaks and eddies
Of old and brief affections. You dream
And startle awake but never cease,
Upon realigning your narrow confines,
To marvel that all your companionless life
You have been blessed to sleep in small rooms,
The near approximations of a warm embrace.

The Last Troubadour

All the women at the nursing home
Adore him—when have they ever had a man
Recite poetry, tenderly kiss their hand,
Eyes closed, and say with conviction
You make my going not too bitter.
When they trim his nails
They sit on the side of his bed
And say, if only you were ten years younger
And some days he imagines he is
Wearing again that bottle green jacket
He wore to the scholars' recitation,
Worn collar adorned with a polished rondure
Of blood jasper on a black string tie.
Some nights he is certain he can hear
The bells sounding curfew at Sewanee
And some young lothario gamboling
Along the serpentine paths
Life-drunk and singing.

Han-Shan on His Ninetieth Birthday

The white cottage gleams, the wavering round
Table a coruscation of cups and bowls and gold foil-
Wrapped caramels for the girl who brings the noonday meal.
In the window a sprig of jewelweed winks from the cobalt blue
Bottle pocketed some years ago in the village tavern.

All in all, not a bad fate, superannuated to the provinces,
And even though his green idyll is gliding to its close,
He never ceases to delight in molding the feckless plonk
Of the bamboo chime, swish and scratch of sparrows
In the neglected garden into a respectable iambic pattern.

Too frail-jointed now to greet Shi-Te at the gate,
He waits fastidious on the porch, gladdened by the hollyhocks,
By the bold bituminous stare of a crow poised on the eave
Like a glazed roof tile from the Imperial City. When it lifts,
He deems the clatter of wings a spirited applause,

A singular ovation cancelling that light tapping years ago
By the nonplussed citizenry of his hometown, an old opprobrium
As distant now as the carbon fragment wafting heavenward
At the same seeming speed a feather pirouettes
In freefall, an unexpected honorarium.

Passing Through

Suspended between sleep and China,
The Tang poets long abandoned
On the nightstand, I pause to watch the moon
Glide behind clouds, the same moon—imagine—
Lu Chi watched set over the edge of the forest
Seventeen hundred years ago when he stopped
For the night at the Monastery of Good Omen.

This old Cold Mountain book of songs
Delighted you until the last, reducing troubles
To a windblown gourd rattling from the eaves.
You are done now with cockcrow and evening bell,
All the etesian fluctuations in this moonspun world,
Leaving the last house of refuge, looking ahead
With still childlike wonder at the darkening pines.

Donna J. Long

Sago Mine Explosion

       January 2, 2006, Upshur County, West Virginia

Forty-eight hours in the dark, Weighted
with hope. The news just what no one knows, but

we listen. Silence is unbearable.
When twelve men are pulled from the deepest place

in the mine, a bad line translates "none are
alive" into "all are alive": None. All.

Like words sounding our desire. Imagine
thanking God for three hours before learning

the truth was a bad line

We who fear any way of dying try
not to imagine what a coalminer

knows in every descent: air thin, gases
invisible and lethal, whole tunnels

subject to a fragile physics. They knew.
Scribbled notes to assure loved ones dying

there, each exhale swallowing more oxygen,
was like falling asleep. No words for prayer.

Silence the blessing among them. Safe
in the truth that they are good men, generous,

even as air pinched off, without violence.
Imagine they all embraced, they clasped hands,

clicked lights out. Sure in the other side and
strong beyond the poisonous need to breathe.

Hanging Audubon's Flamingo I Discover a Late Poem for My Mother

> *Flamingos . . . obtain their food from the water and mud
> by means of highly specialized filtering structures . . . in
> the bill, which is held upside down.*
> —The New Dictionary of Birds

Audubon was wrong about the flamingo's smile.
He drew the bird with head askew. Could he not see
beyond those boa-pink feathers,
the slender dancer's neck? In truth,
flamingos know only how to frown. Lovely still

I hang his print, aim hammer at nail and neatly
smash my left thumb. Curse, laugh, aim again:
I think of you in this way.
We share narrow lips, yours drawn for thirty years
around a cigarette. Unless we caught you unaware,

in photos you smiled, a scarlet trauma that relaxed back
to a frown carved by early grief, slow dismay, disappointments
deeper than I could see, leaving, finally, questions
I didn't know how to ask. I worry the purple stain,
curing my thumb's dull ache until the pain splinters,

salting wounds a kind of proof I'm your daughter.
Twenty years needling grief
to keep you from being quite gone. Too late
I wonder what you hid, sitting hours
in the dark. I would ask now—how you grieved

when your mother died and if you liked birds or
simply believed knowing bluejay from mockingbird
from mourning dove was knowledge worth having.
I would ask which Elvis you would choose to post
on a stamp, and if the bitterness you wore taut as wire

recalled the one long muscle your waist was
when you married. How soon did you learn
young love goes wrong? And in one breath
children bless and condemn? I dream my wrists thin, squeeze
one uncharted genealogy of vein wide and blue, a river
flowing through valleys of bone, a river feeding

acres of sweet corn, alfalfa, the memory of a mare
we bought because she'd been barbed wire torn
fetlock to flank, shoulder to poll, because she'd healed
alone and bore with grace her ragged river of scar.
We share hands that look like work. Did you,

like me, dream your skin smooth, dream long

nails red at night, pink by day, white halfmoons
you could hold up to the sky, pretending
everything could be set right, turned round,
deserved the second shot, more careful aim, or

like me, did you love the well of blood
becoming wound, the ruin of skin, scars shaped
like stars, like wings, like every mistake ever made.

Denton Loving

Under the Chestnut Tree

What strange light filters through the sex
of a chestnut tree, leaves and catkins
blooming and softly falling, sickly-
sweet smell pressing into the warmth
of thick July. Whatever's dropped,
I heap into piles and set on fire.
Flames engulf, then slow to a smolder
that keeps the gnats at bay. Smell of smoke,
smell of sex. Sips of whiskey bewitch
shade into dusk the way burnt offerings
lure out stars and lovers.

Feller

This is the white oak that grew among other oaks and beech,
pine and hemlock. This is the tag that marks the tree.
This is the saw with whirring blades. This is the sawdust
that thickens the air. Praise the machine and the task it achieves.

This is the creak of the trunk splitting. This is the fracturing
of fibrous limbs as they bend and break. Praise the thunder
of the falling. Praise the quake of the earth accepting its weight.

This is the log hauled to the sawmill, cut into lumber, measured
by board feet. Praise the planks that will shape a dwelling.

This is the crown of the tree. These are the branches left to rot.
This is the wood's cellulose and lignin that replenish the soil.
These are the fungi, the beetles and the earthworms that flourish
in the oak's remains. Praise decay and decomposition.

This is the feller who brought the tree down. Praise the worker
and the work of felling trees. Praise the quickening pulse
and the flowing blood.

This is the first green leaf from last year's acorn, taking root.
This is the light that enters the woods and cleanses the wound.

Praise the wood and the woods. Praise the light, praise the wound.

Robert Wood Lynn

Not Hell

but damn it all froze over
anyway. This road winding
up Spruce Knob. Its ice not invisible
but almost, like two phones
back to back and video chatting.
By the time I realize this,
above the last switchback, I'm out
of ways to turn around
without sliding my little truck
over the side on down. Okay. O keep on
to the top. Keep wondering
if it's steep enough they'll never
find me, snow swallowing my tracks
as the ravine swallows me,
greedy birds scaring each other
off the feeder. Robert, you've done it
again embarrassed yourself
in front of whatever *they* there is
that looks for the foolish lost.
No one knows I am here, almost
not even me. I just wanted to be
the tallest living thing in West Virginia
today. And at the peak, even that
I fail: the spruces poking above
the crest of my observation tower.
Below, wisps of snow blow low
over the asphalt, turn over
with the shame of a lover
waking up alone. I'm here,
no one knows. O terror, O joy
of that. The sun spraying us dark
as it too slips off the ridge.

The River New

November in its shirt sleeves, drawing
its own precise undoing, leaf by leaf.
The way for decades I told people I was certain
I'd die in one specific place at one specific time.
Said it to strangers, lovers, anyone who'd listen.
It's still decades ahead but I drove here anyway,
just to check on it, how you would a stove burner
you remember using but not turning off.
When I got here the clouds hung exactly as low
as the gorge rises. I arrived to find so many people
getting married. Or not getting married
but pretending to, dressed like ancestors
and taking the photos they'll remember later
as the real thing. The mountains stay perfect.
Oranged less like fire, more like a man walking
in the woods hoping not to get shot. The past is all
how you remember it. Hunting season is all next week.
I can hear the sad rifles practice their practicing.
The rain, too, not yet eloped with the prettiest leaves.

George Ella Lyon

Where I'm From

    –after Jo Carson

I am from clothespins,
from Clorox and carbon-tetrachloride.
I am from the dirt under the back porch.
(Black, glistening
it tasted like beets.)
I am from the forsythia bush,
the Dutch elm
whose long gone limbs I remember
as if they were my own.

I am from fudge and eyeglasses,
        from Imogene and Alafair.
I'm from the know-it-alls
        and the pass-it-ons,
from Perk up! and Pipe down!
I'm from He restoreth my soul
        with cottonball lamb
        and ten verses I can say myself.

I'm from Artemus and Billie's Branch,
fried corn and strong coffee.
From the finger my grandfather lost
        to the auger
the eye my father shut to keep his sight.

Under my bed was a dress box
spilling old pictures,
a sift of lost faces
to drift beneath my dreams.
I am from those moments—
snapped before I budded—
leaf-fall from the family tree.

How Sunday Went

The first thing was, I woke up
singing *Verdi Prati*, "lovely meadow,"
which I'm working on for singing class.
Then I looked out the window and found
it hadn't snowed and wasn't snowing
which it has been a lot, like living
in the bottom of the bowl below
the sifter. I made coffee and toast,
wrote and read by the fire. Buxton,
the all-orange, lay on my writing arm
so words would not tug me, some
strange angel, into the sky.

I swept—broomwise, Swifferwise,
vacuumwise. I dusted. I Pledged.
I descended and ascended many times
with the dirty and the clean. I sorted
and folded, fed the fourfoots,
washed my hair, during the drying
of which, I opened my mouth to sing
Verdi Prati, but a different song
came out, starting with Grace Paley's
words, "Every time you speak the truth
you're making justice in this world."
The tune was wobbly as a just-dropped
foal, but I licked it over and over until
it could stand. Then, hair not as dry
as it might be, I ascended farther
and wrote the words down.

I paid the bills. Made notes for a talk.
Read three poems. Went to singing
class. I told my mother, I always called
you on Sunday but I can't, you know,
because you're dead. You understand?
And she said, *Of course. But did you see
that piece in the paper about hospital-
borne infections?* Yes. They've proposed
a bill about reporting them, including the kind
you had. *Well*, she said. *That's good, isn't it?*
Yes, I said, but the roads to Frankfort are slick.
Those roads are always slick, she said.

Report Card

I failed Yard—again.
Barely passed Broom & Mop.
In Skillet I scraped by.
In Salad I showed some improvement.
Dust? I was all over the chart.
Windows? The outlook is dim.
While I kept up in Grocery and Dishes,
in Company I fell behind.
Laundry was a washout.

I know, I know: if only I'd
do my homework each day.
Aghast in Heaven, my
grandmothers nudge my
mother. She can't be
bothered. She's reading.

Vocation

I don't know why I have to go
or what, when I get there,
I will do

Only

that something just to the left
of birth, says *Go*, and
I am going

Jeff Mann

Mountain Fireflies

The long drive home from lovemaking—
mountain roads, catalpa bloom, mists rising
in the first rush of rain. Axe-cleft,
memory still moist with our mingling,

I stop at my aunt's for coffee. While rain shakes
the black walnut leaves, she ladles out stew,
slices coconut cream pie—recipes used for generations.
In her eyes and face and hair my grandmother lives still.

I listen for hours, tales that ended under headstones
just up the hill, the Ferrell family graveyard.
A bowl of wilted lettuce hurled at a husband's face,
the slow carcinogens of mismatched marriages.

The wife, discovering adultery, who wrote Roosevelt
and had her husband transferred across the continent.
Men staring at the gunrack, staring at the fire,
hearing the awful river ice snarl and crack.

The great-aunt, who outlived her husband
by forty years—graying alone in the Richmond
home they'd shared, leaving his shirts still neat
in the drawers, his hat and coat still hung in the hall.

Under all those gravestones, small sagas
as intense as mine. How you haunt,
how I cherish the touch we thieve
from time—their dust pulsed as such.

How the heart splits in half, dull buried
bulb with its own serendipitous seasons
rising slow and aching into petal and scent.
All as axe-cleft with love as I.

I leave after the storm subsides,
looking once towards the hilltop, where
I will cease the heart-long and hunger,
the rush and cling and spin.

All about me, mountains and pastures
my ancestors worked, distant treefrogs

chirping, darker peaks of barn against
meadowed sky. And fireflies everywhere,

constellations to match the sparks
above, as if I strode the Milky Way,
pulsing with the gravitationals of stars.
Fireflies rising from the wet grass,

spiraling about the chestnut trees.
Galaxies drifting up from graves,
dispersed consanguine fires.
These fragile linkages of light.

Creecy Greens

Christmas shopping in Roanoke I saw them,
sandy spiders for sale in the farmers' market,
a treat few outside Appalachia would recognize.

From the barren flats above the cliffs,
those riverbank rocks time raised to mountainside,
you gathered creecy greens, age and autumn
stiffening your spinster stoop. Over the sink
you hunched them, rinsing off grit.
How long they simmered I do not know,
the shy child I was choosing the affections
of moss and oak, the elfin fancies of ferns.

Like the Mann farm, slopes too steep for surplus,
you were too stern for me, slapping my back
your only touch, made formal by poverty.
Perhaps you thought me weak, loving
books over gardens as I did. I preferred
the Ferrells, my father's other family branch,
all the abundance that permits warmth,
the closest to landed gentry West Virginia ever had,
huge bottomland farms portioned off
and lost long before the deed descended to me.

As you died long before my manhood,
long before I knew how few are arable bottomlands
or any abundance, how the sediments of solitude
may silt up a lifespan like yours or mine,
the way a small pond slowly fills with sedges
and cattails. It is your mountain blood that allows
this endurance, as I clean meticulous a batch

of creecy greens, snow blowing in again beyond
the steamed windowpanes. I am strong enough now,
boxing away a silver ring, raking leaves off graves
as frost seizes the limbs, as silver petals
in my weary beard. This skill you embodied:
how to live on weeds, how the wilderness feeds us
if we know which plants to pluck. How to season
spareness with fatback, how rich pot-liquor is:
with homebaked biscuits we sop up every drop.

Digging Potatoes

Toxic odors of Jimson weed.
Ragweed's gold-dust, pokeweed's garnets,
foxtail dew. Amidst all this useless
richness, we seek out the final
hills. Fogs of the equinox fumble
over pastures, spiral over ponds,
settle like eerie birds in the walnut
boughs already bare. We have come
for the last gifts of the dying.

Look for shriveled limbs. Then fork
beneath those consumptive splays, lift
and shake. What parts poisonous,
what parts edible—for that knowledge,
the past paid, for these safe harvests.
Gold buried does not bud, corpses
do not sprout, tendrils breaking
from fingertips and crawling towards
the light. Only potatoes. And memory.

Today we are archaeologists,
psychoanalysts, digging the dark lobes
for something lost long ago to force
our blood-fires through the snow.
Irish ancestors shove through my shoulders,
curse the tuber caught on a tine, the bushel
handle cutting its load into the palm.
Against heart's famine there is
no proof. Against the belly's,

potato cakes, Dublin coddle, colcannon,
chowder. We hum, exhumations over,
one hunger we can hoard against,
hefting baskets to the basement.
Now we need a little less.

Maple Syrup

1

The masking tape on the jarlid says
1973. Heaviest snow in my memory—
about the house the heap of two feet,
exhausting the flexible spruce,
so we mix buttermilk into buckwheat flour
and from a cellar cupboard after twenty years
retrieve this long-forgotten jar.

At fourteen maple syrup was nothing special,
something everyone else must be accustomed to,
and too much work. Wearisome, lugging zinc
buckets of sugar water down the wintry
hills, gathering wood for the fire.
And so little yield—from forty gallons
of dripped sap one meager gallon's syrup.
I expected more sweetness from the world,
bliss uncoaxed, not distilled with long effort
and one's own roughened hands. I knew
worth would accrue results, honorable love
in all justice would be returned.
It was a relief to shut down the sugar house:
I had easier things to do.

Amidst the crystalline ruins of winter,
one West Virginian manhood, I pour
what I recognize now as costly, as precious,
a few tablespoons from that small jar,
that last jar, onto a pile of gritty, sad
buckwheat cakes. I bite into this history:

those mornings split between winter and spring,
when sun against the maple flanks conjures up
the sap's ascent. All that charcoal-gray silence
in the sugar grove, a flicker rapping remotely.
About me the tiny plink plink plink.
Siphoned up roots from the mountains' rocky flesh,
the rain and ground water some alchemy in maples
makes sweet. Dripping from spiles of elderberry
in summer broken and carved, freed of pith. Each drop
ignited by early sun trembling pendant on the spile-
lip before the silver shudder and fall. Zinc buckets
propped on sandstone stoops my great-grandfather set,
the bark pocked with vague scars he drilled
in the Februaries of another century.

We stayed up late, simmering the great oblong pan,
skimming off the scummy froth, sitting long
on banks of windfall limbs, searching
for the Pleiades, between which branches they nested,
searching out certainties in the North Star,
stretching chill-stiff palms as if in hope of
lasting blessing towards the fire. Even the air was sweet.

2

I lick the last drops of maple syrup from my lips,
knowing again a moustache moist with manna beneath mine,
ecstasies after which so much is merely wait.
A face still vague with sleep is dwindling
in the seconds between doorjamb and door.
Matched mysteries, eyes meet. On mumbled goodbyes
the door closes with a switchblade snick.
Years lost, a bliss too brief to be jarred and sealed.
I finger-scrape the last sweet crumbs from the plate,
taste a body memory has finalized as Michelangelo
did marble, as my great-grandfather's memory
held some woman's body long loved.

The long evaporations, the patience, years
of simmering off, the distillation of decades.
Some syrup is consumed in a season. We are left
with sticky fingers and lips, satisfied with nothing
less, knowing how paltry all attempts
to preserve so intense a sweet.

Goldenrod Seeds

complete the decade beyond your death.
Stemmed flumes of river fog, pasture fog,

these gray gauntlets lining December's
mountain backroads, lining the family

graveyard's link fence. Feasts are what
I remember most, dinner tables where

good food was love made solid,
offered by those too shy or proud to speak it—

buttermilk biscuits and country ham,
cobblers rich with blackberries

thicketing the dell below the cemetery.
I brought daisies, your favorite flowers,

to your deathbed, then tried
to forget what you said—

a dream in which you died,
and what woke you was not fear

of death but worrying
how afterwards I might survive.

No one knows which breath is last
until that breath is over,

as if silence defines
all that came before.

We men who are too stern,
we carry the weight of each refused tear

like stones. Our hearts are leather
bags slowly filling with river-smooth gems—

agate, smoky quartz, snowflake obsidian.
We own our griefs, will not let go,

for sorrow is solid, something to hold hard,
to stroke, remembering gifts given by those

we have lost. Grandmother, I brush
winter leaves from your marker. I puff

a seeding stalk of goldenrod out
along the wind—its gray trails match

my breath, your breath rising, heat
from subsiding, shimmering sunlight.

Each seed a breath,
each breath a stream of stars.

Homecoming

Today, mid-November, my lover, my sister, and I,
we're carrying box after box of Ball jars to the basement,
riches my father has grown and canned. Lime pickles,
spaghetti sauce, green beans, tomatoes, strawberry jam.

Hinton, West Virginia, is much the same, that Appalachia
my teenaged years so wanted to escape. There's a storefront
preacher shouting about perversity, a bookish boy with a split lip.
There's a gang outside a Madam's Creek farmhouse shouting
"Come out here, you queers. We'll change you."

Now I know only five hours away, amidst D.C. traffic,
crowded sidewalks, men are holding hands along 17th Street,
buying gay novels in Lambda Rising, sipping Scotch
and flirting in the leather bars. But I want to be here,

in West Virginia,
where my ancestors worked their farms, where, today,
we form this assembly line from kitchen to basement.
John hands me a box of bread and butter pickles,
I lug it down the cellar stairs. There, amidst cobwebs,

Amy's lining up the jars, greens and reds,
with their masking-tape dates, joining other summers
packed away. I want to be here,
where first ice collects along the creeks,
where the mountains' fur turns pewter-gray,
and my father mulches quiescent gardens with fallen leaves.

Early evening's hard rain, hill-coves filling with mist.
After pinto beans, turnip greens, and cornbread,
John's drowsing on the couch, I'm finger-picking
a little guitar by the fire. There on the coffee table,
gifts Amy's left for us: a jar of spaghetti sauce, a jar of jam.
There on the mantelpiece, my mother's urn.

The boy who fled Hinton twenty-five years ago,
he's here too, the boy who dreamed
of packed disco bars, summers on Fire Island,
fascinating city men, the boy who did not yet know
what family meant. His hair is thick and black,

his beard is sparse, still dark. He shakes his head,
amazed that I've come back willingly, even for
a weekend. An ember flares up, fingernails of freezing
rain tick the windows. The boy, bemused, studies
the lines on my brow, shyly strokes the silver in my beard.

Locrian

Where is there to rest?
Not the pasture, where the ground-cherries plumped,

where, in late summer, ironweed pooled.
Not the forest, where the flicker hammered,

where we walked among the emerald,
illicit hand in hand, where we sucked nectar

from nipped honeysuckle blooms. Not the loft
of last century's barn, where hay scratched our cheeks

as we lay through the rain, storm strumming
corrugated tin, sipping moonshine from a flask,

beard to beard, post-seminal drowse. Not
the farmhouse porch, or wedding-ring quilt, or the pantry full

of canned peaches, corn relish, half-runners.
You left long ago, for another life,

and tonight I am landless, driving these backroads drunk,
snow swirling in the headlights, and what we owned is gone.

Now strangers yank our oaks from the earth.
Tree roots sprawl against the sky. They gasp like landed trout,

stacked shoulder to shoulder, bier-burnt. It is a blessing now, how
you are not here, how you do not see machines break the moss-

stained stones, stain the streams with vermilion, tangerine, puce,
bury the water deep. My grandfather's pasture is a bowl

of shattered shale, the maple grove a heap of boulders,
a clatter of coal trucks. The well is dry, the farmhouse flattened,

the cornfield a great beast's dung-heap, where it scratches up
dust and hides its waste. There is only the graveyard left,

where, each Memorial Day, we trimmed the spruce boughs
and the weeds about the graves, then lay together, naked

inside May, inside young grass and red maple shade.
Once I hoped we might have ended here, this fret where,

after unrelenting dissonance, a callused forefinger slides
into peace, into resolution. Ferrell Ridge, last tooth left

in a shattered mouth. Headstone bearing one name,
not two. I lean against it, pretending it is a mighty tree.

I sip from the pewter flask you bought me in Scotland.
In Celtic swirls, two warriors share a cup.

Tomorrow the blasting and digging will begin again,
rocks fall from the sky, hills upend themselves, but tonight

it is silent enough to hear the chimes of frost, the slow way
ice marries my moustache. I take another swig. I cannot feel my toes.

Tonight I will trace the stars, stroke the few last trees.
Someone must stay to console the dead, name the mountains that are gone.

Maurice Manning

The Yonder Side of Sourwood

Now I don't know if it's true today,
and I won't reveal the name of the county
he mentioned, but my father recalled
that his grandfather concluded the people
from _____ county were hard-headed,
uncommonly mean, and backward, because
not a one of them had a sense of humor.
Not a single man, woman, or child
in the dark county could laugh with delight.
They had decided to live in the darkness
of ignorance but had yet to notice
their mistake—and couldn't imagine the toll,
which nevertheless rung out and left
a long and lonely shade that fell
behind them like a second shadow.
They knew what they knew and that was enough—
they weren't impressed by anything new
and never noticed anything
surprising, curious, or strange—
and being in such company
was about as exciting as stubbing your toe.
It's hard to reason with a person
for whom laughter is but a concept
murkier than muddy water
with nothing underneath the mud.
In fact, the old man continued,
I'd rather converse with a dead possum
than shoot the breeze with anyone
from _____ county, because they're not
the kind of people who shoot the breeze—
they'll shoot their uncles, but not the breeze.
You could spin the one about the man
who confessed to stealing a rope, but convinced
the judge he didn't know a mule
was attached to the other end of the rope,
and the judge decided if a man
would go to such lengths to steal a rope
he ought to keep it and fully deserved
to keep the bony mule as well.
If you rattled a tale like that to a man
from _____ county, first of all,
he'd believe it was true, and then he'd say,

I never had much like for a mule,
with a sour, benighted pout on his face,
as if the point of the story was
the mule and not the clever defense
of a man who aspired to steal a rope.
Now that's a profound absence of humor,
I said to my father. You know it, he said,
some of the gloomiest people ever
are fetched up in _____ county—
granddaddy had them pegged.
But that old judge did his best to help,
because I gather he believed
the human condition could be improved,
a belief the people of _____ county
unwittingly conspired to challenge.
One time a wiry heathen who came
from _____ county was being tried
for shooting off his uncle's ear.
The judge's questions received a lot
of Nopes and Yeps, and all the victim
could do was point and mumble, Him.
In the end, it wasn't much of a trial—
the one-eared uncle appeared to take
little notice of his condition,
and a similar indifference dimmed
the nephew's gaze to a faint ember.
With so little to guide his judgment, the judge
simply shrugged and pronounced, Whereas the victim
retains a prodigious other ear,
and whereas said missing ear now confers
on the victim what he so sorely lacked
before the incident, namely,
a speck of curiosity;
and whereas the victim is widely known
as a thief who can't steal anything
of interest, purpose, value, or meaning,
such as a broken barrel stave,
or a cracked and leaky thunder mug;
therefore, if the accused can summon a flicker
of imagination and tell me why
committing injury to the ear
of his uncle seemed a worthy thing
to do—if a tale can be construed
to provide this court a precious moment
of entertainment, I will let
the matter of the missing ear
be recorded as an accident.
The accused may now commence his tale.
Well, he looked at me funny, and I don't like
a funny look, so I shot off his ear.

The boom of the gavel rattled the windows,
the accused and the one-eared victim alike
just stood there slack-jawed and blank.
The judge rubbed his chin. The court,
he said, having seen no evidence
that neither the accused nor the victim
possesses a shred of imagination,
and that, in all likelihood,
a dead possum has more spark—
you dullards can't even exaggerate—
hereby finds all parties guilty
of ignorance, malice, sloth,
overall ineptitude, gloom,
mono-syllabic mumbling,
bunions, bad teeth, dropsy,
and failure to imagine a story—
and invites you both to sixty days
and lonely nights in the county jail,
which I know won't balance the scales of justice
and will matter little to the people
of _____ county and, further, will not
deter either of you in the least
from being so earnestly what you are,
a double-blight, for whom reason has all
the allure of pissing on a turtle.

A Reaching Thing

The Swopes were fine, upstanding people
with unremarkable children except
for the baby, Luther, known as Lute,
who claimed a truth-telling haint
was always following him around
to jump in if someone was lying
or plank-blind to an obvious truth,
because Lute was simple-minded and prone
to fall for falsehoods big and small.
Lute said the haint was Ballard Boggs,
the ghost of a blacksmith who'd died,
a hundred and fifty-two years ago
not at the forge as one might expect,
but from a tree blown down in a storm
on top of the privy where Ballard Boggs
at midnight with a plop of triumph
had lately concluded his final heave
of relief as a living soul in the world.
The ghost of Ball Boggs had, clearly,
conveyed the dire and tragic details

of his demise to Lute Swope
over the course of their long acquaintance
after Ball arrived in ghostly form
to serve Lute Swope as his protector.
The fact that Lute could speak of his haint
and the sad result of Ball's life
with sympathy and plain knowledge
made Lute's belief in a ghost persuasive.
Nobody doubted Ball was real.
He was a powerful help to Lute
in school, especially when the answer
to a question was either True of False.
When that was the case Lute Swope
stood high above the other scholars—
thanks to the wisdom of old Ball,
there was a brain and a half between them.
But matters got pinched when Lute went to church,
as he often did with his humble folks.
They'd sit in the pew for the preacher's blast
against every happiness in the world
and some no one had ever heard of,
like the sin of loving the world, and the people
would fall out crying because they'd learned
another thing they shouldn't do,
but likely had done it a time or two,
so they wept in shame. And then old Ball,
the ghost, would lean in the ear of Lute
and say, he's wrong, he's got it wrong—
that preacher's awful loud, but he's wrong.
The spirit is a reaching thing,
and reaches out from all Creation,
wherever you are it's bound to find you.
To shout that the only thing to do
is to ramble sad and broken down
the road of suffering because
that's all there is in the world—sorrow
after sorrow until the joyous day
of death—is a damnable bane of the truth.
He's preaching the Gospel of Misery!
So, eventually such instruction prompted
young Luther Swope to speak, after
the preacher strutted and cried in rage
and sent the congregation to Hell,
ending with a vicious amen.
Now, Preacher, I've got a haint named Ball,
killed in an outhouse accident,
who speaks to me and says you're wrong,
he says you're preaching pure deception.
You've made us all feel terrible
and told us the world is only a place

to suffer out a pitiful life.
And now you're fixing to pass the plate,
to pay you for making us feel helpless.
But all around us here is hope—
grass-heads toss in the wind,
an old mule finds the shade,
a seed pops up out of the ground
on its way to climbing up the pole.
Brothers and Sisters, I ask you now,
does that sound like misery to you?
I wasn't blessed with brains, but thanks
to Ballard Boggs, my haint, I've learned
how to see the world for what it is,
the Life that makes our lives have meaning,
because it reaches out to us
and claims us all wherever we are.
And the world reached out for Ballard Boggs
in the outhouse that night when the tree
fell down in the storm and mashed him flatter
than a railroad penny, a moment
after Ball delivered his last burden
down the old hole, as they say,
and received his final recognition,
but in that instant he knew he belonged.
My fellow believers, why shouldn't we
also belong? Isn't that our call,
to belong to the world we're in right now?
And isn't that a comfort to hold?
To belong to each other and the world—
that's what I've learned from a haint, who loved
the world so well he came back to it.
And so the witty, Luther Swope,
out-preached the regular preacher that day,
though, of course, he didn't gloat, because
a witty is never the kind to gloat,
it's something that isn't in his nature.
Lute's themes, as you might imagine, did not
sit well with the preacher, who simmered and fumed,
because he didn't believe in ghosts,
and later assembled the grave deacons
who struck the name of Luther Swope
from the rolls. They kicked him out, and told him
with sneers, to go into this world
he was talking about—if he could find it.
But moseying along, Lute did,
and the ghost of Ballard Boggs went, too,
and left those people to themselves
if all they wanted was misery.

Jeff Daniel Marion

The Unexpected Guests

to my mother

Morning in May and the promise of green
all around me, windows down on the drive
to your house, an invitation to memory
as the road unwinds, familiar as lines
crisscrossing my palms. What could be more
welcome than a morning such as this, no matter
losses of past years, a family dwindled
by death to three—but once three held
magic: three Marion brothers married three
Gladson sisters, and I the one child
shared among them. Now three widowed
spouses. I entered the backdoor into the kitchen
welcomed by the aromas of food cooking, a pot
simmering on every stove eye, cast-iron skillet
of cornbread ready, and you, hand to head,
exhausted, in your living room chair. I smiled
as you looked up. *Why so much food?*
"They're all here," you replied, waving
a hand toward the bedrooms. "They're back
there and they'll want to eat." I turned away,
hoping you wouldn't see what I was afraid my face
presented. *Who?* I asked, and you began to name
the long dead: my father, Uncle Gene, Aunt Sally.
"I've tried to get them to come in here—
but they won't." I helped you prepare the table,
seven place settings, and the two of us sat down
to break bread, the living and the dead communing.
"Why won't they come and eat?"
I tried to pacify your dream, illusion so real
you stared at me in anger. *They'll come when they're ready.*
I told you my week, stories to bring you back,
leading finally to talk of the dead in the past tense.
How could I understand then—your losses
a depth I could not fathom but only stare into?
Not until five years later when all of you were gone,
households of sixty years and three families broken,
goods sold and scattered to the winds, did I know:
rising from bed in the middle of the night, a cold
sweat on my brow from a dream of your return,
the dead come back to their houses and my knowing
I must tell you there's no place for you here—
you're no longer welcome. I ache to see

all of you disappointed in me, turning away,
I suppose, to some faraway promise of a place
where many rooms have been prepared for you.

Short Wave

to my uncle, Eugene Marion

June dark and the first stars were beginning to appear:
we took our places in the lawn chairs, your short wave
radio between us. *I always like radio best this time
of day and late at night.* Static of a dial searching,

then the music began, voices harmonizing in a language
neither of us knew, but its longing clear as the cicadas'
constant call. We settled into the song and the coming
of night, the radio our ship sailing toward unknown ports.

The land you knew behind you then, those forty acres
farmed nearly half a century before the bypass
divided you against yourself, leaving house
and barn as island between two roads.

Behind me growing darker as lightning bugs lifted
their lamps like a futile invitation, my childhood spent
wandering those fields, chasing rabbits flushed
from the wheat at threshing time, hours of unequalled

freedom in that country lost to time. What lay ahead
was even greater loss, but the ship plowed on, our silence
broken only by an announcer's voice who, for all we knew,
could have been foretelling the future then softening

its impact by the next song, lamentations in a strange
tongue for the unknown about to happen.
We heard no songs the December night my father
died, only our voices struggling to comfort one another.

I didn't know it would be this hard, you wept,
knowing that you, too, were dying of cancer
but never spoke of it, holding steadfast night by night
in a week-long vigil for your most beloved brother.

And come October of the next year, I would be
keeping vigil for you, remembering your words,
our evenings spent listening to summer sounds
and songs from faraway in a better time.
I never knew it would be this hard, I remembered,
reaching toward the radio dial when I knew—

ah, death was with us all along: in those sad,
sweet songs of a foreign tongue when we were most

alive, death sang for us, waiting to claim us as his own.
So there in the silence it was as clear as this night
with its brilliant stars, so far away yet close enough to touch.

Ebbing & Flowing Spring

Coming back you almost
expect to find the dipper
gourd hung there by the latch.
Matilda always kept it hidden
inside the white-washed shed,
now a springhouse of the cool
darkness & two rusting milk cans.
"Dip and drink," she'd say,
"It's best when the water is rising."
A coldness slowly cradled
in the mottled gourd.
Hourly some secret clock
spilled its time in water,
rising momentarily only
to ebb back into trickle.
You waited while
Matilda's stories flowed back,
seeds & seasons, names & signs,
almanac of all her days.
How her great-great-grandfather
claimed this land, gift
of a Cherokee chief
who called it "spring of many risings."
Moons & years & generations
& now Matilda alone.
You listen.
It's a quiet beginning,
but before you know it
the water's up & around you
flowing by.
You reach for the dipper
that's gone, then
remember to use your hands
as a cup for the cold
that aches & lingers.
This is what you have come for.
Drink.

By the Banks of the Holston

Come a Sunday in October
& old man Tilley will be hobbling
down out of Shady Grove,
his gallon bucket chock to the brim
with chinquapins, glinting in morning light.
How his hands dip into the amber
yield, sift the tiny nuggets,
cupping them on the scales of his palms.

His fingers are like wands
always witching the hollows,
dark with wells of possibility.

And now on this morning
by the river where he poles
his skiff out into the mist
letting the current ferry him down,
he disappears into those wings
of water, shedding a husk of weight
like voices rising to one song:

for the dark loam of hidden coves,
for the river's shifting eddies & shoals,
let there be hosannas,
hosannas forever,
hosannas forever & ever.

The Lost Nickel

Just yesterday I fished in my pocket
for coins to lay in the clerk's outstretched
palm. One clattered to the floor and rolled away,
a wheel off on its own journey. What came back
was a July day over fifty years ago. My grandmother
had sent me out across the fields and up the dusty
road. "Bring us back something ice cold to drink."
Running up the steps, a nickel in each hand,
I stubbed my toe and fell, sprawled on the porch
of the store. Only one nickel remained
in my clenched fist. Inside, I sat and slowly
sipped my drink, letting its iciness salve
the sting of sweat. Barely eight, what did I know
then of an old woman's needs, blind and listening
for the familiar creak of the front porch steps,
lips yearning for the cold kiss of a long-awaited
drink? Now in my pocket of memory her laugh
and question still shine bright as any new coin:
"How did you know whose nickel was lost?"

The Dying Art

"You're in the zone of particularity,"
the radiologist said to the intern,
staring at the moon-disk screen,
socket and bone of my hip
his lunar landscape. The needle eased
into the narrow groove, left its message
to heal, rise from the table and walk.

Restored and reprieved but with no physician's
skill, I'll take up the fountain pen to probe
that zone of particularity, the address
of both letters and poetry.

E-mail won't suffice—I want
that handwritten page, ink as blue
as this morning's April sky, cursive letters
sweeping across the distances to some
mailbox, long-awaited words alighting,
perched in a safe nest.

So it's been called the dying art,
attempts to revive it as fruitless
as trying to raise the dead.

Nobody's got the time now;
let instant messaging pop up on screen
or text message, or even better
call on cell while scanning
grocery shelves, evening's dinner
and conversation just arm's length away.

Didn't Emily say so long ago
"These are my letters to a world
that did not write to me"?

What I need to say is in that narrow
valley, the zone of what I had no chance
to say to all those long gone.
It's not their answers I seek,
but my need to remember,
and in so doing raise the dead,
let words rise and walk into flesh
before I cross into their country,
shade among shades,
with no forwarding address.

The Man Who Loved Hummingbirds

Once I saw my father
   lift from last fall's leaves
     below our wide picture window

a hummingbird, victim
   of reflected surfaces, the one clue
     a single feather clinging above the sill.

He cradled its body in his cupped
   hands and breathed across the fine
     iridescent chest and ruby throat.

I remembered all the times
   his hands became birdcalls, whistles,
     crow's caw from a blade of grass.

Then the bird stirred and rose
   to perch on his thumb.
     As he slowly raised his hand

the wings began to hum
   and my father's breath lifted
     and flew out across the world.

Michael McFee

For My Sister, Dead at 54

I've spent all summer trying to start the elegy
I know I ought to write,

looking through the dingy waterstained boxes
of stuff you left behind,

keepsakes kept for who knows whose sake,
hoping to remember

long-ago happinesses; but I can't, I'm sorry,
there's simply nothing there

to see or feel or say, we were too far apart
for far too long, Leslie,

all I can give you is guilt disguised as words,
this spray of dried-out weeds

extended toward the silence where you now are,
the part of you that's not

ashes scattered along the Blue Ridge Parkway,
your box of gritty dust

emptied off an overlook, a failed puff-cloud
eager to be grounded,

or dumped beside a trail for animals to sniff
in the fog, in the dark.

Robert's Lake

Less a lake than a homemade pond, less a pond
than a big muddy puddle locals mocked as "Bob's,"

nevertheless my sister dragged the family there
and landed a crappie and managed to get it home

alive enough to plop in tap water in the bathtub,
naming it "Robert" after its place of origin—

a Biblical fish, or Scottish, Robert McRoberts.
It (or, briefly, he) swam a few wobbly victory laps

then rose to the surface sideways, floating, stilled,
so dad scooped him up and bore him to the toilet

and Robert circled the porcelain vigorously
on his way down and out of this dazzling world,

leaving our neighborhood, Royal Pines, never really
regal or (once cleared for houses like ours) piney,

joining the French Broad (so called not for a dame
but for settlers) just before the shallow river passed

below Robert's Lake, a modest body of water
that was home to our modest fish for a little while,

its name his memorial, as every name is: an epitaph,
a plot in the map's cemetery, the briefest elegy.

Arcadia Dairy Bar

Sometimes I think I dreamed it,
that little lunch place far out in the mountains
not really on the way to anywhere,

whose meals came fresh from the family farm
you couldn't help but smell
as the screen door snapped shut behind you—

cold sweet milk that left a mustache to lick,
fries sliced from a huge potato
and shining like golden fence posts on the plate,

crisp bread-and-butter pickles
and kitchen-garden Vidalias and ripe tomatoes
stacked on a handmade patty:

even plain vanilla ice cream
filled the mouth like heaped-up frozen manna,
whether licked from deep cones,

spooned from bowls, or gulped in aching gasps
from milkshakes somehow
both liquid and solid, miracles of consistency.

The Smathers ran it, grandparents and parents
and litters of cheerful kids.
I don't know why they opened it, why it closed,

or why I can't find where it was
when I go back home and wander the countryside
now planted in subdivisions,

but I do know I've never been happier
to be hungry than in a booth at Arcadia Dairy Bar
after ordering a burger all the way,

looking out an open window at the row of cows
across the narrow road, staring in
and making that room resound with wide-eyed moos

as I waited to fill myself with homegrown plenty
and savored their ruminative air,
the valley pasture, those blue peaks huddled beyond.

Sorry

I hated horseshoes but played anyway,
trying to hook good luck
around the distant iron stake with a clang
that would thrill the halter-top blonde
and cause her to press her chest against my strong bicep,
her sweaty hero, but no,

I never rang iron and lost and sulked off
with dusk, my fellow loser,
scuffling down that mountain dirt road
until good old-fashioned fun was out of earshot
and I heard a creek at the bottom of a steep bank saying
I should come splash my face

so I slid down, and did, and liked it there
in that ditch so deep
I thought no one could ever discover me:
I cursed the party, and the unwon girl,
and the farriers who decided horseshoes could be a game,
and was about to climb out

when suddenly the dimmed air shifted
above and behind my head.
Long deep growl. Shotgun-cock. Pause.
"What the hell do you think you're doing on my property?"
Just feeling sorry for myself was the answer
but I couldn't say that,

my city-boy body and its smart mouth
were stone-cold frozen

there in Bloody Madison, a county where
meddling outsiders could turn up dead,
hog-tied in their cars. Would the hungry fish rise to drops
of blood as if to bait?

"I don't know, sir," I finally said. "Sorry."
Hands up. Hackles. Pulses.
My retreating back was a pale uphill target
they couldn't miss, that dog and god
I never saw, who never lost sight of me, who never allowed
anybody back into paradise.

Bear Jam, 1951

Big grinning head turned in profile,
a black bear poses inside the barrel
as if to mock its stencilled warning:
PLEASE PLACE TRASH IN CANS.
People point as they slow their cars
along the steep Newfound Gap Road,
stopping for a closer look or shot,
a happy traffic jam in summer woods.
My sergeant-uncle takes this picture
with a camera brought from Germany;
my pregnant mother later borrows it
and documents the pre-me family
all staring toward the hungry bear
except Aunt Jo, always ready to eat,
who's turned her back to the comedy
and started setting out a picnic lunch.
When Old Blackie finishes his snack
then clambers out of the stinking can,
somebody says "Go!" and she turns
to see his dense stormcloud advancing
toward the loaded plate she's balanced
on the Ford's hood: rheumatiz cured,
she runs to the back door and jumps
inside with all her laughing kinfolk,
slamming and locking the heavy steel
against rude nature up on its hind legs,
the black bear clawing new black paint
as he finishes her food then, sniffing,
moves on toward other ripe humans
backpedaling to their abandoned cars,
sealing themselves behind tempered glass.

Saint Lucy

She wears the Western Hemisphere
like an enormous halo,
its flat circle shining behind her
on the lumber mill office wall:
Canada is cold dark smoke
haunting the crown of her head,
Brazil is a flamboyant wing
of hair she simply can't control,
but most of the backdrop map
beatifying this young woman
who's never seen a beach or wave
is ocean, ocean, ocean,
empty water crossed by vessels,
submarines and ships and planes
trying to end the unholy war
that stranded her here keeping books
deep in the Smoky Mountains.

Every day at this plank desk
she wears the Western Hemisphere
where their finished trees are shipped,
where a soldier-husband fights,
where a dreamed-of son may travel:
its nimbus weighs her shoulders down
but still she offers a neutral smile
and poses for the photograph
with her long pale fingers poised
on the adding machine handle,
ready to tally another sum
as the calendar tallies black days
in December 1943,
its bird dog pointing unseen game,
its single advertising word
glowing like a nightmare caption
her hand makes singular: EXPLOSIVE.

Rose McLarney

Realizing

> "Silver seems to dominate in the Carolinian dream, when it is, of all such dreams, the one least likely to be realized." – Popular Science, 1892

Silver does dominate my Carolinian dream—recalling
granite run with metallic seams, creek beds sparkling,
glitter in graded banks and gravel roads of the mountains
I come from. My mind goes back, not to precious metal
explorers sought, but mica's shine. Mica the mineral

made into insulation for toasters and vacuum tubes,
felt, paint, roofing, joint compound. Mica the comfort
in new houses I move to, flung all across the flatness
of the map. Mica as filling in wallboard, fragments of
the Appalachian chain, linked, companions to me yet.

As when I played in old mine pits. Lowered my body
down into the ground. Lingered there, peeling layers
from solid blocks of mica called *books*. Looked through
single, translucent sheets, thin enough to admit a little
light, but not to give a clear view. My vision didn't reach

to India, Brazil, sites of more successful mines, where
mica spangles wrecked land and the lungs of its people.
Seeing far, or ahead, is difficult still. The original lens,
material from home soil, confers both focus and blur.
The page is already written when first lifted to the eye.

Remains

Burning fuel but not to travel away,
boys cruised circles around town. Then,
came back, to park at the gas station
where they began. Girls stayed in the lot.
Waiting for men with powers endowed

by time. Strangers of age to buy liquor
would do for a while, until the local boys
grew up enough, got ready to realize claims
on the land where, already, roads, schools,
and cemeteries bore their names. So we

could take, or be taken by them, too.
It seemed our staying, boys' circling, were
the continuation of all that was ever done.
We didn't consider the figure standing
across the street, as it had for a millennium:

the mound, built by people preceding
the Cherokee. Where the townhouse
of that ancient civilization would have been.
What might be lying beneath. Or legends
of sacred fire buried and still blazing there.

Neither did we yet know what the town founded
this century had interred—oil tanks. Which leaked.
While we struck matches, dropped cigarettes, and
watched boys' hands at rest on the steering wheels
of leased trucks, eager for their next move, fingers

of combustible seepage reached in the direction
of the mound. Yet we were spared flames. Allowed
to go on, speaking of *we* (unaware of all it didn't hold),
a little farther into what young history we'd heard,
loitering on the surface of that earth.

Kelly McQuain

Dolly

At ten even this boy wanted to have them:
what older girls in training bras
had taken to padding we manufactured
with balloons swelling our t-shirts
as we sang, my younger sister & I,
to Dolly Parton on the car radio, the slosh
of automated car-wash rollers slapping
against roof & window, & Daddy
for once not yelling at our backseat
performance. I was falling in love
with Dolly, that hillbilly Valkyrie,
her platinum hair-do a spun-sugar miracle,
her hummingbird voice a God-given weapon
against heartache, life's missed takes,
hardscrabble lessons about getting
the things we weren't getting but wanted—
Dolly, the doll I could never have,
her songs hungry & angry & funny—
a golden-throated spiritual connection
to the busty Daisy Mae hidden inside me.
My Dolly-pops squeaked as I rubbed
their knotted nipples, the car wash's
soapy water and brushes almost through,
& Dolly still singing "Here You Come Again"
as Daddy strummed the steering wheel
and lit a cigarette, while Dolly offered
a quick wink, all glitter & glue,
with eyes that could tell if a man
was a happy drunk, a sad or mad one—
& me, a balloon-breasted boy still singing
for a tender bosom to lay his head upon.

Jim Minick

Clear Blue Spring

Her mother leans against the windowsill,
nuzzles peach-fuzzy head, and holds

the newborn to the light. Even then,
days into this world, the Scotch-Irish

blue of Ruth's right eye begins
to disappear under a fold of skin.

The lid grows like a glacier covering
the landscape of her eye. By age three,

the glacier halts, becomes a bulging fold,
a small mountain with a trickling blue spring

seeping from underneath. At night, her parents
whisper their worry, but they can't name this

without a doctor's help. Years later
when a relative offers, the mountain is scarred

by scalpel, but not moved. The surgeons release
an avalanche of family despair. Yet

for both graduations, Ruth smiles
and looks straight into the camera.

She does the same with her sixth-graders
even though they snicker behind her back.

What did that seep of blue see? What coolness
of the underworld did it come to know?

She married late, hesitated at that,
a man sixteen years older.

Did he ever touch that eyelid,
see himself looking into that spring?

Ruth never talked about her eye,
even with sister or best friend,

never explored surgery again.
The doctor at her deathbed hissed,

"Don't you know what this is?
Neurofibromatosis,

the elephant man's disease,
an easy operation today."

Ruth pushed on in those last long nights
diving into the spring, spelunking through

that coarse mountain, searching for the source.

Her Secret Song

Her eyes they had that blue of dawn
before the chiseled night gives up
and owl still hunts that thin line
of new light. Their blue was of
winter too, pale and cold
as frozen sky, a spark of sun
on each new flake, a reservoir
of fire. Sometimes her eyes became
the color of water—pebble pearl
and dart of silver shimmering
and dimpled—a seep welling up—
a spring that sings her secret song.

Waspy Apples

Ruth always feared them, Dick and Mike
and Bob, their very snorts enough to
set her back, even though her father
chuckled and clucked at this fear, gentled
the horses into their stalls, each nuzzling
his neck like a lover, snuffling into his ear.

But her sister Alma loved these giant
friends, scavenged apples from the waspy
grass, brushed their coats while her daddy
threw down the hay and fed them oats
after mowing the pasture on an August day.

And sometimes in the field, he'd hoist
tiny Alma onto Mike's bare back,
her legs rubbing the sweaty hide. She'd
grab the knobby hames, listen to the squeak
of traces while her daddy's steady banter
circled them and calmed the canter.

Ruth watched this from a distance and snapped
a black-and-white hoping to capture for once
her daddy's smile. But at the last moment
he hid behind the horse. And the film all spent.

Ghost Stump, Sun Music

A stump is the ghost
of tree, empty
shoe of one long leg
that could dance
to any waltz of the wind.

But this spider has spun
a ghost of a ghost,
a dew-covered web flat
atop fleabane.
In its circular trap,
the green orb weaver has outlined
all of what once was,
the slip of web
the smooth plane
of an old stump,
each strand a ring, a year
this ghost dancer
traced overnight.

Or is this spider
also a musician?
Looked at sideways,
the dead-level web
becomes an old record,
LP of invisible vinyl,
strands circling,
spider a diamond needle
capturing shining light,
releasing it
to smooth grooves
the sun's own music.

Thorpe Moeckel

Bartram's Trail

To follow Bartram's trail upstream, past Tugaloo,
to cross the Chattooga River at Earl's Ford,
to go up the Warwoman Valley,
up past the cascades & bridalveils of Finney Creek,
up along the Continental Divide
between Rabun Bald & Hickory Knob,
is to crawl, is to hopscotch
between the doghobble and the yellowroot,
the rhododendron and the laurel, hand over hand,
inch by dirty, glistening inch;
to follow Bartram is to squirm, prostrate,
under the lattice-work of limb,
the umbrellaed variations of lanceolate,
the way the lungless slip like tongues
through the tiny, moss-flamed grottoes,
oblivious to four-legged jesuses
walking on the water's white-lit roostertails;
to follow Bartram's trail is to go
wet-socked, knee-weary & briar-inked,
is to limbo under shadows
mosaiced and three-quarter domed;
to follow Bartram as far as the end
is split, past the leastmost echo,
past the hiccup of wild mint and galax,
the azalea, the teaberry, the trailing arbutus;
to follow Bartram into the shade of the giant poplar,
across the intersection of trunk and root,
across the blighted chestnuts,
is to find the place
where no pattern goes unrepeated,
the place where the first ashes were spread.

The August Listener

But I was trying to think in bug time,
as though a day was a season and a season was a life.

For instance, it was Saturday,
humidity flat-lined & flush,
                    some lather, more drool. Gullied.
The clay-matrix damp, frenetic stillness of roots

tangled, a post-flow affair. I mean the ambient,
I mean a blister nuthatch gnawed at.

Not
a drill, August's language, but a pupa. I touched
my forehead, there—& knew it.

        *

Woodwind, pincher, antsoul.
Or this: skimmer & glide,
            glissando & shimmer—
summer's music,

scoops of rice in a paper bag. It entered me
like a sleeping breath, not quite lungful,
        nourishing all the same, sun on skin, skin
            on water; the clouds gladiolaed & close,

damselfly's air traffic: the vectors, the orbits,
the thrift.

        *

Toward afternoon & catbird preened from the edge
            of something, forgetting
maybe, or lassitude. But there was a girl making
        a spongeball of scum at the edge of the pond,
her arms like slivers of moon. *I'm going
to throw it in the water*, she said,
                    and see what it does.
At once, green heron began a song
like knocking
on wood.

       *

If sweetness had a sound,
                            and sweetness had a sound,
it dipped my heart in summer's butter
      a while. Well,
it did. It fried me good.

       *

Because the air had let go
of emptiness, because folly's a hard sell

in such a groove, because even the soil settling
had a rhythm beneath hearing. Or because the frogs
needed to boot up like that. Like that.

Or because they didn't and belief's a kind of headphones. But more
likely because it's a girdle, no, a corset of sweat & light.

       *

In pairs, or in funnels of three, as if in chase,
the dragonflies stirred summer's soup. I doubt they meant to,
or even sensed
the haze where webs clammed like loss & finding
in the ur-radiance, juicing
the phloem anyway. Then the rasp
and hoofthump of whitetails: said *listen*,
said *go*.

       *

Sweetgum fruit a gleamworks of nub & flay,
nearly neon with wantjuice, as when skink flitted
like seeing out of seeing, a tailwhip into crevice–

and so each night by the pond the chorus began.

       *

Butterfly
on buttonbush, the pond a green glaze. I didn't mean
to be hugged. I didn't want one more thing,
not the chalksplotches
of blossoms on the far shore,

not the pine fallen across the cove, its scales or

the brown needles still
on the branch. But the whirr
and skitch, I'd take that, and the birds' bubbles & rouge,
their lime. Yes, color to make me blind.

      *

So the ears

grew eyes and ceased to sweat. How amphibious even
      the sky in its slow fade, lavender to taupe, blueberries

and ream. As if each day, too, the world fluffed its pillow.
Yes, in wanting nothing, I wanted more. You see,

I wanted nothing but the slow pulse of evening,
cantata of katydids, the frogs saying *this, this, this*.

And the bats, then, to hear like a bat.

Janice Townley Moore

Windows Filled with Gifts

> *Then everyone*
> *Crowds to the window*
> *To watch the falling snow*
> *—Derek Mahon*

No snow this night,
Only November's curled leaves
Wind-whipped across Blood Mountain.

I am a party of one
In the trafficless late hours
Where sounds are few:

The comforting bass of the motor
Pressing against the steep assent,
The slight singing of tires

On the hairpins going down.
The earth is older than four billion years
And maybe too is this mountain.

There have always been,
There will always be
The slaughtered and the slaughterer.

How is it that I should be alive
In this minuscule window to hear
And rehear on the long drive home

The magnetic measures of your voice
Still reading how snow fell on Nagoya
So many years ago?

Robert Morgan

Prophet

The weathered trunk of bristlecone
that twists in ancient whirlwind flame
on highest ridge of continent
and leans in the prevailing roar
is reaching for the lee country
and lower slopes and distant plains,
a relic of momentous war,
persisting since the glacier.
Now it's outlived all things that grow
upon the planet. See, it holds
out like a torch of sparkling green
the needles on one withered arm
to pass on to the next eon,
a word still spoken from the root
of spinning elder burning heart,
the history that is also prophet.

Horse Fiddle

To keep the squirrels from fields of corn,
and crows also, those farmers made
a kind of windmill out of rags
and rusty parts. Old wires and bits
of iron would scrape and scratch, screech out
like owls or ghosts when a faint breeze
would touch the rough contraption.
A scarecrow for the ears, the thing
they called a 'horse fiddle' would cry
out loud and shriek like fiddlers mad,
or nails jerked on a blackboard. The rig
repelled the critters and the crows
like music in reverse. The air
was poisoned with cacophony.
But when the wind died down the noise
would stop and corn-attracted ones
slipped back from woods or flapped from pines
high on the ridge to savor milky
kernels, and the music's absence.

Burning Spring

In the mountains of Virginia
when a ridge was stinking with
the gas that sighed from deep in rock
and bubbled out of dogwood springs,
and lightning set the breath aflame,
the fountain on the mountainside
spoke fire, spoke light, that lit the woods
at night and scared the bears away.
When Indians came and looked in awe
the bush of fire would dance and sway
in wind, now blue, now green, now gold,
and seem a prophecy sent forth,
as if lightning had found its root,
as if the rock might speak a truth
with fiery words from deep in earth.

Apple Howling

Way back in Anglo-Saxon times
the young men of the countryside
would gather New Year's Day in groves
of apple trees to shout a rhyme
and blast a horn and rap the trunks
with sticks, saluting dormant trees
in what was called a wassailing.
The tribute to the orchard begged
the trees to bring a richer yield,
a harvest weighing boughs of gold
down to the reach of children, bright
as jewels, the aromatic flesh
as cool and white as frost that turned
to foam on tooth and tongue, though now
the sugar slept in roots beneath
the snow and tracks of circling boys
who called the cidery sap in veins
to rise and rise and glimmer forth
as sun soared back behind the earth.

Translation

Where trees grow thick and tall
in the original woods
the older ones are not
allowed to fall but break
and lean into the arms

of neighbors, shedding bark
and limbs and bleaching silver
and gradually sinking piece
by piece into the bank
of rotting leaves and logs
to be absorbed by next
of kin and feeding roots
of soaring youth, to fade
invisibly into
the shady floor in their
translation to the future.

November Light

November light is like a dream,
no winter brightness yet, and fall's
extraordinary tints are all
receding, gray and brown, and seem
subdued as animals asleep
in dens and hollow trees and deep
in mud beneath the pond; the lint
of thistle, milkweed, goldenrod
lies white as frost and opalescent
on dying grass, at side of road.
A switch has been turned off: a lull
of outer-space and inner world,
this light is like a spiritual
heard underground or from horizon,
Gregorian yet contemporary too,
a promise that some chores are through.

The Years Ahead

When my grandpa took his produce
down the Winding Stairs to Greenville
to peddle door to door, he left
the day before and camped somewhere
near Travelers Rest just north of town.
After cooking by a campfire
he slept beneath the wagon since
the bed was heaped, and listened to
his horse crop grass and watched above
the trees the comet fling its ghost,
portending either ruin or
a century of wonder ahead.
Both interpretations were proclaimed.
Next morning he hitched up and drove

into the streets. He knew to go
to sections of the poor and of
the working middle class for there
they paid the price he asked. The rich
and servants of the rich would haggle
and criticize his vegetables.
But ordinary people paid
more readily and more for beans
and squash, tomatoes, corn and hams.
He sold them frames of sourwood honey
and jugs of rich molasses made
the fall before. Only at the last
would he take the things unsold
to finer streets to dicker with
the servants of the quality.
And when the last jar of preserves
or jam was sold he took the dimes
and quarters to the stores for cloth
and shoes, for cartridges and coffee,
sometimes a book, sometimes a doll.
And then he turned the wagon north
and rattled out the avenue
back toward the hills. And once he paid
a mesmerist who had a booth
beside the road to charm him, but
my grandpa's concentration was
so strong it broke the spell. And once
he paid a palmist to read his hand.
That night he camped beside the pike
but parked his wagon pointed south
to make a robber think he was
still loaded and not headed home
with cash that had to last throughout
another fall and winter. When
he looked up then and saw again
the comet's eerie plume that seemed
to write upon the sky he thought
the portent good and years ahead
as golden as the leaves on hickories,
and future bright as the river,
or line that crossed his callused palm.

Rick Mulkey

High Lonesome

It's the hammered notes of rainwater over dry October;
lost voices conjured from the polished grain of poplar,
the mandolin's tight strings pressed into the memory of wood.
It's the song of wind in laurel, the shifting sun above the chicory of June.
Song of the banjo, sweet loss thumb-picked and bone-strummed.
Songs we don't hear so much as know in heartbeat,
toe-tap, and blood-thrum. Songs hummed in kitchens and bedrooms,
in backseats rollin' in our sweet baby's arms.
Songs of pickups at dusk turning home, the AM radio broadcasting
light on the blackened faces of men heavy with the work of grief.
Songs of the barbed wire fence, the salt-cured sow,
the chicken coop, the stray hound.
Song shaped by hands breathing over gut-string and hog-hide.
Songs of towns whose names imply they might hold light.
Song of stone and storm, weary hymn of the woman
above the ironing board, the shucked corn,
the straw-haired child dancing 'round the apron strings.
Song of creek-cut valley, wind-hewn ridge. Song of the Chevy
abandoned to thistle, the plow gouging the wet pasture.
Ballad of the worm working the heart's deep cave, the shrill a cappella
of starlings in a winter field, wind on a timbered hillside,
the owl offering the half-eaten world on a bed of bones.
Songs that fill the sky above rail yards
with the scrolled promises of falling stars.

Hunger Ghazal

Even lonelier than the owl's question is the whisper of boiling water.
On the table, morning's cracked cup petitions its boiling water.

I wake to the root-bared light of November. While oaks shed
to reveal their truer selves, fog rises from my kettle of toiling water.

False summer, and the honeybee refuses the machinery of bloom and rot.
She sucks out life to form another: black tea transforming boiling water.

As a child, I saw rabbits after the flood spoil in the sun, crucified on briars
in creek side thickets. Empires of flies rose to profit beside the roiling water.

Of course there is the other, the teenage boy who spies the hips of housewives,
each daughters' sprouting breasts. Desire beaded on his lip, a kind of holy water.

My wife adds salted pork to the soup pot's steeped delicacies. Our hands brush gently, as if again we're young lovers walking above the river's rolling water.

To look at us, you'd think we'd been happy all our lives. How much our joy depends on love as bearable hunger, a pot of boiling water.

Toward Any Darkness

It returns, that dream of predatory flight,
soaring above dusk light, claiming little,
maybe the corn snake I'd thought lucky
shedding one body to live in another.
I rise, quiet, camouflaged, becoming one
of those middle-aged men
who watch from safe distances.
The great bird shreds the flesh,
drives its beak into the sinew
of something rank. The offal
ushered and unraveled
like Sunday morning's first hymn,
the notes beautiful and terrible all at once,
and the sweat on the preacher's brow
rising from some place unmentionable,
deep in the blind rookery of the body.
How do I keep the violence in?
Instinct moves me to smell the blood
and bone, hear the muscles' black
roots snapped from joints.
I fear nothing can weigh me down,
keep me from understanding
how this life I craft
could have been different,
could have been more
than bric-a-brac in a cupboard.
I step back from the window.
Wind rattles the outer walls.
In the fireplace flue, the wing-flutter
of startled wrens. Shadows,
roused from the boundaries,
stir toward any darkness.

Homecoming

> *The choice is never wide and never free.*
> —Elizabeth Bishop

It is always September here, summer's crops
hardening into stalks, watering cans, chalk-dry,
left to tarnish. Off Route 460, the town's only factory
stands abandoned. Its weathered smokestack spires
toward the sun; while below, the tractor meant to mow
thistle idles, cast off to the side of the road. Children,
who played hide-n-seek in hedges, vanished years ago.
Front yard deer caught grazing have turned
to stone. Even the jays and cardinals are snapshots,
frozen on concrete, garden bowls. The whole scene
antiqued for auction, for militants who shape
their lives into museums. I tell myself

leaving cost me nothing, but I know that isn't true.
These meadows of wind stained blue and green
with chicory and apple wood, reveal this
is as good a place as any to learn the language
of undoing. I've returned in the middle of this life filled
with doubt and indecision, to witness the end of a town.
Like it or not, the world answers us by discarding what we covet.
Old friends grow bald as babies. Former festival queens,
donning make-up thick as frosting on cakewalk cakes,
can't hide the fact they outlived fame. I forget the names
of streets and find the ones I do remember
won't lead me out. Like memory, they spiral and tangle
until all that's left are maps revealing how far we have to travel.

Devolution Theory

Late at night when I remember the women
who shaped their lips into a perfect "O"
over the burning end of a joint and blew
shotguns into my mouth until our heads
grew as full of static as the AM station
out of Dubuque and we slid naked and willing
into the backseat, I'm amazed I've ended up
this marginally respectable, 401K contributing,
family man. I'm as likely to be caught
today reading *Popular Science* on a park bench.
Or if I'm really daring, you might find me browsing Darwin
at Hot Rodz, the local exotic bar, where $4.50 buys you
a watered-down bourbon and a corner table
far enough back not to be bothered or recognized
but close enough, between paragraphs, to watch the dancers.
There are moments when I allow myself these visits
into the smoke and light of my former life
that I hear my name denounced through the megaphone
of what's correct and decent,
and I rush outside to make certain no one
is photographing my car and license plate
for distribution on the Web under the title
"Perverts and Miscreants of the Carolinas."
It isn't that I've forgotten my wife,
or the women before her I spent whole nights with
arguing the rules of love. I wouldn't
exchange a single one of them for any
locker room myth-fest or testosterone prom.
But I won't renounce that world of men either,
leaning against their Mustangs and pickup trucks,
their hoods lifted like battle flags,
groping beers and engines as readily as anything,
sniffing the exiled edge of a wilderness of their own making.
Maybe this is the best that natural selection can do.
Marking trees and tires with our own pee's scent,
barking out lists of boasts, we dream of wading mouth-
deep in the slough of primordial love, not because we're afraid
to hope for something finer, but because we see
those invisible borders drawn on bodies,
places allowed and forbidden, and growing closer
we hear the robotic clamoring of the soul.
So like any good primate we thrust a hand deep
into the stinging ant's hill because what's hidden there
tastes sweet, and the pain, being this much
alive, sweeter still.

Ted Olson

Baptism

Through that unmanned gap
a bolt struck, sparking
an untended fire.

Defenseless, plants prayed;
creatures with no wings
scurried from wind, flames.

Caught in this hollow
I hurried downhill,
then stopped, watched, inspired...

as life was transformed:
smoke forced my eyes shut,
ash clogged my blood-flow.

I remain here, still—
cooled, cleaned in a creek—
after all is dark:

the sun will return,
yet the pulse I'll feel
will no longer burn.

The Short Leash

Father fenced his garden
(groundhogs were eating
his beets) and poured beer
in a bowl to drown slugs.
Then he went inside.
I was there to help him
harvest what he planted;

I was there to tie down
his old hunting dog
beneath the apple tree
to scare the deer.
I dragged that beast
with his leash, yet he
whimpered and tugged:

my hands already bled
from digging up roots,
so I let go . . . the dog
ran off, and I followed—
together we plunged
in the river, swam
away from shore.

Soon afterward I heard
the scream of a shotgun;
I turned, rushed back
to see Father—a buck
caught in the fence—
standing there panting
"here, boy, here!"

Displacement

Three government men
in soiled uniforms
did what they were told:
torched Father's cabin
while I was at church.

I'm old, not quite dead;
they're young and blind,
can't read my mind
or see the Bible's words
manifested on the land.

They live here now,
that much is clear:
I'm not so sure of
where I, an apparition
to them, will go.

Through choking smoke
I watch them remove
the black skeleton
of Mother's stove,
toss it in their truck;

it'll be disposed
where I'll be taken
with the other ghosts:
a dark place controlled
by all-night lights . . .

Swallows

Alone in this valley of a thousand mountains—
the Blue Ridge Mountains—by the Shenandoah River,
I'm walking,

watching water meander over the old rocks,
wash them away: limestone mostly, some sandstone and shale,
dissolving;

outside the framed farmhouse, I pause, knowing no one
is home this late September evening—I shall step back
in . . . my boots

worn like the door-screen, I stumble, my graceless feet
trampling the floor-boards into dust; now I trespass in
the place of

swallows—they swoop for my eyes, and so I cower
where once I crawled; I recall seeing swallows then but
then they lived

in cavities in banks and trees, not in our house;
and yet, I'm not surprised to find them hiding here from
me—my kin

stole flight from them; and once, for fun, I flung stones at
them but missed, hit only my window—I can't look back
now, can't see

my path as one . . . dissolving; in the darkest room
of the house, I open the curtains: moonlight pours through
broken panes.

Lisa J. Parker

Return

This is home:
overhang of poplars and oaks
where we climbed and ran, snuck cigarettes
and hid them beneath the lush bend of forest ferns,
where we took boys and kissed them until
our jaws ached, rode our bikes past worn trails
to the water tower where we dared each other
one rung higher, ran from packs of wild dogs, and later
sat at the top of the tower, holding hands, making out,
drinking strawberry Boones and wondering what the hell
there was to do in this town.

I made Manhattan home for long enough
to love the city and its noise, the Puerto Rican women
on 96th and Broadway who took my 50 cents, gave me
a Dixie cup of coconut gelado and smiled with gold teeth
like my Grandma's, the smell of heavy yeast and garlic
from H&H Bagels just beneath my gym, the mantra
of the old black man on 104th who called *Jesus! Jesus!*
as if calling him home to dinner.

I made Manhattan home for long enough
to break my heart when the towers fell,
when I trudged through ash with other medics
and stood helpless as all the rest
when they brought us no one.
I stayed long enough to hand a fine man my heart
and have him hand it back, long enough
to pine for fresh air and familiar sounds,
to pack my bags when my bank account emptied
for the hundredth time and my family beckoned.

Now I sit in this driveway, engine off, windows down,
alone until they realize I'm here, run out to greet me.
It has been a summer of heavy rains and already
mosquitoes and horseflies buzz my car, a dove
bends its awkward neck to sip from the standing water
between two hickories, daddy-longlegs are stretched
into corners of the garage, motionless in this heat.
The fields will have to be bush-hogged—too tall
for mowing, too full of thick weed and goldenrod.
It is all overgrown, perfectly entangled.

I Mark This Gone Place With Foxfire

Buchanan Co., VA

At the edge of coal country
I pull the car onto a switchback,
stop where road and hollyhock run together
where used to you could go this road
to the top of Drill Mountain.
I abandon the car to this unkept place,
walk between overgrowth of briar and honeysuckle vine,
walk until I find the crevice—large enough
to walk into—where Granddaddy hid blackberry brandy.
But I am too long in the city, too afraid
of fast-moving critters who covet these dark niches,
I reach in with only my leg, toes pointed,
sweeping the floor for that bottle.

I come away with nothing, gone
as the road we used to drive together,
gone as these mountains, peaks missing, lopped off
by draglines that decapitate it all, leave
this strange, foreign landscape, absent
the rush of the Dismal River, even the creeks dried up,
or gone underground.

I find a poplar stump, sit against its damp wood,
breathe deep and imagine apple blossoms,
patches of pennyroyal, hillsides unvanished.
This place gave you love and children, mandolin
and shaped note singing, a taste for squirrel gravy
and fried bluegill, and those black lungs
that finally slowed you to a stop.

I stand and dig up the forest floor with the toes of my boots,
break this rotting poplar up with my heels and push it in chunks
beneath the ground, cover it over again. You taught
me this trick. You said,
I know this to be true: sometimes
when you bring up things, rot and all,
you get a queer thing of light,
glowing even as it dies.

Linda Parsons

Driftwood Found on the Greenbrier Trail

Something to mark the day, you said, digging it out
of the bank, as big and worn as a work shoe. We'd come
from Knoxville, an hour or so on Hwy. 441, to see anemone
and wild iris. Hickory like this will burn all night, and here
it's come down from Pisgah on the Carolina side, hollow to
headwater, hank of whorled wood near-buried in the rushing

cold map of the mountain. Maybe once a table, virgin planks
cleared pretty as you please, set with lamp and oilcloth, hearty
smells carrying out to the bald, the men plowing till dark.

Later on, every man called off and leaving in gray homespun.
The women staying on, tending to Hannah, her time nearly come,
soaking the bed for thirty-odd hours, the baby not breathing,

her man and his brothers shot down at Shiloh. Then the table
and the bed busted up for the two boxes, the women digging
till dark. The next day loading the wagon, leaving the chickens

for whoever came along. Maybe going as far as Wears Valley,
maybe on into Knoxville. Their men's hats pulled over their eyes,
their mouths set against weeping.

I Dream You Speak the River

Not yet hip-deep, I wade in and out of shadow, sleep of middle
age a foothold not slipping away. You sit on a stool in the kitchen,
your shirt autumn rust, elbows in pools of rose and black granite.
I dream you speak the river—not how the Holston feeds Horseshoe
Bend, nor the day in 1955 your Explorer troop rafted down,
bound briefly by youth and sheepshank knots—but the river itself:
green light of Tennessee snagged in your sentences, reeling
as they splash the countertop. Eddy and flow of trout freckles,
blue cold snaking the crooked stride from Clinch to Norris,
fat of the land clear-cut by your grandfathers set out at Mooresburg,
logwalkers dead before your birth riding poplar and shoal
to the Knoxville lumberyard, their homegoing road a-jingle
with silver. Water, water, until there's nothing left to say,
the late hour rising higher around us, this current everlasting
of house and deep night, river that courses memory that carries you.

Rosemary, for Remembrance

Said in garden lore to clear the head
and make the heart merry, try to breeze by
without stirring the pot of old suppers,
or lotion on a cherry bureau, or an airy porch
painted robin's egg blue–sachets mislaid
in the drawer of your mind. This fragrance
catches my breath, lingers like smoke on sleeves
and pants. My fingers feather down the soft-needled
stem. Prickly oils stick thumb to forefinger, shine
places I have shunted from light–the sorrowful
palm, the afraid place on the pale inner wrist.
Behind each ear I dab some like *Evening in Paris*,
pinch a sprig for minted lamb and red potatoes.

No rosemary in my grandmothers' backyards
or kitchens. They cooked country, lard
and bitter greens, calves' brains scrambled
for breakfast, sugar mixed in their rice. At tables
set with gravy boats and tea-stained linens,
this bears remembrance: Their steam under my ribs
carried me through the pinewoods of childhood.
I awakened to the gloss of morning, finding
I had wintered the worst. Across flagstones
I bristle like a mane, fierce in the memory
of their flowered dresses and reticence in all things
but pan-fried chicken and the sweet victory
of Jesus rising into clouds. Brush past me,
yesterdays, brush past.

Hands

She got right in there, knuckle to wrist, meatloaf
    and salmon croquettes, her fingered sieve doughing
the plain wedding ring with the night's plainer meat.
    Marie lived by those hands, kneaded broadcloth through
needle at the lint-snowed garment factory, never hesitated
    to hunker down in the mixing bowl, rail at the drunken
misdirection of my grandfather. Unflinching in the world's devilry–
    my mother's shenanigans with a married man–she grabbed
me up, paid dimes and nickels to sweep the porch, whiten
    tea stains with Bon Ami, until all was made straight
in His wondrous sight. She bequeathed them to me:
    long and flighty, they hem perennial seams with silver
trowel, dig and delve, pat and mound the mineral fabric,
    stitch me wholly in grandmother earth.

Repossessed

The chaise floated on hot gravel, my mother
in short-shorts, turned to the stare of Sunday sun.
A sweaty Pabst cooled her copper thigh, then cheek,
then brow. She lounged next to my stepfather's
baby-blue DeVille, tailfins and power windows
I had never seen the likes of.

That day I jumped from the preacher's car, afire
with the Savior and life eternal. Brother Clyde
said I was a wanderer no more, but had strapped on
Jesus' sword, dipped in His precious blood. Heat
glanced off the grand and sinful car, off my mother's
oiled legs. In the gospel light she covered
what she could of her shame.

That handsome man dragged her down, she later
claimed, down the unrighteous path. Their glory
road outshone even memory's awkward remains:
a man revving his passions, one day the Cadillac
burning rubber; the next, repossessed by the bank.

Did I see you get saved? she asks now. No,
but you were there when my head went back,
immersed in the Father, when temptation
sucked us both under—mine few and uncomplicated,
yours seared beyond blame or repentance—
when my robe rippled to the surface,
nigh as the wayward lamb to deliverance.

Jarflies

Low in the grave of rooted earth
they tick off the wait, spring night,
spring day, until wet-winged emergence,
exhale midway in June's throat, a racket
like hunger to my ears, a passion young
and ancient to imprint our mirrored selves.
Their rasping chord, the goodness
that suspended me in childhood—bellows
of grandmother's quilts pressed breath
from my chest, the ton-weight slight now
as I dream us back in that old, cold house.
Jarflies, she called them, scales of night
falling limb to glider to porch, as oak
and catalpa thrummed indiscernible verses,

multitudes of the many and the one.
Missionaries of summer, convert us,
white-robed in the garden, arise from
that dark continent we all must return to.
Immerse us in lingering dusk, sweat
of beanrow and clotted clay. Our lives
lengthened by their short stay, iridescent
roar that brings me to the doorstep
with caught song. Whir of singing
circles rock, bark, leaf—bodies
sacrificed to remembrance.

Charlotte Pence

At Opry-Mills Mall with God

People-watching outside The Gap,
we smell the anxious
celebration of Saturday night:
food-court fries, skins that hint
of chlorine and musk.

We try to decide if I'm sad.
I tell him how most nights
I blink in the dark, worrying about
what I need to do. He says
I don't understand what's normal,

sadness only a perspective.
But then he tugs on that oversized
ear lobe of his, takes a breath,
and suggests maybe always wanting more
has finally hurt me. What can I do

when told an unpleasant truth?
I change the subject to his faults,
tell him he's never had enough ambition.
He sighs, bums a dollar to buy
a big pretzel dusted with garlic.

We share it and lick our fingers
while we watch the sales clerk
call her boyfriend when she thinks
no one's looking. She says, "I can't wait
to get out of this god-forsaken place."

After Two Weeks Without Rain

When Demeter grew too tired
       to keep searching, she trusted herself
              to sink down beside the dirt road and cross

one thin leg over the other,
       and mourn—not for the dead,
             for the living no longer with her.

She's like me this morning as a muttering surrounds:
       tinny ping from seeping gutter-seams;
            splats slide off rhododendron leaves;

First mockingbird call. Second.
       World quenched momentarily.
            Once everyone wakes this morning, once you

wake in your house away from mine,
       this rain will have become
            invisible difference. I, too,

want to become one of many
       filtering drops into earth,
            be all that's damp, settled—the fatigue

of Demeter. Such relief in giving up.
       Beige ripples of skirt folding
             in beige dust from the road.

Edwina Pendarvis

Melee

the mood of a comic book
and all the diligence of a summer's day
crowded with whoops and cries
from the woods around us
a tattered dog, ticks on its ears

giant zucchinis lie scattered
like green clubs dropped after a free-for-all
both sides too fagged
to shoulder their weapons and carry them home

along the sunniest ragged edge
of the forest, thorny blackberry bushes
green and red leaves, red and black
beads shining like snakes' eyes
overpower the barbed-wire fence
and sprawl across the rusty bedsprings in the pasture

onto the highway and down the dirt path
we steal through weeds and bushes, through trees,
drop our towels on a rock and walk down
to the bank of the man-made lake—
itself a medley

on the concrete bridge high above
where we're swimming
cars and trucks whiz by
out on the lake a blue jet ski zigzags after a red one
Penny points at an oil slick and a dead fish in the water
close your mouth she says

Scarab

How things change over time.
The great are brought low
(though the low are somehow never
raised high).
Take the scarab: talisman of ancient Egyptians.
We thought these clumsy bugs were toys,
beautiful but comic in their wrecked, lumbering flight.
With the sun glaring down on us,
we slung the summer beetle,
its leg tied to a string,
around and around, a buzzing wheel.
Unaware of the importance of our prisoner,
we twirled in the green heat,
while far away—in cool underground chambers—
pinned to the still, muffled chests of pharaohs,
the June bug's brilliant cousins lay poised,
ready to bring back the dead.

While We Sleep

> Sixty percent of the population believes in angels.
> —Newsweek

Salamanders, startled into being,
flicker far away; through the banked fires
of autumn moss and leaf litter,
they arc across wooden synapses
of yellow birch
and red spruce
on mountain peaks lifted from an empty sea.

Triumphant myriads—scarlet, brass-flecked, jet-black
and muddy (autochthonous as Adam),
sluggish or coursing through the boiling streams—
their shiny skin, their tiny hands
twinkle into and out of starlight,
auguring
not a millennium

but a *kind* of joy.

Patrick Phillips

The Rules

The first rule was that he made the rules.
The second: we obeyed them.
The worst rule was that rules changed
unpredictably if he was losing.

There was a rule that split us into teams.
A rule about no starting over.
According to the rules, our mother,
forced to choose, always chose him.

And though the game was nameless,
we could have called it Abraham and Isaac.
My brother hauled the wood, the flint, the knife
as our father made a bonfire of his anger.

There was a rule about the first-born son—
the lone, unbroken one that saved me.

Lynn Powell

Fragments of a Lost Gospel

1.

April at floodstage, and the mercury
rising to the occasion—the blind pond healed
of its cataract of ice; the sky's
white hemorrhage stopped.

And who was there when the stone
of winter rolled away?

A glossolalia of geese.
Magdalenas in the orchard repenting of their nakedness.

2.

No suet in the feeder. No chime in the wind.
The loose magnolia singed by frost. And nothing
for me again in the blue satchel of the mailman.

And my own heart stubborn as a love letter
written in the passive voice.

3.

What is this shrub with flowers in its hair?

Country cousin to the rose,
slut in a white dress,
it flatters the barbed wire, then throws
itself at the trees.

Along my path, there is a throng of it—
chaste fragrance with a hungry reach,
and soft, ambivalent thorns.

4.

That mockingbird can aim its song at me,
batter its bravado against the open pane.
It can gossip to the grapevine,
mooch the music of the sparrow, festoon
the silent pillars of the dark.

But that bird can't argue me out of my loneliness.
It can't filibuster
the tongue-tied stamina of my grief.

5.

The green's turned to a familiar passage.
I set aside my shears and bow
my mind to the *lectio*.
What other way is there for me to know my heart?

If I listen, I can hear the small, crimson
creed of the cardinal.

If I wait, I can watch my shadow
wade into the light.

6.

The yard's still head over heels in purple.
But once it is plucked, what exactly
can you do with a violet?

Place it on a page,
and send the weight of half the language bearing down.

7.

The sky has a mind so clear it can read itself.
I wish I had a mind like that:
one sharp-shinned thought at home on the updraft.

Down here, the wind stirs up a dry
dervish in the unsown field—a godforsaken god
scuffing her heel in the dust.

Indian Summer

1.

Dawn bailing out the sluggish dark as if
the day still might right itself in the wake
of the equinox—

in this season of the second thought,
with its clear blue falsetto sky and flashbacks to crimson.
Like spring, in a bolder key.

2.

By now, each day's an anniversary of something—
a first or final touch, or kiss, or blow . . .

back to a split-level girlhood in the Appalachian South:
pom-poms and curlers and a red-leather Bible
embossed with my gold name.

I left home with a pedigree of Pentecost
and *Do unto others as you would have them do unto you.*
Which I did, in my earnest and wanton way.

3.

Last night a cake on fire and plastic cups of champagne.

Today, it's drunken bees in a wheelbarrow of windfall rot,
and poison, tit for tat, on the poison ivy.

Think what you wish for, they cheered
as I blew the decades out—
think, think.

4.

A storm front slips across another state line,
moist touch to the cheek of the rain-starved air.

And who could begrudge the geese and the asters,
the last field of corn shriveling in the October sun?

Yet I keep my eye on the conscientious oak
and, closer, the slender limbs of the locust,

trifling with the wind through my bay window glass.

5.

The pang that passes understanding—
and, all morning, a cello's mahogany grief.

Where else but in this small white room can I weep,
not wronged or widowed,
forgiver or forgiven?

Outside in the breezy yard, the sun blusters on,
and hard buds tighten on vines—

little think tanks,
with their farfetched scenarios of pink.

6.

The days slide round again to this one, drawn back
as if to the scene of a crime,
and the heart still sifting through the evidence.

What did you mean by the pronoun 'my'? chides the wind,
unraveling the maples with its Buddhist hands.

7.

The sky shakes out a scribble of starlings,
then erases them
from its lavender slate.
Why are they more real once I want to tell you of them?

Grief, love, anger—which would I send
as a swoop of starlings over shattered fields?

And beyond them, in a nonchalance of dusk, the moon

full again and face to face
with the trembling light of Venus.

Kind of Blue

Not Delft or
delphinium, not Wedgewood
among the knickknacks, not wide-eyed chicory
evangelizing in the devilstrip—

But way on down in the moonless
octave below midnight, honey,
way down where you can't tell cerulean from teal.

Not Mason jars of moonshine, not
waverings of silk, not the long-legged hunger
of a heron or the peacock's
iridescent id—

But Delilahs of darkness, darling,
and the muscle of the mind
giving in.

Not sullen snow slumped
against the garden, not the first instinct of flame,
not small, stoic ponds, or the cold derangement
of a jealous sea—

But bluer than the lips of Lazarus, baby,
before Sweet Jesus himself could figure out
what else in the world to do but weep.

April & Ecclesiastes

> Vanity of vanities, saith the Preacher, . . . all is vanity.
> —Ecclesiastes 1:2

Windflowers edging their way out of the garden,
violets hinting to the plush grass, bluets
lazing in cloud nines—wherever
you are, you can sink
to your knees in lapis and lavender.

Even the scraggle of woods, rank
with snowmelt and leaf rot,
wades into drifts of sorrel, pools of trout lilies,
while peepers make a ruckus
and, one by one, the iridescents hatch.

It's a swig of Eden, a rendezvous
of promises, the luxuries of lust
before anybody gets hurt—

and only a spoilsport who's been
around too few or too many times would
want to point out the waste it all is coming to:

just beyond hyperboles
of sweet pea, the brassy
glamour of goldenrod,
the cattails' last delirium of seed.

Revival

I'd gotten used to the goldenrod rattling
its empty cup, the bony maples, the prostrate
garden, the wind bothering the oak
for one last brown indulgence of leaves.

Now the yard's changed its hair shirt to velveteen,
and dogwoods tire quickly of their legend, tire
of blood-tipped crosses they have to bear, heavier
than the redbud's, old Judas tree redeemed in pink.

There's rejoicing among the violets
when the backslid earth comes home to the green gospel.
I want to lie down and let them lay their hands on me;
I want to take April as my personal savior.

Consider the tulips, washed in the blood,
the forget-me-nots blue-eyeing heaven,
the privet, the briar, the prodigal weed ready
to be born again, and again.

Etudes, for Unaccompanied Voice

1.

Is it better to be the crocus,
speaking up too soon, putting
a purple foot
in the snow's white mouth,

or to be the mum, mulling
over its maroon, holding out
for the last dark word
on the subject of summer?

2.

April, and every apple tree's a diva,
our little orchard smug with Dolly Partons
and the chaste arias of *La Boheme*.
The rest of the season they'll eke out
only a few whole notes for the yellow jackets,

but nobody's a no-show for this brief, white run.
Look at them: bending and bowing,
each one sure the tumult rolling in
from the back row of the horizon is
meant for only her.

3.

The frost-tired ground's in the mood for mud.

And maples in strips of curb lawn, redbuds
poised in side yards, dogwoods stalled
between the porch and the open gate—
they're all trying out
their red and pink opinions
after the large, gray, censorious season.

And before green clouds gather in the branches
to drown them out.

4.

At first you think a bird's gone
berserk in the dark maple,
that blotch of black against the sprinkled stars.

Nobody around here ever goes out on a limb like that,
this late or this loud.
It's a robin on steroids, a starling
sweet-talking its way into the dreams
of finches and cardinals . . . .

When you find yourself mocking
the mockingbird, stumped by its southern riff,
you know you've lived too long
at the wrong latitude.
What cynic misnamed that bird, anyway—
that earnest DJ of spring?

5.

Everything has its say.

Small gray birds chip
at the silence.

Forsythia belts out bright arpeggios.

Even the magnolia, alone
in the dark, corroborates
the moon's white lie.

To all of which the frost
takes cold exception,
in a gloss of asterisks.

6.

The body throws itself at the mind's problem,
shrugging out of desire
or despair
with a squall of tears.
And so, for a while, each thought
is solved, relieved of what it knows.
All afternoon, a storm shook
the pear tree at the edge of the orchard.
Now it lingers in the mist,
the way a woman lingers
in the soft
euphoria of the well-wept.

7.

Bring in the loudmouth tulip,
the white vow of the lilac,
the iris in its velvet pleasures.
What can fit in a vase, can fit in a voice.

The wind hurries by
in its scarf of birds
and spent petals, undoing both
the naked magnolia and the bold
proposals on top of skinny stems.

Even out of the wind, nothing scarlet stays.
But what would we be without
bright slips of our tongue-tied hearts?
Granite, with a grudge against the weather.

Rita Sims Quillen

Sunday School Lesson

for Teague

"What is the chief end of man?"
I ask,
But the boy doesn't hear.
His serious brown eyes
Sweep the hurrying water
For bluegills and suckers.
We walk this way every Sunday
Along a quick, clear creek
Watching for the grouse—
The same one, we're sure—
Who startles us to silence
Each time he rises,
A sailing miracle
Heading for a lightning-struck mulberry.

"I don't know," he finally says.
"What do you think
About this God stuff?"
So he was listening.
I glance at him
Notice the keenness
I admired from the start
Thinking again
How each of my children
Resembles someone long dead
As if God had run out of new faces
And started over.
The girl is her great-grandmother
Right down to her fused toes
And unbending will.
The boy is my father
Reborn
With red hair.

"I think God is something
Different to each of us."
I consider what more to say,
But he answers,
"I think God is up there,
But he expects us

To do for ourselves."

It took me 26 years to figure that out.
We watch two frogs
Leave the shadow of a peeling log
And the boy smiles at the day's bounty.
He stoops
Pokes them with a stick.

"So what is the chief end of man?"
He asks.
"To glorify God," I begin
But I realize
I asked the wrong question.
What is the chief end of boy?
To fish, catch frogs,
And laugh at snakes.
To read the waters.
To answer the right questions
And walk in dusty grace.
To enjoy forever.

My Mother, She Was Very Old-Fashioned

My mother
She was very old-fashioned
Pink toilet sets and white cotton undies
Fried chicken and meat loaf ready
When Dad got home. A wife
Was supposed to live inside
Herself, only her children took her
Away from the sound of a monotone
Monologue running, running
Constantly inside her head
All day. Dad had no idea
What she felt, needed, wished. I
Can't imagine the hurt
If he'd known she was so
Quiet because she was waiting
Always all that time for him
To die. She didn't believe
In divorce, had no reason anyway
From such a good kind man
Who loved her, but
Just couldn't connect anywhere
But at the hips.
It wasn't anyone's fault.

Sometimes they fought
Sort of, my father backed down
Quickly because he knew not
To uncover, to expose the rusted metal
Scaffold of marriage. I think
He could hear the wolf
Cry in the back of her throat,
Knew she shouldn't belong
To him but that she would
Stay, keep the home fires burning
While her soul turned to ashes
Never knowing the closeness
The connection to a twin heart
Because she was very old-fashioned
My mother.

Passing Suite

for Ann Richmond

1.

Among all the things
Ann wished for at the end:
Two white shirts
Her book of Shakespearean sonnets
And the sound of his steady breathing
Napping in the chair at her bedside.
She dreamed snap peas and raspberry vinaigrette
Tall dahlias, snapdragons, nasturtium
The yellow-fringed orchids
She hiked three miles to see
Spoke soft vowels
Carrying Carolina Wrens
Eastern Bluebirds
Ruby-throated Hummingbirds
The white crane
That took out her father's eye.

2.

There's aesthetically appealing Death:
The face of a dying foal
I have just liberated
From leathery placenta with a butcher knife;
The performance art of a Kingsnake
Majestically digesting

A whole nest of baby Bluebirds
Framed in the perfect background
Of azure sky and emerald hill.
And the real inheritance of Mother Nature:
A skeleton with skin
Gasping loudly for air
Lungs filled with cancer's froth
The air heavy with a sister's wailing.

3.

I am resigned
To a thickening waist
Deeply lined skin
Surprised in my mirror
By my wrinkly smile.

Wild gray hairs
Sprout like little exclamation marks
All around my face
Fitting punctuation
For little daily epiphanies.

I relax into a soft pillow of years
The body fades
So sense and spirit can flourish—
Middle age is molting season.

4.

My children are strong
Beautiful, confident, defiant
But plain blind ignorant—
Life has not paid them a visit yet.
When they were home
They put up posters
Collages of images from magazines
Where they could be Creator
God.
My daughter called today
To say she was moving to New Jersey
So she wouldn't grow up
To be me.
(She didn't actually say that last part.)
In New Jersey they aren't pathetic
Provincials: they know wine and design
And nineteenth century Parisian art.
Up there things move so fast
Death can't even blow a cold breath

In a room, let alone grab hold of you.
There's no silence to be found
So she's safe.

5.

Will they say I made a good end?
Even if I don't, I think
I'll copy her—
Ask for the shirts and sonnets
In case the Bible and fiddle music aren't enough
Pray for grace and peace,
For once in my life
Try to go natural, right, and quiet
As a summer storm passing.

Melissa Range

New Heavens, New Earth

Hammering down around the bends of TVA lakes;
twisting in the grip of grannies' hand-wrung *land sakes*;

oozing from pump handles and bent cans of Luck's
beans; hooting from nests in rusted, gutted trucks;

grazing on coneflowers; cropping up in landfill-stands
of chicory and timothy: such are this land's bands

of angels, its chiggers, its scarecrow fodder,
its prophesying sons and daughters

hollering in ditches of purple thistle,
in the windward caterwaul and whistle

of my blood, my twanging tongue, gauging
scrapped tobacco fields, hexed factories, raging

past backroad Jesus junkie whitewashed crosses,
crying out from razed mountaintop rock the losses

they'll not tell, by God, in anybody's books—
the Wal-Marts and bright highways and ground shook

open for coal, sleek ores, and all the rest
that shines. But they sing, in miners' chests,

in tractor treads, *we are here, we are making
all things new*; they poleax fences, they spring

from slurried wells; they burrow to the hearts
of crows; they wreck the dead tree's death, the banker's art;

they throb in graveyards, haybales, cohosh, clover,
with the vengeance of this land, which is never over.

Bloodroot

Mountain reaper, with your weepy roots
seeping red, you're an altar clotting the dirt
of Tennessee, ground like a Bible to me,
full of blood and wood and divinity,
peopled with exiles, saviors, horses,
trees that clap their hands before they're cleared,
mountains blasted into scree, and a god
with a name that means "mountain,"
the only god of my beckoning, buried
unmarked like an arrowhead, lost
past all reckoning. Where other
would I worship? And worship what
unless it grow native and unspeakable?
Blood brother, your raiment's red and white
like my cracked eye, which sees a mountain
in my sleep and in my waking;
I'll see you below after I am dead
from the root that wraps and wraps around
my heart and twists the red sap out of me.
Will see you every day in that other land
where there are no such things as days, no such work
as digging to remember the names
of flowers, gods, a breaking line of kin.
Bloodroot, bloodhound, blood shed
beneath the surface of the world,
stain me red, and bury me with my people.

Ron Rash

Three A.M. and the Stars Were Out

When the phone rings way too late
for good news, just another
farmer wanting me to lose
half a night's sleep and drive some
backcountry wash-out for miles,
fix what he's botched, on such nights
I'm like an old, drowsy god
tired of answering prayers,
so let it ring a while, hope
they might hang up, though of course
they don't, don't because they know
the younger vets shuck off these
dark expeditions to me,
thinking it's my job, not theirs,
because I've done it so long
I'm used to such nights, because
old as I am I'll still do
what they refuse to, and soon
I'm driving out of Marshall
headed north, most often toward
Shelton Laurel, toward some barn
where a calf that's been bad-bred
to save stud fees is trying
to be born, or a cow laid
out in a barn stall, dying
of milk fever, easily cured
if a man hadn't wagered
against his own dismal luck,
waited too late, hoping to
save my fee for a salt lick,
roll of barbed wire, and it's not
all his own fault, poor too long
turns the smartest man to stupid,
makes him see nothing beyond
a short term gain, which is why
I know more likely than not
I'll be arriving too late,
what's to be done best done with
rifle or shotgun, so make
driving the good part, turn off
my radio, let the dark
close around until I know

a kind of loneliness that
doesn't feel sad as I pass
the homes of folks I don't know,
may never know, but wonder
what they are dreaming, what life
they wake to—thinking such things,
or sometimes just watching for
what stays unseen except on
country roads after midnight,
the copperheads soaking up
what heat the blacktop still holds,
foxes and bobcats, one time
in the forties a panther,
yellow eyes bright as truck beams,
black-tipped tail swishing before
leaping away through the trees,
back into its extinction,
all this thinking and watching,
keeping my mind off what waits
on up the road, worst of all
the calves I have to pull one
piece at a time, birthing death.
Though sometimes it all works out.
I turn a calf's head and then
like a safe's combination
the womb unlocks, calf slides free,
or this night when stubborn life
got back on its feet, round eyes
clear and hungry, my I.V.
stuck in its neck, and I take
my time packing up, ask for
a second cup of coffee,
so I can linger awhile
in the barn mouth watching stars
awake in their wide pasture.

The Corpse Bird

Bed-sick she heard the bird's call
fall soft as a pall that night
quilts tightened around her throat,
her gray eyes narrowed, their light
gone as she saw what she'd heard
waiting for her in the tree
cut down at daybreak by kin
to make the coffin, bury
that perch around her so death
might find one less place of rest.

Watauga County: 1803

Night falling, river rising
into the cabin, a hound
howling on the porch, and then
an unbuckling from bank roots,
no time to lantern children
up to loft or higher ground
as the cabin, current-caught,
filled like a trough before lodged
on a rock, and when dawn brought
neighbors and kinfolk the hound
still howled on the porch, allowed
no one to enter until
shot dead by a flintlock pressed
against its head so men might
drag out those drowned in the harsh
covenant of that failed ark.

In Dismal Gorge

The lost can stay lost down here,
in laurel slicks, false-pathed caves.
Too much too soon disappears.

On creek banks clearings appear,
once homesteads. Nothing remains.
The lost can stay lost down here,

like Tom Clark's child, our worst fears
confirmed as we searched in vain.
Too much too soon disappears.

How often this is made clear
where cliff-shadows pall our days.
The lost can stay lost down here,

stones scattered like a river
in drought, now twice-buried graves.
Too much too soon disappears,

lives slip away like water.
We fill our Bibles with names.
The lost can stay lost down here.
Too much too soon disappears.

Good Friday, 1995, Driving Westward

This day I feel I live among strangers.
The old blood ties beckon so I drive west
to Buncombe County, a weedy graveyard
where my rare last name crumbles on stone.

All were hardshell Baptists, farmers
who believed the soul is another seed
that endures when flesh and blood are shed,
that all things planted rise toward the sun.

I dream them shaking dirt off strange new forms.
Gathered for the last harvest, they hold hands,
take their first dazed steps toward heaven.

Speckled Trout

Water-flesh gleamed like mica:
orange fins, red flankspots, a char
shy as ginseng, found only
in spring-flow gaps, the thin clear
of faraway creeks no map
could name. My cousin showed me
those hidden places. I loved
how we found them, the way we
followed no trail, just stream-sound
tangled in rhododendron,
to where slow water opened
a whole to slip a line in
and lift from a well bright
shadows of another world,
held in my hand, their color
already starting to fade.

A Preacher Who Takes Up Serpents
Laments the Presence of Skeptics in His Church

Every Sabbath they come,
gawk like I'm something
in a tent at a county fair.
In the vanity of their unbelief
they will cover an eye with a camera
and believe it will make them see.
They see nothing. I show them Mark: 16
but they believe in the word of man.
They believe death is an end.

And would live like manure maggots,
wallow in the filth of man's creation.
Less than a mile from here
the stench of sulfur rises
like fog off the Pigeon River.
They do not believe it is a sign
of their own wickedness.
They cannot see a river
is a vein in God's arm.

When I open the wire cages
they back away like crayfish
and tell each other I am insane—
terrified I may not be.

Others, my own people, whisper
"He tempts God," and will not join me.
They cannot understand surrender
is humility, not arrogance,
that a man afraid to die cannot live.

Only the serpents sense the truth.
The diamondback's blunted tail is silent,
the moccasin's pearl-white mouth closed.
The coral snake coils around,
my arm, a harmless bright bracelet,
in the presence of the Lord.

Mark A. Roberts

Of Local Habitation

A thousand species of vegetation merge
to make a mountain side, where I imagine oaks thrive—
white, red, and poison, where the curved praise of hemlocks
green skyward above acerbic complaints of political pines and
the low groans of hackberries that bend with currents of wind.
A thousand species of vegetation merge to move the mind
to embellish the singular fullness of any specific thing.

But in the local habit of the yard, I trace veins
of red and yellow maple leaves that lead to sniffing
pungent rotting walnuts beneath their skeleton walnut trees,
to caressing the knotty chestnut hybrid and rub my own
knotty knees, followed by a spectacular tackle
of the boy who rolls in alfalfa and dresses in soccer green.

Veering from the vague haze of the mountain range,
beauty parades in specific things:
one rebel lock, old and gray, breaks from its tie, to tickle my ear,
while the smirk you strike near the patch of pokeberry
I notice is particularly fine.
We pluck together—me from my head, you from the vine.

Pleased to ignore the imagined pageantry of the mountain side,
I ease into the curved back of the Adirondack, to mourn sweet
apples I let fall from pregnant trees, and adjust to the chill
of a late October breeze and the coming winter it portends.

Jane Sasser

Scavenging

At night she roams this house
where she has lived for fifty years
to find what secrets it now yields:
a cotton baby's cap, just which child
she cannot recall, a plastic corsage,
a yellowed letter tucked inside
a leather book. She picks up
each china cup, turns it
in her claw-like hands: nothing
in this house remains unbroken.
Around her, the roof springs leaks,
paint sloughs like fragile fingernails,
timbers sigh toward weary earth.
My mother sits on the sofa.
She thumbs through an old church directory,
touching faces she tries to call back,
reclaiming again and again
what can be saved from the dark.

Second Shift

Sometimes, now, words fail
to fall from memory to tongue
the way upholstery fabric
spills from the spool across the table
and she checks it for snags,
for patterns gone missing, awry.

How long has this been her job?
Her mind sorts through wisps
like lint that drifts, catches light—
diamonds' flash on winter afternoons.
Second shift. The tang of polyester,
slide into evening, darkness' call.

He'll be waiting for her outside.
Pearl, he'll say, take her arm,
though sometimes even his name
floats away. He'll take her home,
she'll slip into sleep deep as black velvet,
richer than dupioni silk.

A Catalog of Lost Things

The name of their dog, that Kansas spring.
His letters from France. Her Easter hats,
a rainbow of lace and froth. The phone number
for home. The fork in the road where her parents met,
the evening they eloped. The hollow where
wild ginger grew. The call of the Stanfield train,
its whistle long and sad, the stillness
of snow in the air. Blackberry dumplings.
The morning her brother died.
Her mother's favorite Psalm.
The first time she rode in a car. The sound
of the cotton mills, the roar and clacks,
the whiteness of lint in her hair.
The smell of dirt, the seeds going in.
Her children's faces. The way dust motes
caught light, winter mornings in the barn.

Elizabeth Savage

Forgiveness, West Virginia

Sopping and steep
        this unexpected earth
fenced by hand

buckling with trees
        is fantastic enough
for the durable—

a welcome arrest
        for the patient
among pines

        wider than inequity
        vivid as weeds

but when western people
        come here they go
crazy from warmth

with their fog
        each morning
makes less sense

and the sky is either
        broken or lost
even when it's right

        on top of them

January

Deer wander through the back yard
on private errands

their quiet courtesies
disturb the everyday—

              and cats—some stray—
roam or claim the front porch
refuse food
beg to be touched.
              The snowplow will distinguish
                intricate slopes from sidewalks

      but the easement tangles
      overtaking guardrails and fences.

Here, between the city and what's beyond it

wildness is an order
of freedom for the disowned
        and choosing this I know
         my house holds all that is mine
                to give
against the appetites
the outside bears

George Scarbrough

Singularity

Because he had been one of nine
In his father's house, Han-Shan
Has never been able to use plurality
Wisely. "One man makes a poor team,"
His father opined. But the son
Had dissented. Consequently Han had
Not lived easily in the plural world.
"I'm a man of sense not census,"
He says grimly. Dismissed early
From the capital because of his
Singularity, he had come here.
Remembering his father's house as
He walks under the trees on Exile
Mountain, "A whole plantation," he says
"Is beautiful and good to see,
But a solitary pine jutting out
From a headland is also fair
And commendable."

Drouth

Squeezed in foreskins rolled tight as iron,
Okra pods grow phallic in the garden,
Hardening in the hard light.

As always Han-Shan weeps for the infant ones,
Paralyzed in their bracts, stifled
Before emergence, into the first glory.

The birds come with immaculate feet to the bath
Skimmed with dirty water. When they fly again,
Their white feet become paradigms of mud.

The Postman, (O God, the Postman), stops
At the gate, ponders the number on Han's door,
Shuffles his letters and goes, leaving nothing.

All things are unfinished:
Heart's pulse, love's instrument foreshortened,
Withered pod. All day the raincrow has cried for rain.

Monday

Han-Shan loved churning day—
The bashing clashing dashing lashing
Mashing smashing nattering battering
Pattering spattering splattering
Neaping leaping sweeping heaping
Backing hacking tacking quacking
Tracking cracking packing slacking
Racking pounding sounds rounding
Grounding founding flavoring savoring
Clavering favoring wavering muttering
Spluttering uttering buttering—
The whole messy mattering—

While his mother wove
Another sort of magic at the stove:
Bread making
Always set his teeth aching,
His legs quaking,
And his back breaking.
Han-Shan thought he would smother.

He adored his mother
And his mother adored Han-Shan:
That is, as much as a mother can
Running between stove and churn
As loving mothers will,
Lest something spill
Or something burn.

After what seemed an eternity
Of dash and commotion,
What they looked in to see
Floating on a calm ocean
In the summer sun
Was the golden islet of Hesperide.

And the golden bread was done.

Monday II

Han's mother taught him what her
Own mother had taught her: to sand
A floor for scouring but to disdain
The crunch underfoot.

Old preachments keep surfacing.
Han goes for the grain in the wood,
Strings the nerve of board and vein
To bare exhilaration,

Scrubs his own pits raw,
Scumbles stench with lavender.
Yet he has not attained the godliness
She subscribed to,

No, not in time enough
To have entered the trinity
As a rinsing mist among those
Landmark stars.

Ancientry

These days, at broadest noon,
Han-Shan has sleep in his eyes:
At the well, tiger lilies
Are blobs of indistinction.
By the gate, peonies are white
Ducks circled on the grass,
Inert as silence.

All the world draws faintness.
Once piercing eyes hardly
Prick the nearest distance:
Han thinks of an old gray horse
He once saw browsing upmountain
He September mist.

Dragonfly

Last night I dropped my famous
Crystal cup into the spring.
This morning it is nowhere to be seen.
I've dazzled by eyes with looking.
My knees ache from the kneelingstone.
Even on my table it was invisible,
Empty until shaken, so great was
The clarity of what it held.
Only a dragonfly with isinglass
Wings, and sand grains spinning
Now make a little something of the light.

Roots

Han-Shan says:
Consciousness is the first hurt;
The word springs from the wound.
After that the first red flower;
And then the land itself, humid,
Intense with cedars, heavy with
Keen water and the purple smear
Of mountains and white stone's
Weight. The length of a meadow
Lays on a stripe, and the wind
Singing alone in weathered grasses.
But these are common hurts. It is
Love that denounces happiness, and
Friends who cast the first stone.
I write them this note of thanks.

Vivian Shipley

Alice Todd, Outside Cecelia, Kentucky

Born at the head of Rough Creek
in half-dovetailed logs daubed with mud,
my mother claimed one window to watch
two woodpeckers clash for a nesting cavity
in a dead oak: one golden shafted flicker,
the other she couldn't name, blue-black
and white with a ruby velvet head. Even
as a girl, she chased out dirt in that house;
odds were against her. She counted white-eyed
vireo, grosbeak colored the lapis lazuli I dreamed
reading Robert Browning's bishop order his tomb.
I would not marry back to naked barnyard.

Ocean was in early morning fog resting heavy
on ridges in Hardin County; diamonds in frost
ribbing a blackberry bush's leaf. Building castles
in damp yellow sand, my bare foot shaped a tunnel
where water could escape and it didn't cave in as I
slowly pulled out. Fearing the fall into the creek full
of crawdads, hornyheads and jackfish, I'd ignore
the log, hang on the rope over the swinging bridge.

I cannot string those boards together, bruise
myself a crossing for the quiet smell of ashes
or a drink, my hands cupped under the clear cold spring
where the creek began its long journey to South Fork
to join North Fork then create the Kentucky River
outside Beattyville, a town my mother never saw.
When traps set by furriers on Rough Creek's banks
snapped, there was no way to escape. To get free, a fox
or muskrat had to gnaw away a leg for the creek to swallow.

Savannah Sipple

Get Out While You Can

I can still see my mother, sitting in a chair on our concrete slab of a back
porch, cigarette in hand, legs crossed—one foot shaking to the beat. Loretta sang
for minimum wage women like my mother, those who worked hot hours
to come home only to wrangle the kids and dinner before they went to hoe
long garden rows. If I close my eyes, I can smell the Doral 100s and hear
Mom hum along. If she was mad, her foot shook faster, her inhales deeper. I know
when Loretta said, "you ain't woman enough to take my man," she meant
"I'd like to see you try," but as I got older and watched my parents' marriage fall
apart, I wondered if, when my mother ever sat there, chain smoking and drinking
Pepsi by the cupful, she ever hummed a new lyric to herself. I wonder
if there was ever a moment where Loretta or my mother or any of those women
uttered to themselves, "honey, you can fucking have him," before they put out their smoke,
took the last drink, and heaved themselves into the house to sleep and start it all over again.

Triptych of a Drowning

I.

If God is in the fingers of the craftsman
who build mandolins by hand, if God is
those fingers as they tune each string
and break out into the trill of Poor Wayfaring
Stranger, why did He send waters rushing
down the mountains? Was it really to cleanse
sins away?

II.
What if God isn't the fingers or the strings or the water? What if he is the mountain,
blasted apart? What if God is the seam, the black stitch that holds it all?

III.

A hundred and thirty miles from Hindman, my students tread water,
overwhelmed by new laws that tell them where they can pee. They ask
me who will save them in this world that wants to wash them out. How do you
reinsert a stitch? If God sees the rainbow as a promise, when did it turn
into a threat? Can you tell me, who will be left when these dark waters recede?

Arthur Smith

Easter

Early April, there are still
Mindfuls of furred snow
Smudged in the gutters,
Like dough that gums up

Corners of the bread pan
When the soft hot loaf's
Rocked out
And you look inside.

It's like that every spring—

The sheer dumb thrust of it—
The earnestly uttered
One-toned notes,
The color-criers and the wet spikes

Bright with the green
Blood of God
Driven through from the other world—
Every winter of a day I forget,

O first of all—

More Lines on a Shield Abandoned During Battle

The one time I said something
Awful to someone
I didn't know the meaning of,
It hardly mattered to him how empty
My head was
As his three younger brothers jumped
Down from the barn loft they slept in
And closed ranks behind him.

The hen he'd been about to kill
Rejoined a few others feeding
Near the stump.

—Are you talking to me? he said.

And it's true,

As you and anyone who's ever scattered knows,
And usually sooner, someone or something
Will ask what you mean—
The quicker
The world lives in a person,
The earlier he learns
To ask.

I'm trying
To imagine racing over
Someone's countryside, and raping its riches,
As you and your brief nation did,
Then coming up
Face to face
With one of them better-armed.

I'm glad we ran, both of us, having
Straddled that line
Beyond which
There are only dogs' jaws
Candid
About the river of death,
And how there are no limits to its length,
And how someone had better live
To tell the others.

Kudzu in Winter

Nothing as dead as, dead-beat,
Beaten back—vines like pylons
Limb to limb, rigging

On a ghost ship, the dead and living
Webbed as far as the eye can see—
Fog on the hills, and netted pines,

And a few stumps like dock pilings
After the dock's rotted and the engines
Everywhere have blown and the heat's

Seeped out and is gone, the silence
Louder than the engines ever were.
—And whatever being right had to do

With anything, and whatever beauty,
What on earth made me think it wouldn't be
Just like this at the heart of winter—

Everything not bitten back burned
With cold, and everything not burned
With the cold, feeding from it?

James Malone Smith

First Freeze

I.

Any cold rain
and you lie beside me mumbling.

Once, you sang out—
Martha Allengood, sweet sister,
Martha, Martha Allengood.

Or the wind shrieked in the pines.
"Hear that?" you whispered,
pulling the quilts loose.

And a freezing rain nails
everything shut, house and heart.

Nights, your rough cold feet
restless against my legs
long into the drizzling nights

until at last your rigid body
drifted into darkness like snow.

II.

"Of what?" my father demanded of me.
"What are you afraid of?"

He rummaged through dark closets,
threw back heavy drapes, swiped
under the bed with a broom. "Nothing."

And he held his hands up empty, tired
of proving the same thing over and again.

III.

I could not keep you warm enough,
grandfather, could not sleep until you slept.

How stark that morning, the year's first freeze,
hoarfrost on the grass,

your face as lightly stubbled.

How pitiless, whatever you could no longer
look away from.

How you had sat by the woodstove
each day of those winters
patting your foot,
Martha, Martha Allengood,
patting your right foot all day long.

Harm's Way

Measles, mumps, chicken pox—
a rhyme you learned at school.
Do you smuggle them home in your lunch box

like bombs? You gave the cocker spaniel
fleas, an exotic strain from your class hamster.
Frantic, her hind leg thumped the floor.

You borrowed a little boy's comb;
the doctor said *itch*, and we scratched,
smearing hot ointment, boiling bedclothes.

You catch disease easily, a fastball in your mitt,
easy as clamping lids on jars of fireflies—
your skin a jaundice glow last summer.

And you spread it . . . like the grass fires
you set, when we forget to hide matches.
I've joked these years, but some things will catch you,

the surprised face in the mirror, much too old.
I watch you bike down different streets,
a vicious dog always at your heels.

When I grab a stick and run after, it turns
on me. How to infect you with just enough fear?
Sharp things bring blood, deep water drowns.

For now I try to quarantine the world,
things you touch, things seen and heard—.
My words, charms and chant against all hidden harm.

ring a ring of roses round

I could hold you each morning until your joints grind
like the gears of the big yellow bus,
its red lights flashing.

Hen

Day took fire at her bidding,
the stove down to coals, almost cold,
bacon drippings in the coffee can
white as ice. She would prod embers

until flames bit at her fingers,
glut the open mouth with fat wood
and slam down the iron lid
as if she were rousing some monster.

Then she scrambled an egg for me.
But all this had happened forever
when one morning I dawdled in
as she dredged ashes, crisscrossed kindling.

The stove is out. She lights a match.
I sit at the table and wait.
Morning light flutters and stills
on the chipped enamel of the white sink.

In it, spraddled headlong (but headless!),
a large plucked chicken
in all its galled gooseflesh,
a single bloody feather stuck to the faucet.

I startle as the stove lid clangs into place.
With a flourish she reveals an immaculate
brown egg in her powerful hand
and pauses. Long enough to make sure

the break will be clean and even,
the yolk full, and heavy,
the rest as clear as water—
then cracks the world apart.

Noel Smith

Ada's Poem

Sweet Crude, I cannot help
who I love, you and your
creaky house whose huge logs
were notched, hoisted and chinked
by those first Morgans.

You nailed the logs over
with tarpaper and siding
but you could not cover
the humble hall stairs,
each step shiny and swayed
from centuries of feet,
tread up and tread down.

And in the rooms, all that
junk from another time.
I cannot help who I love
the prize rattler skin
eight feet long, hung over
the honkey tonk bar, that
plastic coal miner's lamp.

And all that stuff put in wrong,
like the upside down front door,
the kitchen window with the
bottom pane at the top
and the top pane at the bottom.

I cannot help who I love

When we go into the upstairs bedroom
named for me, our feet crunch
a carpet of dead ladybugs.
On the bed, beans dry on a screen
which you gently lift. You close
the door and "I Luv You" drips
from the back in purple spray paint.

I can't help who I love

Sweet Crude they found coal
under your house. They've yet

To find gas though I'll bet
it's there and when they do,
you'll be slick and rich

just like the others.
Will you take down the house
to get to it? Some think you will,
some think you won't but you'll leave
That to your sons and they will.

They got no use for land, Crude
As you do. Sure, they'll keep
"Papaw's" house standing
for the first year or two
And then they won't fool with it.

They'll leave the old Ford truck
full of feed and old lumber
To rust in the weeds, the coke cans
and junk mail choking the windshield,
right there with the empty cartridges,
but right now you bump and rattle

along the creek bed and through
the water, grab the corn from the back
and hold it out to the horses.
They eat right out of your hand,
Sweet Crude, and so do I.

R. T. Smith

Mockingbird

    (Gettysburg: November, 1863)

That next autumn the Weaver Brothers
with their camera bigger than a hatbox
caught us at Bull's Tavern in parade dress
half-snockered on cheap oh-be-joyful.
They promised each man a half-dollar
to pose on Devil's Den where the slaughter
we'd survived in the recent summer
had been too gruesome to summon
to mind full sober. So we trooped out
into the brisk weather and reclined,
artful as a squad of studio models
tricked out as the dead, while a pair
of doctors in smart frock coats stood
over us like Satan's angels claiming
souls on the threshold. *It's all theater*,
jested the photographer's helper,
now that Lincoln and the multitudes
had remembered and cheered and gone,
but I'd be there for the big scrap—
crouching, shit-scared, firing wild.
I couldn't quit flinching, not back in July
nor in the cold and quiet. Our Corporal
Billikin, knock-kneed in his cups, kept
singing from his ghost pose a popular
ditty called "Listen to the Mockingbird,"
about the bird trilling high in the willow
by the grave of poor Halle. *We want
the look of fresh dead*, one Weaver
shouted out from under his camera hood:
*Cut out the hayseed concert, fellow
and pretend to asleep, if feigning death
seems to you reckless.* It was reckless,
but I was soused and sprawled across
the altar of the pinnacle rock to watch
empty limbs pointing out our tableau's
lie: not summer at all, but frosty season.
Fool Billikin kept warbling his somber
song, as if it was a funeral, as if we'd
not all soon head back to the tavern's fire.
Making history again, we were glad

but Sergeant Archer scolded the boy
to drop his chirping: *Secesh marched
out to that tune. It's a killer's rhythm,*
and suddenly we were all cold sober,
avoiding each others' eyes, dead solemn.
We'd had all the art a man could bear.

Mallard

Something of an arrow in him,
and something of a flower.

I brought him down just after dawn
in cold and pearly weather.

The echo from my Wingmaster
ripped blue air asunder.

In the hound's mouth his gloss was fading,
eyes still embered, amazed, reflecting

sunrise bloody on the quiet river,
wingtips sharp against my fingers.

I shiver now as I remember
reading: when you're ready to cross over

they'll judge your heart's failings
against the weight of a feather.

Steve Sparks

Vespers at the Bishop

> "I scarcely dared to look
> to see what it was I was."
> —Elizabeth Bishop

1.

Blunt and abrupt as a dropped hymnal,
it is a clear spot among shaggy pines
at the foot of Goat Mountain.
To the left of the oldest graves
through a mesh of briars and underbrush
slumps a vast, abandoned apple orchard.
At the end of summer when the fruit
rots on the ground, the air shimmers
with the smell of cloying decay and the hum
of a thousand wasps and yellow jackets.
The noise is like the roar of some giant engine.
Almost loud enough to make you believe
that if you could make it through the scrub,
you would find a rent in the earth
and the true machinations of how it turns.

People from within the city limits don't know it
by my family's name. They call it the Bishop
after a gravestone shaped like a chess piece.
Legend says if you back your car up just right
and shine your lights on the ecclesiastical stone,
the face of the Devil appears. Then your lights die,
and you're left in the dark with the knowledge
that all those stories you were told are terrible and true.
I went on foot with a flashlight to see for myself.
The gravestone, one of the oldest in the cemetery,
was nameless and dateless—worn blank and shiny
by decades of wind and grit. All I saw reflected there
was my own light and the top of my hornless head.
Walking away through a December night as cold
as the stars above me, I still thought I could hear
the great engine of the world—grinding, grinding.

2.

Why do I return here?
Where the pines grow thick and tall
and empty their pockets of cones,
I can hear the whistles as they fall,
cover the graves. When the wind is up,
the trees creak like wooden ships on high seas.
This world I work in, this world I walk in
buzzes and vibrates. Green drips from the leaves,
brown leeches out of the dirt, and when I reach
into the sky, blue smudges my fingers
like newspaper print. When I'm here,
I wish I'd remembered to bring a blanket.
I would throw it out across my family,
lay with a book sprawled over my chest,
and drift into the dreams of the dead beneath me—
scenes of lives unextraordinary: a lunchtime
debate on a tailgate in the parking lot
of the chicken plant; or a summer dusk's sit
on the front porch telling tales and watching
the fireflies mimic the skies.

3.

this place looks the same
in winter as in summer,
evergreens everywhere.
I walk grave to grave:

beloved father
littlest angel
not forgotten
in heaven now

through my fogged breath
I see this cold world.
Ghostly vapor
not from the graves
I read but from me.
It freezes
in my lashes and brows,
thaws in the car,
trickles down my face.

4.

I remember my aunt at Noccalula Falls Park
wading across a koi pond on a Sunday
after church. We were there for a picnic
of cold chicken and deviled eggs when suddenly
my stoic aunt stands knee deep in pond water,
daintily holding up her dress hem,
still wearing her shoes and stockings,
pursuing a sprig from an exotic flower
blooming in the middle of an islet.

This is where she lays.

The speckled fish waved their fins like silk underwater
and didn't flee my aunt's big feet. They seemed
enthralled by such an unexpected intrusion.
Next to her, my Uncle Red who died three months
to the day after my aunt drowned in pneumonia.
"He just stopped living," the doctors said, "We can't explain it."
I don't remember seeing them display one moment
of affection, one look or slight brush of a hand.

5.

I return though I've taken as much as I want from this place,
inhaled it like sandalwood or clove smoke—
a sweet sting in the nostrils, too much more could make me sick.

Maybe I could learn more but I refuse to feed the ghosts,
the ones who demand blood, stand akimbo
with their transparent mouths swirling with murder ballads.
Uncle Farrell who killed a man in prison
over a boiled potato,
or G.W. Rainwater, cousin never known but shot dead
by a heartbroken secretary in a honkytonk
called the Do Drop Inn, or the bruised and furious children
of second cousin twice removed Eddy.
Their need to sing hangs in the air like a stench,
and they are patient. They know I'll be back.

Henry Spottswood

Fall Cleanup

A twig held fast, rallied
its leaves in clinging to a post,
with my leaf blower full blast.

Annuals refused to leave
their pots, to become compost.
Their roots gave me a tussle.

Yard junk, a leaky hose,
plastic bags snagged in rose bushes.
A solar light I thought was dead.
In the dark bottom of a garbage can
it gave me back the summer sun.

Life in the Mountains

A deer drinks, and then listens.
Five turtles share the sun on a log
that juts at an angle near the bank.
They shine like a string of scarabs.

He gazes across the stream, and up
to the polished granite faces of the cliffs.
He may wonder when the next boulder
will tumble and crash into trees.

He may consider how each turtle
convinced the turtle ahead to climb
one turtle length higher.

Darius Stewart

My Mother's Hands

For some time I'd known
my father's knuckle prints

in the cement wall painted over.
My mother's lip purpling,

a touch of pink
where the underflesh

bloomed
through the bruise.

I wasn't so young
I couldn't reason. & so

wondered how long the scars
would last. Not those of her face.

But the daily routines she continued,
saying nothing while she

opened mail with the blade
of her index finger, loaded

laundry, detergent unrinseable
beneath hard water of the kitchen

sink, a permanent stain
her hands felt even as she smoothed

wrinkles away from my pants,
before the hot steam of the iron,

& skeptical
whether she was getting it

just right. Her hands were
meant for grounding

onions & bell peppers
into meat for a loaf,

for gliding the glass up
a patient's chin, slaking off

drool running
from his lip,

but mostly for holding
my face after a week-long

trip to camp, a gesture
so beneficent

she should one day have them
appraised. These

were my mother's hands, that
even curled into a fist would not

fit the indentations
in the wall

she scrubbed
until paint chipped away,

the brick sunken in like tiny caves
a face makes of itself

from malnourishment,
or a sickness that withers flesh

from bone—
a blueprint of the body that,

when I see it, I consider
how it all happened—

by which, I mean, her touch,
& how, after all these years,

it feels amputated,
& memory unable to mend

what the mind has unstitched.
I might one day come to understand

the mind forgets
what it doesn't want to remember—

like my father's hands searing

the day
into my mother's face.
How she shielded herself

her hands a latticework so tight
no light could enter through.

Self-Portrait as Future Third Person

His face becomes mammal-skin,
        parentheses
drawing shut the eyes.

        When he smiles—
half-moon bags.
        A terrible pallor

courts color
        away on holiday,
across deserts where

        sand dunes become his
shoulders drooped, his back
        a monastery housing

monks weighing him
        in prayers.
Mirrors are a road-

        map to lies—yester-year's—
or what he's come to know
        as the best

of his thighs. This
        is survival of the fit,
though he is the age

        of bovine milk, his body
a heavy stone
        he casts into a well—his

wish to crumble
        like ash, an ember
that burns inside

        out: a star no longer
gaseous

        but a swell

of brittle bones.
        This is the life
he'd live if only

        he could sleep
a thousand years,
        awakening when cows came

to pasture
        beside primroses
the color of after-

        glow. This allies him
to simple pleasures
        he'll plant like wild

flowers in the flesh
        that soon becomes
soil, a field blossoming,

        a harvest. The reason
he remembers to breathe.

Statues in the Park

Toward the end of day & wishing
again for daylight. What's discernible is

evening's impending gloom. If we'd admit it,
this is a sad occasion:

us perched at separate ends of a park bench;
block-headed statues in the dark looming

behind us holding so dearly to one another.
This is what makes art. What art makes of us:

models for statues battling stubbornness.
We try to one-up the other without too much effort,

since that would lessen the impact
of the plan. Which would be what, exactly?

To wax sullen in the afterglow of day gone awry
is to hold our tongues as best as we can.

As for these statues, they bear no resemblance
to any human frailty; though their actions speak

as much about truth as any whose skulls are shaped
to resemble childish drawings of perfect squares.

Perhaps this suggests there is kindness
in our obstinacy—each of us somehow regarding the gift

of winning as if it were the daily courier
arriving with news the earth is no longer a viable place

to live. An absurdity, yes; though a game two men can play—
holding & holding on, as if forever, to silence,

fearing what becomes a man who
clings only to what's left standing.

The Ghost the Night Becomes

Tonight a boy is lost,
his shadow the only companion
sharing moonlight along the stretch
of dirt road. Away from this boy
the road dusts & winds, & where
he travels, it collects flakes of him.
He wonders how he got to this place,
wonders how his body slips between brush
not wide enough to avoid gnarled branches.
& one hand crosses the other as if to soothe
the pain as one tree fallen in the forest
shoulders another. He walks deeper
into this dark place, whimpering
as a child does, hands braced before him.
Beneath his feet, twigs bend & break
a trail behind him, & somewhere
some living thing cocks its ear & knows
that in this forest a boy is lost, & the trail he's making,
some dead thing is covering it up.

A. E. Stringer

April Snow

Sudden whiteout, here and now
in wind and mud. Not so rare how
spring's moods and old news
come to a chilly agreement.

Red buds out and dogwoods just
about, this baby squall is maybe
a frosted mirror, winter's echo.
Was it not this past October,

relishing green, that I likewise
groused, summer's fruition
withering under the bright,
chill omen of sky? These fits

and atmospheric skirmishes
remind us of us, boomerangs
at equinox, wavering between
gone by and come back, every

flake a memory, late and soon.

My Father Asleep

As evening broke, family chatter over,
my father retired to the news, his body
spreading on the couch like milk
spilled into a saucer. He drifted off,
he had to, wrung out by telephones,
boned of the day's unnatural shocks.
We lived it up all through his house.

Now understand, while the clock circled
the office tower, he worked the years
into shadows that I might lie down
tonight in his age, exhausted in my own
living room, bathed in the glow
of prime-time shows ever implausible.
I can't keep his eyes open.

Dan Stryk

Hawk in the Kudzu

for John Roland

John, whenever I glimpse the photo that you framed
    for me—the one, after those serene months

of Oriental lit at our small rural school, you *knew*
    I'd "want"—I think of the day you'd visited, eyes

down, your gold curls that had dangled like two
    sunlit vines, close-shorn. And how you'd told me

of your lack of funds—the only option, for a while,
    of a military life. Your father's and his father's

line, before him. But at least, we'd thought, you'd
    have the chance to use that art, long nurtured

like a plant, to keep you, slyly, from destructive
    ways—photographing regions of the embattled

world from a reconnaissance warplane's distant
    height. Far from strife the Tao condemned,

among the pillars of blue sky. Hidden, like a Lohan,
    by the sea of floating clouds. As we saw it, then.

But after dwindling visits over years—uneasy, glum—
    fidgeting with the briefcase you now carried

at all times, I hear from you no more, lost protégé
    in spirit, thought, imagined ways of the T'ang

recluse. Idlers in bamboo groves, sailing poems
    downriver, folded into elfin boats imbued

with both our breeze-tossed thought, free from
    the "world of men." No more do we meet, now,

on the green hill of the mind. No longer crouch
    in the summit temple shade, to converse,

with wine, about the thing you claimed to be my
    gift to you. A way of finding words—or fecund

silences between—for things you'd always *felt*.
  The luminous, but quiet, truth of Wang Wei

and Li Po. But still, my friend, I glimpse, as now,
  the photo that you framed for me before

we parted ways at the temple gate—the redtail's
  white-fluffed chest protruding like a tiny pearl

from the great chaotic sea of green which cloaks
  a Southern hill. A massive darkness, spread

in monochrome, around that fragile sigh of peace.
  The one I've propped against my lower wall—

emblem of the life we dreamed—among my
  withered sunflower heads and dusty deer

and heron skulls. That beauty in the frail
  and still. Which I yet dream. And showed

you once. Not knowing you'd returned
  for the last time.

The Mountains Change Aspect Like Our Moods

Deep in the Appalachian foothills where, Midwest bred,
  I never thought I'd be, my eyes again are pulled along

the familiar grain of my oak desk, up through my study
  window in the rust light of late afternoon, no longer to see

stubblefields of corn, those familiar miles of frost-etched
  loam, but the golden highlights on the hills, each bare limb

of the leaning oaks now kindled by late sun. That moment's
  fleeting brilliance I've come to wait for at this time: and

then the cold return of winter's drab, as shadows lengthen
  on the evening mounds gone solid as great tombs.

                    And now, at last,
  as the night falls: like faces dim and featureless,
    dark harbingers of dawn.

The Smell of Wild Onions, Mowing

> *The world declares itself.*
> —Robert Penn Warren

Unfailingly, each early May, the work
    year flown for a brief spell, I'm moved by

the deep thrill their keen scent wakens,
    as I shove my mower, whirring, through

the shaggy yellowed grass come back
    to life. Patches of their tiny white-bulbed

heads peek from the grasstips. Pungent
    spies on my elopement into months of

simple tasks around the yard. Of earth
    concerns, alone. My duties rough beside

the careful gardening of my wife—the
    flower borders and new grass seed that

she begs me, scowling, not to mash in
    my deep mindless trance. Our closest

time. And then when all is said and done—
    my mower, stripped of mud and roots,

housed in the shed—their juices wavering
    fuller in the air, declare themselves,

forgivingly, where my smoking metal
    dragon's singeing teeth have scourged.

Their odor, sweetly sour, now spreads
    everywhere. Meant to throw me back,

I think, to something rank and whole:
    when I lived closer to the earth, but can't

recall. Yet the feeling's *oh so close*, like
    déjà vu. Another smell (or sight or sound?)

that must have waked me, for a moment,
    to the world. *The piercing gusts of seaweed*

on a dory in Japan? Rustling of cornleaves
    on a lost Midwestern farm? Precisely when

or where no longer matters. In these
   summer months, ahead, I've *lived before.*

Red-Eyed Cicada

> *Regard the swell of waking souls—*
> *unfettered by the high or low—*
> *as all distinctions fade...*
>   —Bhagavad Gita

I fall asleep, in local woods, in the vast
and pulsing hum of red-eyed locusts. . .

                         Arising
from those tiny earthen holes of sleep
at the end of May,

         like sorcery their thirteenth year,
they float to the treetops,
mate, and die.

            Awakening now, in the late day,
I float upon their boundless, hollow pitch,
touching every corner of the woods (it seems
the World).
            The spent ones' husks and corpses
dangling from the grasstops. Clasped to firmer
roots and bark.

               Mind adrift in that throbbing whirr,
I wish to rise from my own torpor, time,
and fear.
         Join the *atman* of my own small trill
onto their total sound.
                Then disappear.

Larry Thacker

Called

We can find ourselves
sometimes called to the quiet woods,
not for beauty, or for pleasantries,
no, for nature is a guiltless killer,
and some dreadful for the living.

That familiar rotten scent, fetid and sweet
as it may be, can tempt us,
from well off the beaten trail's safety,
singing pretty false promises,
chanting bright futures,

of warmer-blooded times, then spilled, the buzz
of dying hives crying out like a prophesy,
gloaming woods gone still with last goodbyes.

And what are we doing out here, anyway?
Such days, the strangeness hunting us
threaded back through the forests,
to behind closed windows, eyes clenched

against our own cold winds,
our own dangers.

Hold out our plates of earth, salt, fear.
Hold out our hands to pray before sleeping.

Remain in the hug of silence, hidden,
as long as the stillness remembers
your name. Your arms and breath.

We're here to walk away when done.

To never be complete.

The Rune of Out-longing: Wanderlust

Aaron felt as soon-to-be-shorn of this town
as every kid who ever threatened to shake
off the place once three or more beers sloshed
in his gentle belly. He had long passed caring
what everyone else's dreams held. They all
rang the same. Everything sounded that way.
Unbelievable and dull. So damned repetitive.

All but the song. The endless song hummed
its call through the classroom air vent,
through the plate glass no one bothered
wiping clean, through the hayfield mowed
only once a year, over the river swimming
with summer mud, and to the farthest bank
into the unfocused blackness. *To that spot.*
There was the only place it ever stopped.

A wide spot of emptiness called from there,
up the steep bank of root and mud and vine.
After a hard summer rain, on the hottest days,
fog would catch and pool there, curled up
like some thing hid, desiring to inhale
whatever passed by, to own it, craving
the water's pulsing flow and tide, licking
the river's energy into some new form.

The vision of it, would creep into his sight
some nights. Flashes of shapes in the mud,
scratches down bark, thick tree hearts on fire,
black-smeared faces murmuring secret ways
through fingered roots, down the river's guts.
All things he told no one, never put to words.

"Aaron," Mrs. Frampton would speak,
noticing his drifting off at the window.
"Come back to us, son."

"Yes, Ma'am," he would whisper,
finally blinking. Taking a breath.

Eric Trethewey

Frost on the Fields

so heavy it looks like snow at first.
And ice at the edge of the pond, in ditches too.
Everything contracts outside and inside:
sky the cold steel of November,
one more November starving what lives on warmth,
the year gone gaunt with it, the pastures brown,
brown the hillsides and the trees emptied of leaves,
the last of them swept off in a river of wind.

Later, walking, I see the frost has melted.
But the day's hard light does not relent,
reveals all that it touches in keen-edged clarity,
even sodden leaves in the ditches,
a lash of dark birds flicking above the landscape,
bleached grass hugging the earth's skull.
An oak leaf still stemmed to a branch tugs away
and sinks on the air, the landscape's last lowered flag.
Hunkered on a post, a turkey buzzard
flaps into ungainly flight as I pass.

Why are we not better than we are?
All around me the dead leaves lie and shift
as the day exhales one last breeze, subsides
to a stillness in which the germ of what is not yet
palpable pauses and gathers to begin again.

Things

The germ of despair in winterkilled grass
in hungry childhood, and the slither of rats
in a backyard littered with garbage and bones;
the discord of voices, enraged, bruising the air;
the screak of rusty nails being pulled from planks,
all of these things to whose mute solicitations
our senses succumb. The cluttered desk piled high
with paper, a dented car pulling up to the curb,
and the smell of horses, their harness. Think of it,
all of it, a fracas of crows swaggering around

in their funereal garments, a dozen buzzards
hunkered in a vulture tree, crawdads in a bucket,
and the memory from childhood of a handcar
skimming the rails. And yes, even the lilt
of an archaic verb dying on the tattered page
of an old book, or Holsteins adrift on a sea
of high grass at midsummer. And how about
water striders dimpling the surface of a pond,
florets of larkspur, or morning sunlight melting
a ribbon of snow beneath a split rail fence?
And don't forget the redbuds and dogwoods
brightening the hillsides in springtime, the perfume
of mimosa and pear blossoms, the rough bark
of oaks, their leaves, daylight dwindling to dark.
What wouldn't we give not to have to give
up these fading fragments of time? These things.

Sign

Echoing yet with the ache of old time,
the past returns in dreams; what we did
or said or saw comes back as mythic sign

of something still to come. It might be benign—
or foretell a grotesque fate instead,
as echo and portent of the ache of time.

Sometimes I've dreamed in words, retrieved a line
or image from my sleep: A woman, long dead,
whom I once knew appeared, a haunting sign

when she returned in dream, began to climb
an apple tree beside the house where we once shared a bed.
We had eaten the fruit and felt the ache of time.

She returned. She spoke. Was there a design?
Her face wore all the sorrow time had bred,
though still she spoke of love. Was this a sign?

The past returns—more than we want at times;
at times, less than we sometimes feel we need
to salve the mortal ache of passing time,
to give us what we sorely need, a sign.

Lindsay Turner

Dogwood

The flat flowers looked a little childish
But I was grateful for their presence
Like you'd be grateful sometimes
If there were a child present.

In the dogwood the light collected.
Toothy notches in the petals
White as the sheets and pillowcases,
Of which the person I married had many.

Mostly I felt wounded,
Like there was a tiny stream of blood
Leaking but going back in
Before there was too much harm.

Rusty eye of the dogwood,
Pair of cardinals in the dogwood.
With the light in it the dogwood
Seemed to want to make a rhyme.

Tennessee Quatrains

what would it be like to stay here forever

we went up a mountain and went up a firetower

the seasons themselves felt annulled like a marriage

it doesn't matter if it was never gone through with

*

to whom does the texture of a landscape matter

in the hero's landscape it gutters and shakes

the men put their hands wherever they want to

what kind of thing's hiding under this rock

*

heaven forbid you built by the creekside

what kind of mud understructures the house

in some cultures it's kept anecdotal

the singer lay down in the forms of her dress

*

what kind of thing stays away in the mountains

rain only exists in relation to need

sometimes the citizens quake in the mountains

a wash, and awash, and a-wash it away

Susan O'Dell Underwood

Commencement

Help us not to consider our enemies flourishing
like the flowers of the field, as many as the grasses.
Help us not to imagine terror right here
as the speaker's honeyed voice lifts during the middle
of Psalm 103. As he prays, please keep us
from the distraction of the ugly inkling
that we might be deafened in the second millisecond
of the fiery blast that could shatter the gymnasium,
mangle its rage through all the bodies
gathered here in the name of our children.
Lord, help us to worship not you, but this moment
and the one before, this moment
and the one after; fill us with gratitude everlasting
for the silent peace around each word,
for the breaths we take together in congregation.
Help us take for granted the irritation
of crying babies and rude coughing and flash photography.
Fill us up with nothing but the earthy scent of our sweat,
rising up clean under graduation robes and Sunday dresses,
the suit coats of fathers and uncles and grandfathers.
Pour across us the sour smell of a thousand skidding sneakers,
and the sweet odor of floor wax.
Protect us in our boredom as each name is called,
our mild applause and congratulations.
For truly this is a hollow place,
a house meant for shouting hoots and referee whistles
where worship can hardly take hold.
Lord, we are a little people, easily overlooked.
Please help others to overlook us.
Keep us safe from the monstrous in the middle of America.
Far from money and skyscrapers, please sanctify
our mediocrity, our foolish faith that no one
has any reason to harm us.
We bow our heads for the benediction
but can hardly close our eyes
against the beautiful flesh of the maple floor,
emblazoned with our home-team insignia, our colors.
Above us, the scoreboard says nothing, its clock
set at zero hour, and the basketball nets hang empty,
signs as hopeful as any you have ever given.

Specter

Associate those days with hives of bees,
black snakes along the hewn foundations of barns.

It is a conjugation of memory.

We ran through the mowed yard.
We were running and flung the dark aside with sparklers,
singeing phosphorescent lines into the black,
a fleeting alphabet of who we were.

They told us others answered those names before us,
the gruesome old and put-away dead.
No one would ever catch us just by calling.
The grass went cool to easy dew
beneath our pommeling feet.

Sometimes they even said—as if in verse—whose feet,
whose toes, whose eyes, whose hair.
They disagreed.
"No, he looks just like himself,"
someone would finally declare, as if it were a joke,
a lie, a lesson yet to come.

We never owned a toy big as that nighttime,
ignited in frivolity of flesh and fire,
the smell of gunpowder on our fingertips.

Our lights sizzled, white-blinding us
to where they waited,
saying things we couldn't fathom
while we burned the last minutes to pieces,
until finally we had no excuse except to come inside,
but not until every last
shriveled dust of wire was spent.

Doug Van Gundy

A People's History of Randolph Co., WV

Imagine how it used to be.
All that remains now are stones and ghosts. You can't
look at the old topographical maps and see
the places where the miners used to live
even the names of the settlements are missing:
Jeff Scotts, Laurel, Roaring Creek Junction.
If you go there today,
bush-whack through briers and joe-pye.
You will have to
dig into the ground to find anything
to prove that people ever even lived here.

To prove that people ever even lived here,
dig into the ground. To find anything
you will have to
bush-whack through briers and joe-pye
if you go there today.
Jeff Scotts, Laurel, Roaring Creek Junction:
even the names of the settlements are missing,
the places where the miners used to live.
Look at the old topographical maps and see:
all that remains now are stones and ghosts. You can't
imagine how it used to be.

Hymn for Coal Smoke

Praise the antique odor—
        wood smoke compressed and marinated
        in subsea strata and mountain hillsides
        to a richer, sharper smell: incense
        burned on an ancient, animal altar.

Praise the thready column in chilly air—
        slow to dissipate, almost an entity
        in-and-of itself: black stone burnt
        to yellow smoke and snow-
        white ash.

Praise the sweat inside the scent—
        sweetness of the human animal,
        salt of its labor: blood
        smell in the mineral
        dark.

Frank X Walker

Nyctophobia II

When you turn on your artificial lights you might see
thomas edison's white hands gifting you
with an incandescent lamp but not the black fingers
that created the filament that allowed the bulb to burn.

You can flip off your switch, so that you can't see
the coal burning power plants, the now toothless mines
or what's left of the mountains huddled together in the dark.

In the false fluorescence, none of the men you imagine
with lungs full of sulfur dioxide have carbon colored skin,
like the documentaries full of jethros and lil' abners,
the same old closed eyes masquerading as the dark.

Juvenile Delinquents

The wrong path began when we all unzipped our zippers
and peed on the old woman's flowers with glee.

At nine and ten we tipped over garbage cans,
raided gardens and liberated candy

from the neighborhood convenience store.
At twelve we tortured cats, targeted innocent

pigeons with pellet guns and rocks and worse.
Pretending to be older than our green years

we graduated to hanging out at the hole-in-the-wall
learning things they didn't teach in Sunday school.

When we were not the person hit on the dance floor
by the stray bullet. When we crawled out

the backdoor, sprinted up the alley and arrived back
at the front door in time to stare death in the face

it was already clear, God didn't discriminate.
There was no such thing as luck. Little devils had angels too.

Poem as Prayer

I grew up whispering poems into my palms
whenever I felt eyes looking over my shoulders.

Mamma locked her hands and prayed aloud
at every meal, before I tried to start the car and

under her breath if our taxi driver drove like
he was actually in New York City or Jamaica.

I knew a woman who called out to God as soon
as a hint of whisker brushed her inner thighs.

It seems sinful to compare the two, but I never believed
they trusted me enough to find heaven on my own.

Urban Lullabies

> "Let the rain kiss you. Let the rain beat upon your head
> with silver liquid drops. Let the rain sing you a lullaby."
> —Langston Hughes

At first there's nothing except the wall joints
and hardwood floors reaching out for each other.

Then I hear what sounds like an approaching swarm
of bees or the crescendo of passing cars on the interstate.

My ears comb the neighborhood for music like a dial
on an antique radio: no gunshots, no passing sirens,

no angry dogs, no phantom street sweepers, no overly
percussive garbage men, no church bells. . . just silence.

As I catch the first staccato drops of rain, I return home
where the dripping faucet in the next room, the sound

of bodies stretching beneath new sheets, and the call
and response of our own breathing sing me back to sleep.

One at a Time

Staring as we do at our shrinking parents
surrounded by fewer and fewer of their peers,
we watch as they point back at us as if looking
at old photographs of themselves and smiling.

They only see each other at funerals now,
so we give them space and however much time
they need to unearth apologies, bury old pains
and touch the sweet parts of time well spent.

They steal glances around the room, perhaps
surveying their life's work, complimenting
the sermon and each other and laugh about
the importance of a baby's cry at funerals.

Yesterday after the benediction they fell into
a prayer circle, leaned into each other's breaths
as if drawing invisible straws to see who's next.

William Walsh

Ode to the Andersonville Dead

I have flown so far from God
the angels cannot find me
on this Appalachian mountain.
I am a misfit toeing the earth
with one foot dragging, listening
to the world nagging over unimportant matters.

Fog hugged the ground like a Yankee's last breath,
hiding my charcoal heart as I stood
overlooking Providence Spring where lightning exploded
from the clay, a bath of aqua solis. It wasn't enough
for thirteen thousand at Camp Sumter,
the South's Arlington. Headstones rise
out of the mud like teeth.

I was carpetbagging a little too south
of an everlasting light, an ordinary guy
separating the three ghosts of morning,
no longer believing in anything
of substance. The soil shook
loose my bones while I searched for grace
and dignity on twenty-six acres, beauty
in a world where there is none. Everything has changed.

If only I could be more than I am
and not such a disappointment to myself,
here among ruins
slowly dancing
a waltz around the lives
of neglected men. What of this world
has been left behind that is of any good?
To live or die, the day goes on,
but the night stagnates, forever.

Robert West

Presto

What startled me
more

than the squirrel's
nest

crashing limb by
limb

down the old
oak,

catching at last
on

the lowest, was
how

it gathered its
disarray

into an owl
and

retook the difficult
heights.

Lullaby

Come dark the blinds nod
to adagio nocturnes
wrung out by crickets.

Unswayed pines stand hushed,
deferring to breathless wind.

The deaf moon floats free.

Still

And there:
such everyday

odd counterpoint
as birdsong,

a holding
forth (and

out) among
the pines.

Oasis

Shaded by a few
of the few trees left

around the
college drill field,

the little fountain's
abandoned in August

to fainting
battalions of bees.

Jackson Wheeler

Ars Poetica

Because I was sung to as a child. Because my father shot himself when I was ten. Because my mother took in ironing and worked as a janitor. Because, my mother would say, she could turn on the radio and I would lie in the crib and listen, quiet as a mouse. Because there was singing on the radio: Kitty Wells, The Louvin Brothers, The Stanley Brothers, The Carter Family, The Stoneman Family, and when I was older, Saturday afternoons with my father's mother, her dark Indian eyes glittering in the twilight of the room – boxing from Chattanooga, Tennessee, announced by Harry Thornton. Because I watched my uncles slaughter hogs, because I watched my mother kill a chicken for dumplings, because I watched the Rescue Squad drag the Nantahala Lake for drowned vacationers, up from Florida. Because Southern Appalachia was imagined by someone else – I just lived there, in the mountains until I read about it in a book, other than the King James Bible, which is all true my mother said and says, every jot and St. Matthew tittle of it. Because God is a burning bush, a pillar of fire, a night wrestler, a swathe of blood, a small still voice, a whisper in the Virgin's ear. Because my family is full of alcoholics, wife beaters, spendthrifts, and big-hearted people, who give the shirts off their backs. Because their stories lie buried in the graveyards, because their stories have been forgotten, because their stories have been misremembered. Because my father's people said they were from Ireland, down Wexford way. Because my father's father baptized people, because my father's mother bore a child out of wedlock and was part Indian. Because my mother's father got his leg crushed at the quarry, because my mother's mother died of brain cancer in her 50s. My friends think I talk too much, don't talk enough; that I'm too queer for company that I'm not queer enough. My mother's people were Scots and Welsh, three cheers for the beard of Brady Marr, three cheers for the blood on the shields of the Keiths from Wick, three cheers for immigration, the waves of it and the desperation behind it. Let's hear it for King's Mountain and the Scots' revenge for Culloden. Three cheers for extended family, the nameless cousins, all the petty griefs and regrets, the novels never written, the movies never made, the solace of the bottle, the solace of sex, the solace of loneliness of which there is plenty. All hail the poetic arts, and the art of poetry and the knowledge at the heart of it all: *Words bear witness.*

Backhome Story

One summer when I was in college
I worked with Linda Sanouk
From Little Snowbird over in Graham County.
She was dating a man from Robbinsville
Old enough to be her father.
He drove a truck and picked Linda
Up for long lunches from which she returned
With her hair all messed up.

My friend Charlie called the man
A squaw shyster on account of
Linda being Cherokee. By the end
Of summer Linda was pregnant
And not married, so she fixed things
By drowning herself down at Hanging
Dog just where the bridge crosses the tip
End of the lake, leastways that's what
Charlie told me, the last time I was in town.

Which, as it so happens, was the last time I saw
Charlie. About a month later he got in a knife
Fight down in Elijay, where some big Georgia
Cracker cut him good and deep on the inside
Of his leg up near his privates. Nicked an artery.
Charlie bled to death on the back of his friend's
Truck on the way to get help in Blue Ridge.
That same friend told me that all Charlie could say was,
"Oh God, Oh God, that sonofabitch cut me."

Not the kind of last words Charlie's momma or
Anybody else for that matter would want on a headstone.

The TVA Built a Dam

for Ruth Day Wheeler

It is a lake now, what was once a multitude
of different names, not towns really, but
places, lived in for a hundred years.
Submerged now, into one name:

Motley, Topton, Choga,
Hangin' Dog, Tusquittee, Ela,
Balsam, Stecoah, Hyatt's Creek,
Shootin' Creek, Rhodo, and Red Marble.

Word came by wagon and mule. In one place
the TVA sent a Ford car through the creek and up
Bethel Hill to spread the news that everybody,
including the dead, would come away.

But who would speak for the dead?
They had turned themselves back to earth
in wooden boxes, resigned themselves
to the memory of others, had quickly forgotten

the language of kith and kin.
Keith, Mason, Morgan, Marr, my great-uncle
would find their graves by counting mounds
from the corner of the church.

These dead, secure in their knowledge of being
numbered by the God who counts sparrows,
could not mark their graves with marble or granite.
What did it matter? He knew where they were.

When my mother remembers, she says, "They was
ours. All those dead belonged to somebody."
People from far off came back, and the remembered
dead were disinterred by the TVA. Even the dead

who were past memory were brought forth. And
like some behemoth Adam at work, the Authority
gave them all stones with names. Some were taken
to Aquone, some to Andrews, and the water rose

like a great cold shroud over Hewitt, Almond,
Little Choga, and Beechertown, covering tired farms,
clapboard houses, gardens left fallow, oak, chestnut,

pine, sycamore, chinquapin.
My 85-year-old mother dreams about it: she writes
to me in her crabbed scrawl that it is warm, time
to put out a garden, like her mother, and her
mother's mother before her.

She will hoe all day, plant some early potatoes,
red-leaf lettuce, onions. At night she will dream
of her mother's garden, the old farm, her grandfather
with the wild beard, and all her dispersed kin

who have died: women, men, children, and babies
quicken in her memory as though it were yesterday,
some a memory of someone else's memory, and others
who have slipped away into the mind of God.

God, she says, will sort them out, moved
as they were from places like Briartown, Vengeance
Creek, and Sweat Heifer, moved by the state
in trucks and dumped into one common grave,

or so it is believed. She would always say it, on
Decoration Day, standing amid the rows of Gregorys,
Wrights, and Queens. "Lord only knows who's here,
if anybody." And the dead sleep, sorted and unsorted,

disturbed or undisturbed by the waters that came,
more than three feet a day, climbing until the
lake was formed, over the Almond School, the Free Will
Church, over the uprooted lives of men and women

who lit kerosene lamps against the dusk, talked about
weather, revivals, their crops and mules; marveled
among themselves about the stories of electricity
in Tennessee that could make a room bright as day.

Dana Wildsmith

Bones

I.

We walk our dogs through woods still winter-bare
except where dogwoods blaze as white as bone
among old pines and water oaks. This soon
in spring our hill still hums its hymn of sleep,

a dense and dampish lullaby to green,
a tune we can't exactly hear, but feel
as easing in our bones, like sleeping cold
and someone tucks us in. It's an old

song of the comfort of giving comfort, told
by the wood-burning stove that warmed our bones
five months while the sun backed off, a song
for March's sparseness where we walk our dogs

through elms and oaks with no leaves on, past
slants of light like silvered walking sticks.
On such a cleanly beaming morning, is it
any wonder we think our trees are singing?

II.

We pry a deer bone from the hound's mouth,
a slobbery job, and wedge it high in the crotch
of a sassafras, stashing possible death
where we can see it, but the dogs can't.

These messy meddlings get to be a habit:
More and more we walk our dogs past
other morning's purloined bones clacking
in branches like prayer wheels. Lacking

faith in fate, we let our dogs ramble, then
whistle them back, as if wildness
could be tethered, as if our little forest's
orders and bounds were set in place by us

each time we walk these woods, still winter-bare
today except where plums and dogwoods flower
as pink as skin among the oaks and poplars
greening themselves awake with mindless ease.

Speed

Imagine Florida with no interstates,
the century and Granddaddy in
their early twenties, done with war, but ruined
by war for all things soft or pretty. He'd take
from his garage—Harry's in Jacksonville—
some junkers past repairing he'd stripped to stock,
and meet at the beach to use that sand as track,
to race with other vets against their hells.

My daddy, Speed, nicknamed for the cure
his shell-shocked daddy tried, went to war
(another war) and came home stripped to bare,
forever racing brakeless. He settled north
with mountains topping him, their weight
like brakes, in mercy stopping him.

Matthew Wimberley

Materials for a Gravestone Rubbing

I have long wanted to be starlight in spring
& the late snow that lingers there, coming down
at Harpers Ferry over the river or gathered
on a windowsill on third street in Brooklyn
when I was twenty-two—the potpourri
of sky the wind carries after a storm.
The gray darkening on a far ridge. If you are reading this
there is still a way. I can take your smooth palm in mine
& lead you toward a distant city and a night
when you were on the mountain and dreaming of the other world
& we can walk together past the pre-war homes
converted now to low-rent apartments for college students
or workers come in from long days on a road crew,
coveralls draped over the backs of kitchen chairs
the light swaying just so. We can go on—
along the cracked sidewalks above the train tracks
that can't exist again even as the grasses come up between them
& look through a fog and a single pair of headlights
making definite beams in the material cold.
No moonlight to get netted up in on the surface of the water
no traffic at this hour just the scraps of paper blown
into gutters and the electric hum of streetlights,
a few walk down alleys overgrown with briars
creeping vines, their crude latticework
against the brick and the exhale
of a bartender on a smoke break and the smoke
which still drifts. Now it must be all worn through
but then it was barely remarkable though I stop
to look back at the homes and at snow melt on roads
the flat glitter on the black road, the moiré pattern
yet to be captured by language—and for a minute believe
in something as my stepfather believed in the smell of fire
whenever he left in the middle of the night
returning before dawn and speaking to no one, never
waking anyone up. Sometimes I feel that alone,
that pure, as if looking back at myself
through the scrim of time and you are there
standing in our kitchen at this hour and I can almost
hear you and the first singing caught-up there in the back
of your throat. Lately I've stopped worrying about the end.
Each day my hand is smaller on your shoulders. New birds
still return and the hillsides green all around, the stars

have travelled over the horizon and in the blink
of an eye you are here—grape-vine charcoal in your hand;
little hyphen I have become.

Potato Digging at Trosly Farm

Today, I brought up from the earth
the cold potatoes, the living skip-stones
golden as the throats of deer
in late summer. Here and there
the separated roots spread
like remembered lighting through the soil.
Miles away, Calliope asks
Sally, *How long do I live?* though it will be hours
before I learn this—come home
with dirt in the groove of my ear,
the scapha, there under the sunburned
helix. Who knew anything this small
could be made of language like this?
The rain comes on from the south,
gathering in little cells on the radar—
purple as old bruises. I've failed
to explain time, the concepts of yesterday
& tomorrow, and of patience.
Her question lives on
inside me, like the wren making her nest
in the rough frame of an unfinished barn;
like the milkweed which disappears
which returns.

Annie Woodford

The Four Hundred Angels of Henry County

after Philip Levine's "On My Own"

My first cradle was the moss inside
a stump, deep in a forest
where chestnuts still grew.

The wandering cow
found me, led my father
to me & her hidden calf as well

& we came home
in a muddy-kneed parade,
game for the path,

game for the gate
swinging open to greet us,
tick-trefoil hitched

on my rough blanket, the cuffs
of my father's jeans,
the cow's switching tail.

I was held in the crook
of my big father's big arm.
I am told he was happier then.

I kept a swatch of that thin
K-mart flannel for a quilt
I've been meaning to make,

along with the tiny pink rosette
on the tiny pink bodice
of my mother's one bikini,

for I was a baby born on the
warm waters of my mother's
man-made lake, flooded

over an abandoned iron mine
& the old fires rose
through green water

& entered my veins
& though I was a lonely child,
I was also free, my mother

sleeping off third shift
on the sofa while I drew
red birds, blue birds, & robins

beside her. She'd wake
long enough to fix an awkward wing,
curl their feet around a branch

& tell me never to erase.
Dogwood blossoms grew
to full size under my crayons,

my father taking me fishing
when their petals started to fall
on the Smith or maybe I never

fished, but had the rod
handed to me just after
the rainbow struck.

A Long Line of Hard and Angry Women

All our grandmothers and aunts and second cousins
once removed gather around us,
tough jawed and bent upon survival,

they of the tombstone set into the side of a hill,
of the anonymous corporate cemetery,
of the rock half hidden by leaves.

Of the family plot upended by roots.
Womb to womb I conjure
your bleach and lye-bitten hands.

Sylvia Woods

Wearing My Grammar Girdle

Shedding my grammar girdle, hill talk sighs
onto blue lines, fat on the page, word endin's gone
the very words poured out by uncles and aunts
in stories on porches and dinner tables on Double Creek.

Looking the lines like Mama looked soup beans,
I throw out the little rocks and pieces of twigs,
run my fingers over the mess,
and feel the perfect shapes, silky, smooth.

Them prepositions, sister, are the hardest to rout;
like dandelions, they turn up in batches,
pop onto the page and take up lease
as if they have a quit claim deed.

I pull in my gut, wince at what I up and done;
my pen a willow switch, I whip
across lines, scratch away the lazy words,
and scream like my Aunt Alice yelled at the cat
that climbed to the top of the Frigidaire,
"Get down off from up on top of there!"

What We Take With Us

I make them memorize soliloquies,
some lines to keep, should they
be taken prisoner, like John McCain,
in some foreign jail, no words to read,
no paper to write, just the wild ranting
of Hamlet, Macbeth, to take
them through the darkest nights.
I urge them to know Emily,
Wordsworth, Whitman, some Keats,
seal the music in their souls.

High schoolers smirk at me. I smile,
for I know of prisons closer home
where they will need some words
that flash upon that inward eye in times
when solitude is no bliss, those times
of capture, when we all are held
against our wills, in meetings so long
our eyeballs disengage,
in marriages bleak as dungeons,
and fears so dark we see no light,
the only comfort words we know for sure.

Marianne Worthington

The Girl Singer

The A minor chord she strums
on her signature black Gibson
sounds lonesome as an old grave.
She knows she never got her due.
Those men said *we're doing you
a big favor, honey.* On tours,
she was one notch above
the gapped-tooth comic in his
battered derby and checkered
jacket, clowning on the upright bass.
The ghost of their voices rattle
chains in her sleep: *And now . . .
here's our pretty little lady.*

Her fans tired of the mournful
tunes her people sang in North
Carolina: boots of Spanish leather,
Irish seafarers with their chilly
winds, Kentucky miners chasing
an aggravating beauty, all the Aeolian
tunes weeping like orphan children.
Even the cheerful songs with jaybirds,
sparrows and cuckoos fell on idle
ears, served her no more. Besides,
she grew into herself, weary
of all the women killed in those murder
ballads—bludgeoned, stabbed,
drowned—their bodies floating
downstream to the miller's cove.

Every few years some excited
musicologist finds her, tries to revive
her. So she keeps her hair raven-colored
in case she gets a gig, a folk festival,
a reunion show. Like tonight
in the still air of the Bell County
high school gym, she's buried
between The Wilburn Brothers
and Bill Anderson and the Po' Boys.
She sings: *All men are fools*, the notes
in her throat sharp as the Silver Dagger.

The Unclouded Day

Her bedrooms polished and smelling
of Pledge, before another washing
must be gathered, my grandmother
lets breakfast dry on the dishes, drops
her body onto the piano stool and plays
the only hymn she knows by heart.
She could be chopping wood, the force
of her forearms and bosom ample
as her vision of a home beyond the skies.

She doesn't embellish or let her fingers
fly above the melody like a ragtime beat
out in a rowdy saloon. Her hymn is rich
like her pies, clean as her home, solid
as her steps marching through a cloudless day.

Love in the Cold War

My parents traveled from Knoxville to Nashville for their honeymoon
to see the Saturday night music show at the Mother Church.
Little Jimmy Dickens sang "They Locked God Outside the Iron Curtain."
My father misunderstood the refrain: *They locked John where?* he asked.

To see the Saturday night music show at the Mother Church
they sat in the hot sanctuary on wooden pews but
my father misunderstood the refrain: *John got locked up where?*
while Ernest Tubb electrified the cathedral walking that floor.

In the hot sanctuary they sat on wooden pews,
the music of their youth personified in Nudie suits and steel guitars,
Ernest Tubb electrifying the cathedral walking that floor.
They were new lovers holding one life to stand on country songs.

The music of their youth personified in Nudie suits and steel guitars,
the twang and beat of the honky tonk 4/4 Shuffle,
these new lovers held one life to stand on country songs
while Ray Price's "Crazy Arms" lifted them over the moist heavy air.

The twang and beat of the honky tonk 4/4 Shuffle,
Little Jimmy Dickens singing "They Locked God Outside the Iron Curtain"
and Ray Price's "Crazy Arms" lifting them over the moist heavy air
when my parents traveled from Knoxville to Nashville for their honeymoon.

Amy Wright

Part, Mudlick

> "These
> are the chronicles
> of an imaginary
> town."
> —Charles Olson

Amy Wright grew up on the edge of a populated wilderness
she calls the Appalachian sublime for the way it beckons
from the edge of suggestion, beyond the state-maintained side
of Mudlick road. If there is one thing Amy Wright knows,
it's that the mountains just are & the people who live there
would rather not be looked at like fish in a bowl,
for anybody wanting to look at them has to cross several creeks
on a logging road, which Amy Wright did sometimes
on a four-wheeler and sometimes on foot, to cool off
or go on a journey. Amy Wright and her brother made a game of going
on journeys, which meant walking into the mountains
with a pack full of peanut butter to find something
good. It was instrumental for both of them in terms of shaping
a worldview that was equally brave and escapist, that moved
inside and outside in the world. Not being looked at
made it honest & being looked at made it brave.
And looking at it was intimidating, like an RV with the curtains drawn
or a washing machine on the porch with dogs.
Amy Wright was older by six years, which is part
of the reason Amy Wright thinks like a man
sometimes & a mother too. Amy Wright's Granny
had a plaque in her kitchen that told Amy Wright she needed to learn how
to look like a girl and act like a lady and think
like a man. Amy Wright learned how to negotiate like her father
and to walk like her Aunt Diane and to reason
like her mom. Even then Amy Wright knew
she wasn't going to try to learn how to work like a dog
because that seemed too contradictory to acting like a lady. Although
Amy Wright's grandmother was a lady and she worked like a dog,
Amy Wright only sometimes acts
like a lady & works like a dog to swim like a red-eye
away from it all.

Part, the walking men

There were hardly ever ambulances in Mudlick.
So when Amy Wright and her parents drove past an ambulance
at her grandfather's house, Amy Wright's mother had a panic
& Amy Wright anticipated an adventure of some kind,
which turned out to be that a neighbor's little boy had walked
into the woods and gotten lost. Amy Wright looked at Bill Johnstone
Hill and the mountains rolled out behind it, wondering at the nerve.
Amy Wright had run away too, thrown some things in a bag and set off
down the driveway. But Amy Wright's mother was smart
& offered her a granola bar for the road. Amy Wright didn't get far.
That little boy could be anywhere.
Maybe everyone in Mudlick developed the same fantasy
Amy Wright and her brother had—of leaving the world
for the mountains, which at first were actual & later became anywhere
no one could own. Amy Wright got the idea from a stranger who came in
from somewhere else like Pennsylvania and bought a plot of land
on the logging road & lived alone in a cabin without any heat.
Amy Wright's dad picked him up sometimes when he was walking
to or from town, where he worked on engines. He was the first
of the walking men Amy Wright tried to replicate. How
did Amy Wright try to replicate him? Amy Wright went to Colorado
on vacation by herself and then quit her job and moved there.
But first Amy Wright fell in love with another idea
she got in college from Vincent Van Gogh but hadn't really seen
until she saw a man out walking in an orange tobaggan hat,
thin as a fingernail paring. He walked incessantly
from one side of town to the other, to burn off his own fever.
Amy Wright stopped waiting tables to stare
when he walked by, loving how he was so unlike
her or anyone else. Amy Wright felt unlike everyone else
but not unlike enough, so Amy Wright did things that made it obvious,
how unlike everyone she was.
But everyone kept doing the unlikely things
first & Amy Wright couldn't win. Doesn't Amy Wright know
there's no such thing as winning? There's no such thing in the mountains
where Amy Wright wants to go.

Charles Wright

"Well, Get Up, Rounder, Let a Working Man Lay Down"

The kingdom of minutiae,
                         that tight place where most of us live,
Is the kingdom of the saved,
Those who exist between the cracks,
                                those just under the details.

When the hand comes down, the wing-white hand,
We are the heads of hair
                  and finger bones yanked out of their shoes,
We are the Rapture's children.

The Light at the Root of All Things

Splendor surrounds us, as Kafka says,
                             invisible, and far away.
Will the right word reveal it?
Will the right name enter its ear and bring it forth like a sun?

He says you have to call, and not wait—
It's not hostile, it's not deaf.
I'd guess, if you got them right,
           it's like, when it appears, just what's in front of you,

Something inveterate, something indestructible.

The Song from the Other Side of the World

We haven't heard from the void lately.
                               Such *a wonderful spot,*
There's coffee and bananas and the temperature's hot.
So lush a voice, so lambent a tune.

Must be a bad frequency.
Our astral music, however, will come back, and harbor us
As we go gliding, lashed to the mast,
                           into its sensual waters.

Celestial Waters

May 30th, early evening,
                                  one duck on the narrow water, pond
Stocked with clouds,
The world reflected and windless, full of grace, tiny, tiny.

Osiris has shown us the way to cross the coming night sky,
The route, the currents, the necessary magic words.
Stick to your business, boys,
                                  and forget the down-below.

Anniversary II

Dun-colored moth past the windowpane.
                                      Now, he's got the right idea,
Fuzzy and herky-jerky,
                    little Manichaean
Pulled by invisible strings toward light wherever it is.

On the 5th of June, the mother is like a shining,
Blue raindrop the sunlight refracts
                                      on the tip of the spruce tree,
Crack in the bulbous sky the moth is yo-yoed up to.

Outscape

There's no way to describe how the light splays
                                  after the storm, under the clouds
Still piled like Armageddon
Back to the west, the northwest,
                              intent on incursion.

There's no way to picture it,
                              though others have often tried to.
Here in the mountains it's like a ricochet from a sea surge,
Meadowgrass moving like sea stalks
                                  in the depths of its brilliance.

Jake Adam York

Knoxville Girl

> (Traditional) Arranged by Charlie and Ira Louvin.
> Master #15212. Recorded May 3, 1956

The song is one their mother sang,
a campfire waltz on autumn nights
or, alone, a lullaby.
It's the oldest song they know,

and now the tape is rolling,
Charlie on guitar, Ira mandolin,
the way they've done since they were kids,
the heirloom melody—

*I met a little girl in Knoxville,
a town we all know well*—
their voices close, almost one,
the harmony almost gospel.

But this is not a hymn.
They walk the riverside, whittling
smooth that driftwood branch
they'll use to *strike that fair girl down.*

She pleads for mercy, life,
her dark eyes twinkling
like the river in the wind.
But they *only beat her more.*

They grab her *by her golden curls*
and *drag her round and round,*
and *throw her into the river*
that runs through Knoxville town.

In the song, they never pause,
but run on home to bed and dream
her singing hush-now rhymes
while the sheriff fiddles at the door.

And we never see her raised
from the stream's thick water.
But the song is old,
and she has waited years before

in the Thames and the Tennessee
for her miller, her minstrel, her country boy,
to call her back, then strike her down
and lay her in the stream,

her hair a wild anemone,
a millweed that snakes like flame
to light the sheriff's page,
an ancient tongue in guilty mouths,

or moonlight through the bars
of the cinder-block *cell*
where they sit for *killing that Knoxville girl,
that girl* they *loved so well.*

Sweat gleams on the guitar's face.
Ira holds the chord in the mandolin
till the wood is still.
They wait as the tape rolls out,

smoothing like a broken stream
or sky's last light,
till dark's complete and the mic
is quiet as a lullaby child.

From A Field Guide to Etowah County

Alabama

Bluets, larkspur, common violets in the jimson
and queen-anne's-lace, tangles of boxwood
and honeysuckle and smilax in hydrangea and pine,
thick from which Spring Azures drift,
among the first to emerge, then Swallowtails'
gunmetal iridescence, obsidian-with-stars
wings turning like pages in hands of wind.
Thrashers tear in the leaves for earthworms,
salamanders, some morsel, their stipple
of sunlight-in-leaves blending then reappearing
in a crash of meal. If a snake uncurls,
the bird will leaf it in bibles of territory, protection,
and someone's aunt or grandmother, passing,
will slow to note that summer is on us early.
But this one merely stands, its wing in a ray,
feathers a concrete mottle of grain and pebble
like a roadside table turned into brush long ago.
Here, there is no cankered plum or split persimmon,
sap or juice to bead, mimeograph bright,

on the grass's nibs, and the grass does not whorl
in cursives of moonlight and dark each night,
but this is where they found that postman
from Baltimore, walking his integration letter
to Ross Barnett, three hundred miles to go,
shot in his head and neck, copies of the protest
scattered and streaking in the April dew.
It was September, honeysuckle in full perfume,
the woods a riot of grackles and jays,
when the grand jury broke and let the suspect go.
The facts are simple, my grandfather said,
the D. A. said we couldn't make a case,
so the words they never wrote coiled
in field reports and requisitions, and three days later
a church-bomb in Birmingham
blew the stained-glass face of Christ
like a dandelion head in the roadside weeds.
Snakeroot, aster, and blazing star, some
toxic to cows, should not be eaten, though many take
the greens and fruit of poke, more abundant
in Spring, as correctives, small poisons
to set things right. Goldenrod blazes the highway's
shoulders, all the way to Birmingham
or Chattanooga, and starlings gather
like glass, like grackles in the trees, such
sociability an advance of colder weather.
The Swallowtails and Azures have disappeared,
but you may spot the Great Purple Hairstreak
bumbling, slow and easy to observe,
even in the clouds of goldenrod that dust
when they land. The cones are brilliant
but delicate as their gossamer wings. Touch,
and the color's written in your skin.

At Cornwall Furnace

Cherokee County, Alabama

Blown out just after The War.
The stack's granite gapes. Each year
saplings try, as gravity has
longer, a reclamation masonry won't allow.
Lichens and moss do more.

Promises of love and forevers
mural its inside
above constellations of beer cans and glass,
ashes. The lid of sky's diameter

remains the same.

In water only yards away,
confluence of the Coosa and Little Rivers,
mud ebbs from a bed of scoria,
slag I can find in channels
miles south. Algae homes in its pocks.

The friend who has brought me here
stands waist-deep in the rivers,
taking pictures
near a deadwood stump
when her feet find something odd.

Together we struggle from the water
a mass of pig-iron the size of a liver.
It's why Noble's men built it.
Probably a product of the last blast.
Too late. We can imagine

the boys who mined and cut the rock,
brought the hematite, ore, and limestone,
the slaves
sweating in their tunnel under the hill,
but do not. We know what fire

will burn here tonight, what
fumes will rise.
Flawless architecture of a monument.
Silent,
we heft the pig and give it back.

Letter to Be Wrapped Around a Bottle of Whiskey

for Bob Morgan

Water so thick
light just stumbles through
the cordials you've poured,
making a welcome table
of the cedar chest
the glasses lens
in some compound eye
to observe the story
of a rug or a plank
or a glass of whiskey.
Body and plant, body
and land. Conversations

are naturalists
or rivers, knowing
the schist and the batholith,
ginseng and Genesis,
gathering as they go.
Rise into the balds,
following streams
to their first ideas,
and the fork of the voice
will tremble, strike rock,
and draw the flood.
As corn, once wheat-thin,
will rise from any ground.
As it holds its sugars,
days it's concentrated
to such brightness
we distill, thought
to form, in the hollows
where we remembered
how to cut cadence
from a limb, a ballad
from a family
tree. As the maker of fire
brings the guitar
and the country song
from a turtle's shell
and the stomach of a lamb.
As what begins anywhere
started already somewhere
else. Here, in the ridge
and valley of voice
where you draw the well of song,
the spring that's warming now
in your talk, maybe
it is snowing now,
and a string band threads
the bruise of night
where windows are
crocuses offering their saffrons
to the cold and the snake-handler's
arms in the one-room church
antennas raised
to the broadcast Christ,
the zircon in his pocket
shaking the mustard seed
from the mockingbird,
gospel from the air,
the peavine of melody curling
on his tongue an air

the wanderers know,
having passed mouth
to mouth, over the sea,
guitar to glossolalia
in tangled lines.
As from the stalk
the pone and the potable,
from the blue-hole
the bluegrass and the blues,
you keep pouring,
so conversations are naturalists
and rivers, each step,
each stumble an address
to the ground or the stars,
until we are chests,
until we are rooms,
until we are radios
playing all stations,
a ballad on every one.

John Thomas York

Brains

When I was five,
I loved the curly-headed white-faced steer,
though he was no pet:
he only stared
when I called him to the barbed wire fence.

I didn't see him shot, but I was there
on that bright November morning
when the men attached hooks
to his rear ankles
and hoisted his carcass toward a massive tree limb.
They stripped away
his red and white coat,
the meat steaming, smoking entrails falling
into the waiting wash tub.

I played behind the barn, until my father whistled
and I ran to where
I could see him standing behind the truck.
He told me to get in
as he heaved something onto the bed.
I looked through the rear window,
took just a glance of a bloodied face.

Dad took the head to old Mr. Jones,
who was sagging and gray
like his unpainted house.
The man grinned a broad, toothless grin
when Dad said,
"I hear tell you *love* brains for breakfast."
"Shore do!" said Mr. Jones,
and they laughed.
But I didn't laugh.
I was sure the man had a row of big jars
on his kitchen shelf, a dark kitchen,
jars full of brains, like in some movie I glimpsed,
jars labeled *Steer*, *Pig*, *Boy*.

June

One morning, I walked down
the ditch between young corn and shining gravel,
cool white sand

lovely to my uncallused feet.
I shuffled toward the giant trees hanging
over the road,

walked right into a shower of music,
as strange as the melodies picked up by radio
telescopes—music from the stars.

I couldn't see any aliens,
but I knew their hymn—*how wide the sky*
was my rough translation,

or maybe the visitors
were merely chirping, laughing at a dirty
blond boy: *a wingless creature,*

how slowly and quietly he moves.
I could tell they were the true rulers of the universe,
making radiant the worm,

the grasshopper, the morning glory—
the singers' babel a blessing,
telling everything to grow.

Puzzle

My father quit the farm
one piece at a time:

Kate, the old mule, gone one day,
no word of her destination,

then the cows, thirty-five Holsteins,
sold to a man who didn't know their names,

the tractors, the tall John Deere,
the Ford, John's little buddy,

the wagon rolling on slick tires,
a yellow cultivator splotched by rust,

the antique seed drill,
iron-spoked wheels higher than my head,

a disk harrow, a bull-tongued plow,
the tobacco sleds waiting for summer,

the mowing machine whose teeth
chattered through the alfalfa on the hottest days

and the raking machine that churned
hay into orderly rows,

the manure spreader, orange wagon
splattered black, blades clotted thick,

the two-seated tobacco planter,
its twin trays, belts, and hoses,

the sprinklers, the muddy pump like half
a tractor, the irrigation pipes.

I would come home from school
and the landscape would be changed

in a subtle way
I refused to understand,

the pastures, too quiet, the growing
vacancy in the machinery shed.

One cold Saturday,
my father out for a long haul,

my sister helping my mother pack,
I wandered about the farm,

down to the bridge, along the creek,
the pasture fence, the red boundary flags,

up to the highest hill, where I could look
over the farm and see Mt. Nebo in the distance.

I was looking for a missing piece,
the edges invisible but sharp:

the wind passed through me, as if
I were a wood stove, left there by the road,

the door left open, the wind
lowing over a rusty pipe.

Egret

1

Against the black pines,
a great egret, so large, so white, wading,
then freezing above its reflection.

2

Every Independence Day
it returned to our pond where it pretended
to be two reeds and a patch of sunlight,
until the splash, the snaky lunge,
the image shattered, rippled, coming back,
the beak pointing skyward,
the momentary swelling of the neck.
How I wanted to sneak in
for a closer look but had no cover,
so the alarmed bird would spring up,
laboring, beating the air,
circling, then heading over the horizon
to another pond, a quieter place.

3

And I imagined the minnows, frogs, salamanders,
all relieved, all gathering in the dark
to tell horror stories
of Snapping Turtle, Mr. Cottonmouth, Big Daddy Bass—
but saving a shuddering whisper for the Lightning Striker,
Death's Angel,
and proclaiming the name sacred, a secret.

4

But here, smelling the shore mud
and listening to the water, the wind as quiet as bird's breath,
I pretend to be the plumed wonder,
and, solitary, I wade in deeper, one step,
then, another—wishing I were never distracted,
never deceived by the radiant image
(a long beak, hidden wings)—
I concentrate, waiting for what's moving below the surface,
a flicking shadow, breathing, moving toward my feet.

THE POETS

GILBERT ALLEN's mother, Marie Skocik, was born in McAlester, Oklahoma, and drove coal trucks in Pennsylvania during the Great Depression. She met and married his father, Joseph Allen, in New York shortly after World War II. In 1977 Gilbert Allen and his wife (Barbara Allen) moved from upstate New York to upstate South Carolina. He taught at Furman University for 38 years and is now the Bennette E. Geer Professor of Literature Emeritus. In 1982 he was included in Park Lanier's *A Literary Map of Southern Appalachia*, and his poems have appeared in many magazines, including *Appalachian Journal*, *Appalachian Heritage*, and the "Appalachian Poets" issue of *Shenandoah*. He has published eight collections of poems (most recently *Believing in Two Bodies*) and two volumes of linked short stories (most recently *The Beasts of Belladonna*). His honors include the Robert Penn Warren Prize in Poetry from *The Southern Review* and election to the South Carolina Academy of Authors, the state's literary hall of fame. In 2018 he edited the anthology *Archive: South Carolina Poetry Since 2005* with Jeffrey Makala and William Rogers.

MAGGIE ANDERSON is the author of five books of poetry, most recently *Dear All* (Four Way Books, 2017). Other books include *Windfall: New and Selected Poems*, *A Space Filled with Moving*, *Cold Comfort*, and *Years That Answer*. She has edited several anthologies, including *Learning by Heart: Contemporary American Poetry about School* and *After the Bell: Contemporary American Prose about School*. Her awards include two fellowships from the National Endowment for the Arts, fellowships from the Ohio, West Virginia, and Pennsylvania Councils on the Arts, and the Ohioana Library Award for contributions to the literary arts in Ohio. The founding director of the Wick Poetry Center and of the Wick Poetry Series of the Kent State University Press, Anderson is Professor Emerita of English at Kent State University and lives in Asheville, North Carolina.

DARNELL ARNOULT is the prize-winning author of *Galaxie Wagon: Poems* and *What Travels With Us: Poems* (LSU Press) and the novel *Sufficient Grace* (Free Press/Simon & Schuster, Inc.). Her shorter works have appeared in a variety of journals, including *Appalachian Heritage*, *Asheville Poetry Review*, *Nantahala Review*, *Now and Then*, *Sandhills Review*, *Southern Cultures*, *Southern Exposure*, and *Southwest Review*. She has received the Weatherford Award for Appalachian Literature, SIBA Poetry Book of the Year Award, Mary Frances Hobson Medal for Arts and Letters, and in 2007 was named Tennessee Writer of the Year by the Tennessee Writers Alliance.

JOSEPH BATHANTI is the former North Carolina Poet Laureate (2012-14); recipient of the North Carolina Award in Literature, the state's highest civilian honor; and an inductee of the North Carolina Literary Hall of Fame. Author of over twenty books, Bathanti is McFarlane Family Distinguished Professor of Interdisciplinary Education at Appalachian State University in Boone, North Carolina, and is the recipient of the Board of Governors Excellence in Teaching Award. He served as the 2016 Charles George VA Medical Center Writer-in-Residence in Asheville, NC, and is the co-founder of the Medical Center's Creative Writing Program. His co-edited volume, *The Anthology of Black Mountain College Poetry*, from University of North Carolina Press, was released in February 2025. A novella, from Regal House Press, *Too Glorious to Even Long for on Certain Days*, will appear in summer 2025. His volume of poetry, *Steady Daylight*, from Louisiana State University Press, is forthcoming in 2026.

LAURA TREACY BENTLEY is a poet and fiction writer from Huntington, West Virginia. Her work has been published in the United States and Ireland in literary journals such as *The New York Quarterly*, *Art Times*, *Poetry Ireland Review*, *Antietam Review*, *Rosebud*, *The Stinging Fly*, *Kestrel*, *ABZ*, *Crannog*, *Now & Then*, and in nine anthologies. *Lake Effect*, her first book of poetry, was published in 2006. She received a Fellowship Award for Literature from the West Virginia Commission on the Arts, and her poetry has been featured on the websites of *A Prairie Home Companion* and *Poetry Daily*. In 2003 she read her poetry with Ray Bradbury. Her poem, "The Quiet Zone: Green Bank Observatory" appears on posters with a photo of the Green Bank Telescope, the world's largest steerable radio telescope.

NICKOLE BROWN is the author of *Sister* and *Fanny Says*. Currently, she teaches at the Sewanee School of Letters MFA Program and lives in Asheville, NC, where she volunteers at several different animal sanctuaries. *To Those Who Were Our First Gods*, a chapbook about these animals, won the 2018 Rattle Prize, and her essay-in-poems, *The Donkey Elegies*, was published in 2020. She's the President of the Hellbender Gathering of Poets, an annual environmental literary festival in Black Mountain, NC.

KATHRYN STRIPLING BYER was the author of six books of poetry, including *The Girl in the Midst of the Harvest*, *Catching Light*, and *Descent*. She was awarded the Lamont Poetry Selection of the Academy of American Poets (now called the James Laughlin Award), the Roanoke-Chowan Award for Poetry, the North Carolina Award in Literature, and the SIBA Book Award in Poetry for *Catching Light* and *Descent*. In 2005, she was appointed the fifth North Carolina Poet Laureate, serving in that position until 2009; she was the first woman to hold this position. In 2012, she was inducted into the North Carolina Literary Hall of Fame.

WAYNE CALDWELL is the author of two novels, *Cataloochee* (2007) and *Requiem by Fire* (2010; reissued 2020). His first volume of poetry, *Woodsmoke*, was published in 2021. He followed this with *River Road* (2024). Another novel, *Shadow Family*, was published in March 2025. He has won both the Thomas Wolfe Memorial Literary Award from WNCHA and the James Still Award from the Fellowship of Southern Writers.

SHULY XÓCHITL CAWOOD teaches writing workshops, doodles with acrylics and watercolors, and is raising two poodles and five orchids. She is the author of six books, including *Something So Good It Can Never Be Enough: poems* (Press 53, 2023) and *Trouble Can Be So Beautiful at the Beginning* (Mercer University Press, 2021), winner of the Adrienne Bond Award for Poetry. She has an MFA from Queens University, and her work has been published in *The New York Times*, *The Sun*, and *Brevity*.

Author of many books, FRED CHAPPELL received the Sir Walter Raleigh Prize (1973), the North Carolina Award for Literature (1980), Yale University Library's Bollingen Prize in poetry (1985), a literature award from the National Academy of Arts and Letters (1968), the best foreign book prize from the Academie Française (1972), and the Aiken Taylor Award in poetry (1996). His works of fiction include *I Am One of You Forever* and *Brighten The Corner Where You Are*, and a new volume of poetry, *Shadowbox*.

CATHERINE PRITCHARD CHILDRESS lives in the shadow of Roan Mountain in East Tennessee. She is the director of Appalachian Studies at Lees-McRae College. Her poems have appeared in *North American Review*, *The Cape Rock*, *Louisiana Literature*, *Connecticut Review*, *Appalachian Review*, and *Still: The Journal*, among other journals, and has been anthologized in *The Southern Poetry Anthology*, Volumes VI and VII: Tennessee and North Carolina, and in *Women Speak*, Volumes VII and VIII. She is the author of *Other* (Finishing Line Press, 2015) and *Outside the Frame* (Eastover Press, 2023).

MICHAEL CHITWOOD is a freelance writer and teaches at the University of North Carolina-Chapel Hill. His poetry and fiction have appeared in *The Atlantic Monthly*, *Poetry*, *The New Republic*, *Threepenny Review*, *Virginia Quarterly Review*, *Field*, *The Georgia Review* and numerous other journals. Ohio Review Books has published two books of his poetry: *Salt Works* (1992) and *Whet* (1995). His third book, *The Weave Room*, was published by The University of Chicago Press in the Phoenix Poets series (1998). His collection of essays, *Hitting Below the Bible Belt*, was published by Down Home Press in 1998. *Gospel Road Going*, a collection of poems about his native Appalachia, was published in 2002 and was awarded the 2003 Roanoke-Chowan Prize for Poetry. In 2006, he published a collection of essays and short stories called *Finishing Touches*. His collection of poetry *From Whence* was released in March 2007 from Louisiana State University Press. Tupelo Press published his book *Spill* in October of 2007. *Spill* was named as a finalist for ForeWard magazine's poetry book of the year and won the 2008 Roanoke-Chowan Prize. Tupelo Press will publish his book *Poor-Mouth Jubilee* in 2010.

JIM CLARK was born in Byrdstown, Tennessee. His books include *Notions: A Jim Clark Miscellany*; two collections of poetry, *Dancing on Canaan's Ruins* and *Handiwork*; and he edited *Fable in the Blood: The Selected Poems of Byron Herbert Reece*. His work has appeared in the *Georgia Review*, *Prairie Schooner*, *Denver Quarterly*, *Greensboro Review*, *Appalachian Heritage*, and *Now & Then*, among others. He has released two solo CDs, *Buried Land* and *The Service of Song*, and three CDs with his band The Near Myths. He is an Emeritus Professor of English at Barton College in Wilson, North Carolina where he was the Elizabeth H. Jordan Professor of Southern Literature and Dean of the School of Humanities.

GERALDINE CONNOLLY was born in Greensburg and grew up in western Pennsylvania. She has published a chapbook and four poetry collections including *Province of Fire* (Iris Press, 1998) and *Aileron* (Terrapin Books, 2018). She has taught at the Writers Center in Bethesda, Maryland, The Chautauqua Institution in New York and the University of Arizona Poetry Center. She has received fellowships from the National Endowment for the Arts, the Maryland Arts Council, and Breadloaf Writers Conference. Her work appears in many anthologies including *Poetry 180: A Poem A Day for High School Students*, *A Constellation of Kisses*, and *The Sonoran Desert: A Field Guide*. She lives now in Tucson, Arizona.

JOHN CRUTCHFIELD grew up in Watauga County, North Carolina, and now lives in Berlin, Germany, where he teaches Humanities at the Barenboim-Said Akademie für Musik and works freelance as a translator of literary and scholarly texts. He is also co-founder and Associate Artistic Director of The Sublime Theater, for whom he writes, designs, directs, and performs original theatrical works. In addition to plays and other performance pieces, he has published poems, essays, translations, and reviews in a variety of print and online journals.

DONNA DOYLE resides in Knoxville, Tennessee. Her writing and photography publications include *New Millenium Writings*, *Now & Then: The Appalachian Magazine*, *Poets Reading the News*, *Still: The Journal*, *Pulse: Voices from the Heart of Medicine*, *Medical Literary Messenger*, *JAMA*, *CHEST*, *Anesthesiology*, *Shots*, and several anthologies. Awards include the Libba Moore Gray Poetry Prize and the Tennessee Mountain Writers Sue Ellen Hudson Award for Excellence in Writing. Doyle served as poet in residence at Preston Medical Library and is an East Tennessee Writers Hall of Fame inductee. She is an adjunct writing instructor at the Cancer Support Community of East Tennessee.

CASIE FEDUKOVICH is a West Virginia native and Associate Professor of English at North Carolina State University in Raleigh, North Carolina. Her poetry has appeared in *New Millennium Writings* and *Review Americana*, and her academic work has appeared in *Workplace: A Journal of Academic Labor and Composition Studies*, among other journals. Her research explores labor studies, material rhetoric, and academic administration.

HARRY GIEG's work has been published in journals ranging from *Pennsylvania Review* on the East Coast to *Jacaranda* on the West Coast, together with a variety of Appalachian journals and anthologies, including the poetry anthology *Wild Sweet Notes (II)*. Regarding his poetry, the writer-musician and recipient of an NEA-funded West Virginia Commission for the Arts Fellowship explains, "Mostly I'm just singing."

DIANE GILLIAM is the author of four collections of poetry: *Dreadful Wind & Rain*, *Kettle Bottom*, *One of Everything*, and *Recipe for Blackberry Cake*, and a novel, *Linney Stepp*. She has taught in regional workshops and as guest faculty in the MFA program at West Virginia Wesleyan College. She received the Chaffin Award for Appalachian Writing, a Pushcart Prize, and in 2014-2015 she was granted the Gift of Freedom from A Room of Her Own Foundation.

NIKKI GIOVANNI was born in Knoxville, Tennessee, on June 7, 1943. Although she grew up in Cincinnati, Ohio, she and her sister returned to Knoxville each summer to visit their grandparents. Giovanni graduated with honors in history from her grandfather's alma mater, Fisk University. Since 1987, she has been on the faculty at Virginia Tech, where she is a University Distinguished Professor.

JESSE GRAVES is the author of four poetry collections, including *Tennessee Landscape with Blighted Pine*, and a book of prose, *Said-Songs: Essays on Poetry and Place*. He has edited several volumes of poetry and scholarship, including *The Complete Poetry of James Agee*, with Michael Lofaro, from the University of Tennessee Press. Jesse's work has received the James Still Award for Writing about the Appalachian South from the Fellowship of Southern Writers, and two Weatherford Awards in Poetry from Berea College. He was raised in Sharps Chapel, Tennessee, and teaches as Professor of English and Poet-in-Residence at East Tennessee State University.

CHRIS GREEN is director of the Loyal Jones Appalachian Center at Berea College. He has edited *Coal: A Poetry Anthology* and authored *Rushlight: Poems* and *The Social Life of Poetry: Appalachia, Race, and Radical Modernism*, which won the Weatherford Award. He serves the region and nation though his joyful and passionate teaching, scholarship, reviews, his poetry, his advice to presses, and encouragement to writers of all types. Since 2010, he has written about 1,000 poems in the haikai tradition as actualized through his position as a white, cis-male, Buddhist professor living in Huntington, West Virginia, and Berea, Kentucky.

CONNIE JORDAN GREEN lives on a farm in East Tennessee where she writes and gardens. She has published award-winning novels for young people: *The War at Home* and *Emmy*; along with poetry chapbooks: *Slow Children Playing* and *Regret Comes to Tea*; and collections: *Household Inventory*, Winner of the Brick Road Poetry Award, and *Darwin's Breath*. Her poetry has been nominated for several Pushcart Awards and she has been honored with inclusion in the East Tennessee Writers Hall of Fame for Lifetime Achievement. Her newspaper column ran for over forty-two years. She teaches writing workshops for various groups.

LARRY GRIMES's collected poems, *Upon a Slender Stalk*, was published in 2021. His poems have appeared in several magazines and anthologies. He is Emeritus Professor of English at Bethany College and lives near Mesa Verde National Park in Southwest Colorado with his wife, Carol, and Grey the Cat. When he is not reading or writing (he's an active Hemingway scholar), he teases trout. Sometimes he catches fish. Always, he enjoys the streams, eying the drift.

Ohio Poet Laureate KARI GUNTER-SEYMOUR focuses on lifting up underrepresented voices including incarcerated adults and women in recovery. She is a Pillars of Prosperity Fellow for the Foundation for Appalachian Ohio; an Academy of American Poets Laureate Fellow and the founder/executive director of the Women of Appalachia Project and editor of its anthology series *Women Speak*. Her work has been featured in *American Book Review*, *World Literature Today*, *The New York Times*, and *Poem-a-Day*.

RICHARD HAGUE, a member of the Southern Appalachian Writers Cooperative, edited *Pine Mt. Sand & Gravel* for several years. His twenty-plus volumes of prose and poetry include *During The Recent Extinctions: New & Selected Poems* which won the 2013 Weatherford Award in Poetry, *Alive in Hard Country*, the 2003 Appalachian Writers' Association's Poetry Book of the Year, and *Ripening*, Ohio State University Press, 1984, for which he was named Co-Poet of the Year in Ohio.

CATHRYN HANKLA, native to the Appalachian region of Virginia, is the author of sixteen works of poetry, fiction, and memoir. Recent publications include *Immortal Stuff*, *Not Xanadu*, *Lost Places: On Losing and Finding Home*, and *Return to a Certain Region of Consciousness: New & Selected Poems*. She is professor emerita of English & creative writing at Hollins University.

PAULETTA HANSEL's ten poetry collections include *Will There Also Be Singing?* (Shadelandhouse Modern Press, 2024); *Heartbreak Tree* (Madville Publications, 2022), which won the Poetry Society of Virginia's 2023 North American Book Award; and the Weatherford Award winning *Palindrome* (Dos Madres Press, 2017). Pauletta is past managing editor of *Pine Mountain Sand & Gravel*, the literary journal of the Southern Appalachian Writers Cooperative, of which she was a founding member. She was also a founding member of The Soupbean Poets, a West Virginia-based group active in the late 1970s. Born and raised in southeastern Kentucky, Paulettalives in Cincinnati, Ohio.

In June 2008 WILLIAM HARMON became the James Gordon Hanes Professor Emeritus in the Humanities at UNC Chapel Hill, ending a teaching career of about forty years. Soon thereafter he and his wife Anne, a nutrition biochemist, moved to a 100-year-old house in Oxford, NC.

MARC HARSHMAN has authored 14 nationally acclaimed children's books including *Fallingwater: The Building of Frank Lloyd Wright's Masterpiece*, co-author Anna Smucker. His collections of poetry include *Woman in Red Anorak*, winner of the Blue Lynx Prize, *Believe What You Can*, winner of the Weatherford Award from the Appalachian Studies Association, WVU Press, *Dark Hills of Home*, published by Monongahela Books in 2022, and *Following the Silence*, Press 53, NC. Appointed in 2012, he is the seventh poet laureate of West Virginia.

MELISSA HELTON is Literary Arts Director for Hindman Settlement School, a cultural and historic nonprofit in southeastern Kentucky. Her poetry, photos, and essays have appeared in *Shenandoah*, *Still: The Journal*, *Anthology of Appalachian Writers*, *Norwegian Writers Climate Campaign*, *Appalachian Review*, and more. Her chapbooks include *Inertia: A Study* and *Hewn*. She is editor of the literary and arts journal *Untelling* and the anthology *Troublesome Rising: A Thousand-Year Flood in Eastern Kentucky*, which documents and responds to the catastrophic flooding of the region in July of 2022. She is a dual citizen in the United Kingdom.

RAYE HENDRIX is the author of the chapbooks *Fire Sermons* (Ghost City Press, 2021) and *Every Journal is a Plague Journal* (Bottlecap Press, 2021). Her poems appear in *American Poetry Review*, *Poetry Northwest*, *32 Poems*, *Cimarron Review*, and elsewhere. The winner of the 2019 Keene Prize for Literature and the 2018 Patricia Aakhus Award (*Southern Indiana Review*), they have also received fellowships from Bread Loaf, the Oregon Humanities Center, and the Juniper Writing Institute. Raye holds a BA and MA from Auburn University, an MFA from the University of Texas at Austin, and a PhD from the University of Oregon.

A native of upper East Tennessee, JANE HICKS is an award-winning poet and quilter. The Jesse Stuart Foundation published her first book, *Blood and Bone Remember: Poems from Appalachia* in 2005. The book met with popular and critical acclaim, winning the Appalachian Writers Association Poetry Book of the Year prize. It was also nominated for the Weatherford Award given by the Appalachian Studies Association. Jane's poetry has frequently appeared in journals and literary magazines in the southeast, notably *Wind*,

Now & Then, *Appalachian Journal*, *Appalachian Heritage*, *Asheville Poetry Review*, and *Shenandoah*. Her poems have been anthologized in *Migrants and Stowaways* and *Literary Lunch* published by the Knoxville Writers Guild, *Crossing Troublesome: 25 years of the Appalachian Writers Workshop*, *Coal: A Poetry Anthology*, *We All Live Downstream: Writings About Mountaintop Removal*, *Southern Poetry Anthology: Contemporary Appalachia*, *Southern Poetry Anthology: Tennessee*, and *Southern Poetry Anthology: Virginia*. Her work appeared in an anthology of poetry with connections to the poetry of Gerard Manley Hopkins, *The World Is Charged: Poetic Engagements with Gerard Manley Hopkins*. Her "literary quilts" illustrate the works of playwright Jo Carson and novelists Sharyn McCrumb and Silas House. The art quilts have toured with these respective authors and were the subject of a feature in *Blue Ridge Country Magazine* in an issue devoted to arts in the region. Jane retired from Sullivan County, Tennessee schools after thirty years of teaching. Her second poetry book, published in the fall of 2014 by the University Press of Kentucky, is titled *Driving with the Dead*. It also won the Appalachian Writers Association Poetry Book of the Year (2015) and was a finalist for the Weatherford Award. Her critically acclaimed third book, *The Safety of Small Things*, was published by the University of Kentucky Press under Hindman's Fireside Press imprint in early 2024.

THOMAS ALAN HOLMES lives in Johnson City, Tennessee, where he specializes in Appalachian literature as a member of the Literature and Language Department at East Tennessee State University. His scholarly and creative work has appeared in such journals as *Still: The Journal*, *Appalachian Heritage*, *The Valparaiso Review*, *The Connecticut Review*, *Louisiana Literature*, and *The Appalachian Journal*. With Daniel Westover, he has co-edited *The Fire that Breaks: Gerard Manley Hopkins's Poetic Legacies* (Clemson U P, 2020), including his chapter about Hopkins's influence on Appalachian poets. Holmes has work in both the Tennessee and Alabama volumes of *The Southern Poetry Anthology* series. Iris Press published his debut poetry collection, *In the Backhoe's Shadow*, in 2022.

RON HOUCHIN was an Appalachian public school teacher raised in Huntington, West Virginia. His work appeared in *New Orleans Review*, *The Southwest Review*, *Poetry Ireland Review*, *Appalachian Heritage*, *Appalachian Journal*, *Now & Then*, and over two hundred others. He has five books of poetry published from Salmon Publishing of Ireland and Wind Publications of Kentucky. His latest book, *Museum Crows*, appeared from Salmon, September of 2009.

SILAS HOUSE is the nationally bestselling author of five books including *Eli the Good*, *Something's Rising*, and *Clay's Quilt*. House is the recipient of many honors, among them: Appalachian Book of the Year, the Award for Special Achievement from the Fellowship of Southern Writers, Kentucky Novel of the Year (twice), Appalachian Writer of the Year, and the Helen Lewis Award for Community Service. He serves as the NEH Chair of Appalachian Studies at Berea College. He lives in Eastern Kentucky, where he was born and raised.

REBECCA GAYLE HOWELL is a writer, translator, and editor from Kentucky. In addition to publishing, she collaborates with composer Reena Esmail to write works for classical performance, including *A Winter Breviary* (Oxford University Press, 2022), a song cycle regularly performed on three continents. Howell's awards include the United States Artists Fellowship, the Carson McCullers Fellowship, and two fellowships from the Fine Arts Work Center, as well as Best Book of the Year honors from outlets like the Best Translated Book Awards, the Foreword INDIES, the Banipal Prize, and the Nautilus Awards. Her newest book is *Erase Genesis* (Bridwell Press, 2025).

DAVID HUDDLE grew up in Ivanhoe, Virginia, taught at the University of Vermont for thirty-eight years, and currently is the Visiting Distinguished Professor of Creative Writing at Hollins University. He's the author of sixteen books of poetry, fiction, and essays, including *Paper Boy*, *Only the Little Bone*, *The Writing Habit*, *La Tour Dreams of the Wolf Girl*, and *Glory River*. His work has appeared in recent issues of *Appalachian Heritage*, *Redivider*, *Michigan Quarterly Review*, and *The New Yorker*.

CHARLIE HUGHES grew up on a Kentucky farm. He held degrees from Transylvania University and the University of Kentucky. Though employed as an analytical chemist, he had an abiding interest in the literary arts. He was the co-editor of *Groundwater: Contemporary Kentucky Fiction*, editor of *The Kentucky Literary Newsletter*, a biweekly e-mail and online newsletter, and author of two collections of poetry, *Body and Blood* (2010) and *Shifting for Myself* (2002). He was also the owner of Wind Publications, a small press with an emphasis on poetry. His poems and fiction have appeared in prominent literary magazines, including *Kansas Quarterly*, *Hollins Critic*, and *Appalachian Heritage*.

JANNETTE HYPES was a graduate of the University of South Carolina Aiken where she studied poetry and life with Dr. Stephen Gardner, who later became her stepfather by some strange and wonderful twist of fate. Although a South Carolina native, she became an East Tennessean in 1998. Her poetry has appeared in *Breathing the Same Air: An East Tennessee Anthology* (Celtic Cat Publishing, 2001); *The Southern Poetry Anthology, Volume I: South Carolina* (Texas Review, 2007); and *Outscapes: Writings on Fences and Frontiers* (Knoxville Writers' Guild, 2008).

EDISON JENNINGS's poems have appeared in several journals and anthologies, including *Boulevard, Kenyon Review, Poetry Daily, River Styx, Slate, Southern Review, Triquarterly,* and *Don't Leave Hungry: Fifty Years of Southern Poetry Review.* He lives in Abingdon, Virginia, and directs the English program at Virginia Intermont College.

DON JOHNSON is retired professor of English and poet in residence at East Tennessee State University. For sixteen years he served as general editor of *Aethlon: the Journal of Sport Literature.* Johnson is the author of *The Sporting Muse* (2004) and three books of poetry: *The Importance of Visible Scars* (1984), *Watauga Drawdown* (1991), and *Here and Gone: New and Selected Poems* (2008). He also edited *Hummers, Knucklers, and Slow Curves,* a collection of modern and contemporary American poems about baseball (1992). He has also published several articles on contemporary Appalachian poets, a lengthy piece on Richard Ford's novels, an article in *The Southern Review* on Nobel Laureate Seamus Heaney, and a novel entitled *Blue Winged Olive.*

JUDY JORDAN's first book of poetry, *Carolina Ghost Woods,* won the 1999 Walt Whitman Award from the Academy of American Poets, the 2000 National Book Critics Circle Award, as well as the Utah Book of the Year Award, the OAY Award from the Poetry Council of North Carolina, and the Thomas Wolfe Literary Award. Her second book of poetry, *Sixty Cent Coffee and a Quarter to Dance,* was published by LSU press. *Hunger* and *Children of Salt* are published by Tinderbox Editions. She has recently completed a novel, *Broken Days, Broken Hearts,* and a memoir, *My Mama, My Sweet Nelly,* and is currently working on a biography of a woman who helped rescue over 15,000 children from death camps in World War II. Jordan built her own environmentally friendly earthbag and cob house off-grid surrounded by the Shawnee National Forest, and teaches creative writing at Southern Illinois University, Carbondale.

MARILYN KALLET is the author of fourteen books, including *Packing Light: New and Selected Poems* (Black Widow Press, 2009). Her translation of *The Big Game* by Surrealist Benjamin Péret will be published by Black Widow Press. She directs the creative writing program at the University of Tennessee, where she holds a Lindsay Young Chair in English. She also teaches poetry workshops for the Virginia Center for the Creative Arts in Auvillar, France.

LEATHA KENDRICK is a poet, writer, and editor whose poems and essays appear in journals including *Appalachian Heritage, Passager, Tar River Poetry, New Madrid Review, The Southern Poetry Review, The James Dickey Review, Appalachian Journal, Still: An Online Journal,* and the *Baltimore Review,* and in anthologies including *Women Speak* vol. 8 and *What Comes Down to Us—Twenty-Five Contemporary Kentucky Poets.* With George Ella Lyon, she co-edited *Crossing Troublesome—Twenty-Five Years of the Appalachian Writers Workshop.* Her fifth book of poetry is *And Luckier* (Accents Publishing, 2020).

LISA KWONG is the author of *Becoming AppalAsian* (Glass Lyre Press) and an Affrilachian Poet. Her poems have appeared in *Best New Poets, A Literary Field Guide to Southern Appalachia, Anthology of Appalachian Writers,* and other publications. She teaches at Indiana University and Ivy Tech Community College in Bloomington, Indiana. Additionally, she has taught poetry workshops for Writer's Digest University, The Appalachian Symposium, and The Makery at Hindman Settlement School.

JEANNE LARSEN moved to Virginia in 1954, 1961, 1971, and 1980. The last time worked: she still lives in Roanoke County, between the Blue Ridge and the Allegheny Highlands. Her latest book is *What Penelope Chooses: poems,* winner of the Cider Press Review Award. She has also published two other books of poetry (*Why We Make Gardens,* and *James Cook in Search of Terra Incognita,* an AWP award series winner), as well as four novels (*Silk Road, Bronze Mirror, Manchu Palaces, Sally Paradiso*), and two collections of translated poems by medieval Chinese women (*Brocade River Poems* and *Willow, Wine, Mirror, Moon*). Jeanne was the inaugural Jackson Professor of Creative Writing at Hollins University.

Born in Snowflake, Virginia, JUDY LOEST earned her Master's degree in English from the University of Tennessee in 1998. Her poetry has appeared in such journals as *Now & Then, The Cortland Review, New Millennium Writings,* and *storySouth,* and in The Poetry Society of America's *Poetry in Motion* program. Her nonfiction has been published in *EvaMag, France Magazine,* and *Metropulse.* Her awards include the Libba Moore Gray Poetry Prize, the James Still Poetry Award, and the Olay/Poetry Society of America Fine Lines Poetry Prize. She is editor of *Knoxville Bound,* a literary anthology inspired by Knoxville, TN. Her poetry chapbook, *After Appalachia*, was published by Finishing Line Press in 2007; the poem "Faith" from that collection appeared in Ted Kooser's "American Life in Poetry" newspaper column in 2009.

DONNA J. LONG has served as Editor-in-Chief of *Kestrel* since 2008. Her own poems have been published in many journals, including *The Southern Review, Clockhouse, Appalachian Heritage,* and *Fourth River*, which nominated "Eleventh Grade English Oral" for a Pushcart Prize. In 2020, Muskie Press published her chapbook, *Our World Order*. She is Professor of English at Fairmont State University.

DENTON LOVING is the author of the poetry collections *Crimes Against Birds* (Main Street Rag) and *Tamp* (Mercer University Press). He is a co-founder and editor at EastOver Press and its literary journal *Cutleaf*. His writing has appeared in numerous publications including *Iron Horse Literary Review, Tupelo Quarterly, Harvard Divinity Bulletin, The Threepenny Review,* and *Ecotone*.

ROBERT WOOD LYNN is a poet from Virginia. His debut collection, *Mothman Apologia* (2022 Yale University Press) was selected as the winner of the Yale Younger Poets Prize and Kate Tufts Discovery Award and named by the *New York Times* to its Best Poetry of 2022 list. His poems have appeared in *American Poetry Review, the Atlantic, Poetry Magazine, The Southern Review,* and elsewhere. A 2023 National Endowment for the Arts creative writing fellow, he teaches poetry at Juilliard.

Harlan County native, GEORGE ELLA LYON writes in multiple genres for readers of all ages. She has published five poetry collections, a novel and memoir for adults, novels and poetry for young people, and many children's picture books. Her most recent titles include *Back to the Light: Poems* (U of Kentucky P, 2021) and *Time to Fly* (Atheneum, 2022). Her poem "Where I'm From" has gone around the world as a writing model. Married to musician and writer Steve Lyon, she served as Kentucky Poet Laureate (2015-16) and was recently inducted into the Kentucky Writers Hall of Fame.

JEFF MANN has published six books of poetry, *Bones Washed with Wine, On the Tongue, Ash, A Romantic Mann, Rebels,* and *Redneck Bouquet*; three collections of essays, *Edge, Binding the God,* and *Endangered Species*; a book of poetry and memoir, *Loving Mountains, Loving Men*; six novels, *Fog, Purgatory, Cub, Salvation, Country,* and *Insatiable*; four volumes of short fiction, *A History of Barbed Wire, Desire and Devour, Consent,* and *The Sagas of Mann*; and, with Henry Z., a graphic novel, *Highland Moon*. With Julia Watts, he co-edited *LGBTQ Fiction and Poetry from Appalachia*. The winner of two Lambda Literary Awards and four National Leather Association-International literary awards, he teaches creative writing at Virginia Tech.

MAURICE MANNING's eighth book of poetry, *Snakedoctor*, was published in 2023. He lives with his family in Kentucky and teaches at Transylvania University.

JEFF DANIEL MARION published nine poetry collections, four poetry chapbooks, and a children's book. His poems appeared in *The Southern Review, Southern Poetry Review, Shenandoah, Atlanta Review, Tar River Poetry,* and many others. In 1978, Marion received the first Literary Fellowship awarded by the Tennessee Arts Commission. *Ebbing & Flowing Springs: New and Selected Poems and Prose, 1976-2001* won the Independent Publisher Award in Poetry and was named Appalachian Book of the Year by the Appalachian Writers Association. His collection *Father* received the 2009 Quentin R. Howard Poetry Prize, and in 2011 he was awarded the James Still Award for Writing About the Appalachian South by the Fellowship of Southern Writers. Marion served as the Jack E. Reese Writer-in-Residence for the University of Tennessee Libraries, Knoxville, from 2009-2011. In Spring 2013, his work and career were celebrated at Carson-Newman University and Walters State Community College. Marion was born in 1940 and died in July 2021.

MICHAEL MCFEE is the author or editor of seventeen books, most recently *A Long Time to Be Gone: Poems* (Carnegie Mellon University Press, 2022) and *Appointed Rounds: Essays* (Mercer University Press, 2018. A native of Asheville, North Carolina, and a recipient of the James Still Award for Writing about the Appalachian South, he recently retired after 35 years of teaching in the Creative Writing Program at UNC-Chapel Hill.

ROSE MCLARNEY's books are *Colorfast, Forage,* and *Its Day Being Gone*, published by Penguin, as well as *The Always Broken Plates of Mountains*, from Four Way Books. She is co-editor of *A Literary Field Guide to Southern Appalachia*, from University of Georgia Press, and the journal *Southern Humanities Review*. Rose is Lanier Endowed Professor in the Department of English at Auburn University. She won the National Poetry Series contest and received fellowships from MacDowell and Bread Loaf, among other awards. Her writing has appeared in *Kenyon Review, New England Review, American Poetry Review,* and *Southern Review*.

KELLY MCQUAIN grew up in the Allegheny Mountains of West Virginia and is the author of two previous chapbooks, *Velvet Rodeo* (winner of the Bloom Award) and *Antlers*. His poetry has appeared in *Best New Poets, American Poetry Review, The Pinch, Kestrel, Appalachian Review*, and in numerous anthologies. Also an artist, McQuain's paintings have appeared in books, journals, magazines, and galleries. He currently works as a professor of English in Philadelphia.

JIM MINICK is the author or editor of eight books, including *Without Warning: The Tornado of Udall, Kansas* (nonfiction), *The Intimacy of Spoons* (poetry), *Fire Is Your Water* (novel), and *The Blueberry Years: A Memoir of Farm and Family*. His work has appeared in many publications, including the *New York Times, Poets & Writers, Oxford American, Orion, Shenandoah, Appalachian Journal, Wind*, and *The Sun*. He serves as co-editor of *Pine Mountain Sand & Gravel*.

THORPE MOECKEL is the author of several books of poems and prose, and has taught at Hollins University since 2005.

JANICE TOWNLEY MOORE, a native of Atlanta, is Associate Professor of English emerita at Young Harris College in the North Georgia Mountains. Her poems have been published in many journals including *Georgia Review, Prairie Schooner, Southern Poetry Review, Poetry East, Shenandoah, Connecticut Review, JAMA*, and *South Carolina Review*. Among a wide variety of anthologies that include her poems are *The Bedford Introduction to Literature* and *Listen Here: Women Writing Appalachia*. In 2009 she won first place in poetry in Press 53 Open Awards for the poem published here. For a dozen years she served as poetry editor for *Georgia Journal*. Her chapbook *Teaching the Robins* was published in 2009 (Finishing Line). Currently, she serves as a poetry consultant for *The Pharos*, publication of Alpha Omega Alpha Honor Medical Society. She lives with her family in Hayesville, North Carolina.

ROBERT MORGAN is the author of several books of poems, including *Terroir* (2011) and *Dark Energy* (2015). *To Honor the Imagined Whole: New Poems* will be published in 2026. He has published twelve books of fiction, among them the *New York Times* bestseller *Gap Creek*, and, more recently, *Chasing the North Star* (2016), and *In the Snowbird Mountains and Other Stories* (2023). His works of nonfiction include *Lions of the West* (2011), the national bestseller *Boone: A Biography* (2007), and *Fallen Angel: The Life of Edgar Allan Poe* (2023). Recipient of awards from the Guggenheim Foundation and the American Academy of Arts and Letters, he is currently Kappa Alpha Professor of English (Emeritus) at Cornell University.

RICK MULKEY is the author of six collections including *Ravenous: New & Selected Poems, Toward Any Darkness, Before the Age of Reason, Bluefield Breakdown*, and *All These Hungers*. His work appears in the anthologies *American Poetry: The Next Generation, The Southern Poetry Anthology*, and *A Millennial Sampler of South Carolina Poetry*, among others. With Denise Duhamel, he co-edited *Ice On A Hot Stove: A Decade of Converse MFA Poetry* from Clemson University Press. Individual poems and essays have appeared in a variety of venues such as *Crab Orchard Review, Denver Quarterly, The Literary Review, Poet Lore, Poetry East, Shenandoah, Southern Poetry Review*, and *Poetry Daily*. His awards include the Hawthornden Fellowship for Writing, the Charles Angoff Award from *The Literary Review*, the Editor's Choice Award from *Still: the Journal*, and the Gearhart Prize from *Southeast Review*. Mulkey directs the Low Residency MFA in Creative Writing at Converse University.

TED OLSON is Professor of Appalachian Studies at East Tennessee State University. He is the author of three collections of poetry: *Breathing in Darkness* (2006), *Revelations* (2012), and *Blue Moon* (2025). Olson has written or edited several books exploring Appalachian folklore and folklife. For his work as a music historian, he has been nominated for nine Grammy Awards.

LISA J. PARKER is a native Virginian, a poet, musician, and photographer. Her first book, *This Gone Place*, won the 2010 ASA Weatherford Award. Her second book, *The Parting Glass*, won the 2021 Arthur Smith Poetry Prize. Her work is widely published in literary journals and anthologies. Her photography has been on exhibit in NYC and published in several arts journals and anthologies. She has worked in the Department of Defense for more than 20 years, worked as a first responder for 15 years, and currently serves as a crisis and disaster response volunteer with Team Rubicon and ConversaCorps.

Poet, playwright, essayist, and editor, LINDA PARSONS is the poetry editor for Madville Publishing and the copy editor for *Chapter 16*, the literary website of Humanities Tennessee. She is published widely, and her sixth collection, containing poetry and prose, is *Valediction* (Madville Publishing, 2023). Five of her plays have been produced by Flying Anvil Theatre in Knoxville, Tennessee, where she lives and gardens.

CHARLOTTE PENCE is Mobile, Alabama's inaugural Poet Laureate and a 2024 Academy of American Poets laureate fellow. Her most recent book of poems, *Code*, received the 2020 Book of the Year award from ASPS and was shortlisted for Best Indie Poetry Books of 2020 by Foreword Reviews. Her first book of poems, *Many Small Fires* (Black Lawrence Press, 2015), received a silver INDIEFAB Book of the Year Award from Foreword Reviews. She is also the author of two award-winning poetry chapbooks and the editor of *The Poetics of American Song Lyrics*. Her poetry, fiction, and creative nonfiction have recently been published in *Harvard Review, Sewanee Review, Southern Review, Poetry, Brevity*, and featured on *The Slowdown*. A graduate of Emerson College (MFA) and the University of Tennessee (PhD), she is now the director of the Stokes Center for Creative Writing at the University of South Alabama.

Born in Floyd County, Kentucky, EDWINA PENDARVIS writes mostly about life and literature in Appalachia with the exception of four YA dual-language biographies published by the Shanghai Foreign Language Education Press. Poet and essayist, her work has appeared in periodicals, such as *Appalachian Journal, Cafe Review, Eureka*, and *Indiana Review*, and anthologies, such as *Wild Sweet Notes*. Her most recent poetry collection is *Ghost Dance Poems*, published by Blair Mountain Press in 2015. Her most recent nonfiction book is *Another World: Ballet Lessons from Appalachia* (2023) published by the Jesse Stuart Foundation.

PATRICK PHILLIPS teaches writing and literature at Stanford University and is a Carnegie Foundation Fellow and a fellow of the Cullman Center for Writers at the New York Public Library. His most recent collection is *Song of the Closing Doors* (Knopf, 2022).

LYNN POWELL has published three books of poetry—*Old & New Testaments, The Zones of Paradise*, and *Season of the Second Thought*—and a book of nonfiction, *Framing Innocence*. Her honors include a National Endowment for the Arts Fellowship, the Felix Pollak Prize in Poetry, the Brittingham Prize in Poetry, the Studs & Ida Terkel Award for nonfiction, and four Ohio Arts Council Excellence Awards. She teaches in the Creative Writing Program of Oberlin College, where she founded the Writers in the Schools program. Born and raised in East Tennessee, she has lived in Oberlin, Ohio, since 1990.

RITA SIMS QUILLEN's most recent poetry book, *Some Notes You Hold* (Madville 2020) has received a Bronze Medal from the Feathered Quill Book Awards, a finalist listing for poetry in the American Writing Awards, and is a Bonus Book for the 2023 International Pulpwood Queens and Timber Guys Book Club. Her novel, *Wayland*, published by Iris Press in 2019, is the March 2022 Bonus Book of the Month for the International Pulpwood Queens and Timber Kings Book Club. It is a sequel to her first novel, *Hiding Ezra* (Little Creek Books, 2014). Her full-length poetry collection, *The Mad Farmer's Wife*, published in 2016 by TRP, was a finalist for the Weatherford Award in Appalachian Literature from Berea College. One of six semifinalists for the 2012-14 Poet Laureate of Virginia, she has received three Pushcart nominations, and a Best of the Net nomination in 2012. She lives, farms, writes songs, and takes photographs at Early Autumn Farm in southwestern Virginia.

MELISSA RANGE is the author of *Scriptorium*, a winner of the 2015 National Poetry Series (Beacon Press, 2016), and *Horse and Rider* (Texas Tech University Press, 2010). Recent poems have appeared in *Ecotone, The Hopkins Review, Michigan Quarterly Review, The Nation*, and *Ploughshares*. Range is the recipient of awards and fellowships from the National Endowment for the Arts, the Rona Jaffe Foundation, the American Antiquarian Society, and the Fine Arts Work Center in Provincetown. Originally from East Tennessee, she teaches creative writing and American literature at Lawrence University in Wisconsin.

RON RASH is the Parris Distinguished Professor in Appalachian Cultural Studies at Western Carolina University. In 1994 he published his first book, a collection of short stories titled *The Night the New Jesus Fell to Earth*. Since then, Rash has published three collections of poetry, three short story collections, and four novels. Rash's poems and stories have appeared in more than one hundred magazines and journals. His recent collection of short stories, *Burning Bright* (Ecco, 2010), won the Frank O'Connor International Short Story Award.

A native of Southern Appalachia, MARK A. ROBERTS is an Appalachian scholar, poet, teacher, and college administrator. He has published essays in the *Appalachian Journal* and *James Dickey Review*. He currently serves as President at Reinhardt University in Waleska, GA.

JANE SASSER was born and raised on a farm in North Carolina. She grew up in a family of storytellers and began writing her own stories at the age of six. Her poetry has appeared in *JAMA, North American Review, The Sun*, and other publications. She has published three poetry chapbooks: *What's Underneath*

(Iris Press, 2020), *Itinerant* (Finishing Line, 2009), and *Recollecting the Snow* (March Street Press, 2008). Following a career as an English teacher in Tennessee, she retired to Fairview, NC, with her husband and retired greyhounds.

ELIZABETH SAVAGE is Assistant Professor of English and Co-Director of Women's Studies at Fairmont State University. She is poetry editor for *Kestrel: A Journal of Literature & Art*.

GEORGE SCARBROUGH published five major books of poetry and one novel. Scarbrough's first book of poetry, *Tellico Blue*, was published by E. P. Dutton in New York in 1949. Dutton also published two additional Scarbrough books of poetry: *The Course Is Upward* (1951) and *Summer So-Called* in 1956. *New and Selected Poems* was released in 1977 (Iris Press). St. Luke's Press published Scarbrough's novel, *A Summer Ago* in 1986. Iris Press published *Invitation to Kim* in 1989, nominated for a Pulitzer Prize in 1990; Iris Press also re-issued *Tellico Blue* in 1999.

Connecticut State University Distinguished Professor and Editor of *Connecticut Review*, VIVIAN SHIPLEY teaches at Southern Connecticut State University where she was named Faculty Scholar in 2000, 2005, and 2008. Her ninth book, *All of Your Messages Have Been Erased* (Southeastern Louisiana University, 2010) was nominated for the Pulitzer Prize. *Greatest Hits: 1974-2010* (Pudding House Press, Youngstown, Ohio, 2010) is her sixth chapbook. *Hardboot: Poems New & Old* received the 2006 Paterson Prize for Sustained Literary Achievement and the Connecticut Press Club Prize for Best Creative Writing. Raised in Kentucky, a member of the University of Kentucky Hall of Distinguished Alumni, she has a Ph.D. from Vanderbilt University and lives in North Haven, Connecticut with her husband, Ed Harris.

SAVANNAH SIPPLE is a writer, editor, and professor from Kentucky. Her debut poetry collection *WWJD and Other Poems* (Sibling Rivalry Press, 2019) is a coming out story about growing up queer in evangelical eastern Kentucky. You can also find her essays in GO *Magazine* and *Salon*. She lives with her wife Ashley, a librarian, and their two dogs, Lucky and Lola, in Lexington, Kentucky.

ARTHUR SMITH's first book, *Elegy on Independence Day*, was awarded the Agnes Lynch Starrett Poetry Prize and was published by the University of Pittsburgh Press in 1985. That same year, it was selected by the Poetry Society of America to receive the Norma Farber First Book Award. His second book of poems, *Orders of Affection*, was published by Carnegie Mellon University Press in 1996, which also published his third book, *The Late World* (2002), and his last, *The Fortunate Era* (2013).

JAMES MALONE SMITH's poems appear in *AGNI* (online), *Atlanta Review*, *Prairie Schooner*, *Quarterly West*, *Shenandoah*, *32 Poems*, and others. He is the editor of *Southern Poetry Review*, as well as the editor of the anthology *Don't Leave Hungry: Fifty Years of Southern Poetry Review* (University of Arkansas Press, 2009). Smith is Professor of English at Georgia Southern University in Savannah, Georgia. He grew up in the mountains of north Georgia and western North Carolina and attended Young Harris College. He went on to complete his B.A. degree at Berry College and then the M.A. and Ph.D. at Vanderbilt University.

NOEL SMITH was born and raised in New York City and worked in the 1950's in Eastern Kentucky as a medical social worker for Mary Breckinridge's Frontier Nursing Service. Later Smith taught elementary school in Rockland County, NY. She has had poems in many journals, including *New Letters*, *Shenandoah*, *Sow's Ear*, and *Appalachian Heritage*, as well as anthologies such as *We All Live Downstream: Writings About Mountaintop Removal*, edited by Jason Howard, and *Motif*, vols. 1 and 2, edited by Marianne Worthington. Her first collection of poetry, *The Well String*, was published by Motesbooks in 2008.

R. T. SMITH was raised and educated in Georgia and North Carolina, and has lived in Alabama and Virginia. His nineteen books of poems include two Library of Virginia Books of the Year (*Messenger* and *Outlaw Style*) and he has published six collections of stories, notably *Uke Rivers* and *Chinquapins*. *In the Night Orchard: New and Selected Poems* was published by TRP in 2014.

STEVE SPARKS worked as a lecturer in the English Department at The University of Tennessee where he taught freshman and sophomore classes. He was originally from North Alabama and lived in Knoxville. He had published poems in *North American Review*, *New Millennium Writings*, *Potpourri*, *Number One*, and in the anthologies *Migrants and Stowaways* and *Knoxville Bound*.

HENRY SPOTTSWOOD was born in Mobile, Alabama in 1940. He attended Georgia Tech and Vanderbilt University. Later, he taught in the business departments of several universities. He retired in

2017 after 30 years of work in the addictions field. He now lives with his wife Mary and rescue cat Zelda in downtown Cincinnati where he continues to write poetry and cheer for the Reds and Bengals.

DARIUS STEWART is the author of *Intimacies in Borrowed Light* (EastOver Press 2022) and *Be Not Afraid of My Body: A Lyrical Memoir* (Belt Publishing 2024). He currently lives in Iowa City where he is a Lulu Merle Johnson Doctoral Fellow in English at the University of Iowa.

A.E. STRINGER is the author of four collections: *Asbestos Brocade*, *Late Breaking*, and *Human Costume* (all from Salmon Poetry of Ireland); and *Channel Markers* (Wesleyan UP). His poems have appeared in *Antaeus*, *The Nation*, *The Ohio Review*, *Shenandoah*, *Prairie Schooner*, *Poetry Northwest*, and others. He taught Literature and Writing at Marshall University for 24+ years.

DAN STRYK's poems and prose parables have appeared in a variety of literary and cultural journals and anthologies over the years, including *Poetry*, *Ploughshares*, *Shenandoah*, *Appalachian Heritage*, *The Oxford American* (2008 "Best of the South" issue), *TriQuarterly*, *New England Review*, *Poetry Northwest*, *Commonweal*, *Tricycle: The Buddhist Review*, *A Year in Verse* (Crown Publications, NY), *Commonwealth: Contemporary Poets of Virginia* (University Press of Virginia), *CrossRoads: A Southern Culture Annual* (Mercer University Press), *City of the Big Shoulders: An Anthology of Chicago Poetry* (University of Iowa Press), and *A Literary Field Guide to Southern Appalachia* (University of Georgia Press, 2019). His seven published collections of poetry and lyric prose (often mixed-genre fusions) include *The Artist and the Crow* (Purdue University Press) and *Dimming Radiance: Poems and Prose Parables* (Wind Publications, KY). While forthcoming in early 2025, BACK TO THE SOURCE: *Selected Poems & Parables (1980-2020)* will be Stryk's career-covering volume of representative cross-cultural writing, inspired by his widely traveled lifeway as a (now-retired) Professor of World Literature and Imaginative Writing—first in a large Midwestern Institution (west of Chicago), and later in a small Appalachian Humanities College in the foothills of southwest Virginia (where often granted generous leave-time to explore and create in cultures as diverse as England, Scotland, Italy, the Low Countries, and Japan).

LARRY D. THACKER's poetry and fiction can be found in over 200 journals and anthologies. His books include four full poetry collections, two chapbooks, as well as the folk history, *Mountain Mysteries: The Mystic Traditions of Appalachia*. His two collections of short fiction include *Working it Off in Labor County* and *Labor Days, Labor Nights*, as well as a co-authored short story collection, *Everyday, Monsters*. His MFA in poetry and fiction is from West Virginia Wesleyan College.

ERIC TRETHEWEY published six books of poems, including *Songs and Lamentations* and *Heart's Hornbook*. His poems, stories, personal and critical essays, and reviews have appeared in numerous magazines and anthologies in Britain, Canada and the U.S.: *The Antioch Review*, *The Atlantic Monthly*, *The American Scholar*, *Canadian Literature*, *Encounter*, *The Fiddlehead*, *The Georgia Review*, *Gettysburg Review*, *Glimmer Train Stories*, *The Hudson Review*, *Iowa Review*, *The Kenyon Review*, *The Missouri Review*, *New Letters*, *The New Republic*, *North American Review*, *Parnassus*, *The Paris Review*, *Ploughshares*, *Poetry*, *The Sewanee Review*, *The Southern Review*, and *The Yale Review*.

Originally from Kingsport, Tennessee, LINDSAY TURNER is the author of the poetry collections *Songs & Ballads* (Prelude Books, 2018) and *The Upstate* (University of Chicago Press, 2023), as well as a translator of contemporary Francophone poetry and philosophy. She holds a BA from Harvard College, a Masters in film from the Université Paris III, an MFA in poetry from New York University, and a PhD in English from the University of Virginia. She lives in Cleveland, Ohio, where she is Associate Professor of English and Creative Writing at Case Western Reserve University.

SUSAN O'DELL UNDERWOOD has lived most of her life in East Tennessee, where she was raised by school teachers and farmers. Before retirement, she directed the creative writing program at Carson-Newman. Besides two chapbooks of poetry, she has two full-length collections, *The Book of Awe* (Iris 2018) and *Splinter* (Madville 2023). Her novel *Genesis Road* won the Tennessee Arts Commission Grant for Prose. Her poems and works in other genres appear and are forthcoming in a variety of journals and anthologies, including *Oxford American*, *Ecotone*, *A Literary Field Guide to Appalachia*, and *The Southern Poetry Anthology: Tennessee*. She is married to artist David Underwood.

DOUG VAN GUNDY directs the Low-Residency MFA program in Creative Writing at West Virginia Wesleyan College. His poems and essays have appeared in many journals, including *Poetry*, *Guernica*, *Poets & Writers*, and *The Oxford American*. He is the author of a book of poems, *A Life Above Water*, and co-editor of the anthology *Eyes Glowing at the Edge of the Woods: Contemporary Writing from West Virginia*. In addition to writing and teaching, Doug is an award-winning traditional fiddler and banjo player.

Multidisciplinary artist FRANK X WALKER is a graduate of the University of Kentucky and Spalding University. A founding member of the Affrilachian Poets, he is a Cave Canem fellow, and the contributing editor of *Eclipsing a Nappy New Millennium* and *America! What's My Name: The Other Poets Unfurl the Flag*. He is the author of four poetry collections: *Black Box*; *Buffalo Dance: The Journey of York*, winner of the Lillian Smith Book Award; *Affrilachia When Winter Come: The Ascension of York* and *Isaac Murphy: I Dedicate This Ride*. He is also the editor and publisher of *PLUCK! The Journal of Affrilachian Arts & Culture*. A Lannan Literary Fellowship for Poetry recipient, he is the former Executive Director of Kentucky's Governor's School for the Arts, and currently serves as an Associate Professor in the Department of English at the University of Kentucky.

WILLIAM WALSH is the director of the Reinhardt University creative writing programs (BFA and MFA), as well as the editor of the *James Dickey Review*. His ninth book and debut novel, *Lakewood*, was published in 2022. *Why I Wrote This Poem* was published in January 2023 by McFarland & Co., and in 2025, his second novel, *Haircuts for the Dead*, will be published. He lives in Atlanta with his family and three kitchen wolves (100+ lbs. dogs).

ROBERT WEST is Head of the Department of Classical & Modern Languages and Literatures at Mississippi State University. The author of three chapbooks of poems, including *Convalescent* (Finishing Line Press), he is also the editor of *The Complete Poems of A. R. Ammons* (W. W. Norton) and co-editor with Jesse Graves of *Robert Morgan: Essays on the Life and Work* (McFarland). He grew up in Henderson County, in Western North Carolina.

JACKSON WHEELER was born and raised in the mountains of western North Carolina. He attended the University of North Carolina-Chapel Hill. He is the author of two collections: *Swimming Past Iceland* (Mille Grazie Press, 1993) and *A Near Country: Poems of Loss* (Solo Press, 1999) with Glenna Luschei and David Oliveira.

DANA WILDSMITH is the author of a novel, *Jumping*, and an environmental memoir, *Back to Abnormal: Surviving With An Old Farm in the New South*, which was a finalist for Georgia Author of the Year. She is also the author of five collections of poetry. Wildsmith has served as Artist-in-Residence for Grand Canyon National Park and for Everglades National Park. She lives with her family on an old farm in North Georgia, and works as an English literacy instructor at Lanier Technical College.

MATTHEW WIMBERLEY grew up in the Blue Ridge Mountains. He is the author of two collections of poetry, *Daniel Boone's Window* (LSU, 2021), and *All the Great Territories* (SIU, 2020), winner of the 2018 Crab Orchard Poetry Series First Book award and the Weatherford Award. His writing has appeared in: *32 Poems*, *Image Journal*, *Poem-a-Day* from the Academy of American Poets, and *The Threepenny Review*. Wimberley received his MFA from NYU. He teaches in western North Carolina.

Originally from Henry County, Virginia, ANNIE WOODFORD is the author of *Bootleg* (Groundhog Poetry Press, 2019) and *Where You Come from Is Gone* (Mercer UP, 2022), which was awarded the 2022 Weatherford Award for Appalachian Poetry. Her micro-chapbook, *When God Was a Child*, was published by Bull City Press in 2023. She has been the recipient of the Jean Ritchie Fellowship from Lincoln Memorial University and the Thelma Smallwood Scholarship from the Appalachian Writers' Workshop.

SYLVIA WOODS is a Kentucky native now living in Oak Ridge, TN. Her work has appeared in publications such as *Appalachian Heritage*, *Motif 1 and 2*, *Now & Then*, and *Cornbread Nation 5*.

MARIANNE WORTHINGTON, is author of *The Girl Singer* (University Press of Kentucky, 2021), winner of the 2022 Weatherford Award for Poetry. Her work has appeared in *Oxford American*, *CALYX*, *Salvation South*, and *Swing*, among other places. She cofounded and was poetry editor of *Still: The Journal*, an online literary magazine publishing writers, artists, and musicians with ties to Appalachia (2009-2024). Her second book of poems, *Water. Witness. Word.*, is forthcoming from Belle Point Press. She grew up in Knoxville, Tennessee, and lives, writes, and teaches in southeastern Kentucky.

AMY WRIGHT was the current Wayne G. Basler Chair of Excellence at East Tennessee State University. Her nonfiction debut, *Paper Concert: A Conversation in the Round*, was published in 2021 with Sarabande Books. She has also authored three poetry books, six chapbooks, and received two Peter Taylor Fellowships to the *Kenyon Review* Writers Workshop, an Individual Artist Grant from the Tennessee Arts Commission, and a fellowship to the Virginia Center for the Creative Arts. Her essays and poems appear in *Georgia Review, Fourth Genre, Ninth Letter, Brevity*, and elsewhere.

CHARLES WRIGHT was born in Pickwick Dam, Tennessee, in 1935 and was educated at Davidson College and the University of Iowa. His books include *Sestets: Poems* (Farrar, Straus and Giroux, 2010); *Littlefoot: A Poem* (2008); *Scar Tissue* (2007), which was the international winner for the Griffin Poetry Prize; *Buffalo Yoga* (Farrar, Straus & Giroux, 2004); *Negative Blue* (2000); *Appalachia* (1998); *Black Zodiac* (1997), which won the Pulitzer Prize and the *Los Angeles Times* Book Prize; *Chickamauga* (1995), which won the 1996 Lenore Marshall Poetry Prize; *The World of the Ten Thousand Things: Poems 1980-1990*; *Zone Journals* (1988); *Country Music: Selected Early Poems* (1983), which won the National Book Award; and *Hard Freight* (1973), which was nominated for the National Book Award; among others. He has also written two volumes of criticism and has translated the work of Dino Campana in *Orphic Songs* as well as Eugenio Montale's *The Storm and Other Poems* which was awarded the PEN Translation Prize.

JAKE ADAM YORK authored four books of poems: *Murder Ballads* (Elixir Press, 2005); *A Murmuration of Starlings* (Southern Illinois UP, 2008); *Persons Unknown* (Southern Illinois UP, 2010); and *Abide*, published posthumously by Southern Illinois University Press in 2014. Originally from Alabama, he was educated at Auburn and Cornell. He received fellowships to serve as a Poet in Residence at the University of Mississippi (2009), to serve as the Thomas Visiting Professor in Creative Writing at Kenyon College (2011), and from the Mellon Foundation to serve as a Visiting Faculty Fellow at the James Weldon Johnson Institute for Advanced Study at Emory University (2011-2012). He was also a recipient of a fellowship from the National Endowment of the Arts. At the time of his death in 2012, he was an associate professor of English at the University of Colorado Denver and edited the journal *Copper Nickel*.

JOHN THOMAS YORK is a retired teacher of high school English. His work has recently appeared in *Appalachian Journal, Appalachian Places, Cold Mountain Review, Pine Mountain Sand & Gravel*, and several other magazines. His first full-length book, *Cold Spring Rising*, was published by Press 53 in 2012. He is currently working on a second full-length collection entitled *Hungry for Country Dark*.

ACKNOWLEDGMENTS

The editors wish to thank Erika Perez Cortazar, Christina Ellison, Elijah Keith, Miranda Ramírez, & Bonny Tunnell for their assistance with this volume.

For contributors who supplied publication information, details are listed below. All poem copyrights have reverted back to respective authors, listed or otherwise, and TRP: The University Press of SHSU has permission to reprint poems included herein.

GILBERT ALLEN: "Stairways to Nowhere" and "Late Garden" appeared in *Catma* (Measure Press, 2014). "Some Week" originally appeared in *Appalachian Journal*. **MAGGIE ANDERSON:** "Long Story" appeared in *A Space Filled with Moving* (U of Pittsburgh P, 1992). "House and Graveyard, Rowlesburg, West Virginia, 1935," "Mining Camp Residents, West Virginia, 1935," "Spitting in the Leaves," and "Street Scene, Morgantown, West Virginia, 1935" appeared in *Cold Comfort* (U of Pittsburgh P, 1986). **JOSEPH BATHANTI:** All poems appear in *Land of Amnesia* (Press 53, 2009). **LAURA TREACY BENTLEY:** "Closet Appalachians" originnally appeared in *10 x 3 plus: a poetry journal* and "Gas Station" in *Pudding Magazine*, later collected in *Lake Effect* (Bird Dog Publishing, 2006). **NICKOLE BROWN:** "Self-Portrait as Eastern Wood Rat" originally appeared in *A Literary Field Guide to Southern Appalachia*, edited by Rose McClarney, 2019, and *TSR: The Southampton Review*, July 2018. "Parable" won the 2024 Treehouse Climate Action Poem Prize and appeared at The Academy of American Poets' Poem-a-Day and *The Alaska Quarterly Review*. **KATHRYN STRIPLING BYER:** "Drought Days." *Descent* (Louisiana State University Press, 2012). Reprinted with permission. **WAYNE CALDWELL:** "Fence Posts," "Bird Tree," and "Peeper Frogs" appeared in *Woodsmoke* (Blair, 2021). **SHULY XÓCHITL CAWOOD:** "Inheritance" originally appeared in *The Sun* and in *Trouble Can Be So Beautiful at the Beginning* (Mercer UP, 2021). "Another Poem for Donna on a Crowded Saturday Afternoon in Kroger" originally appeared in *HAD*. **FRED CHAPPELL:** "Stopping by the Old Homestead" appeared in *Shadowbox* (LSU, 2009); "All the Good Times are Past and Gone" originally appeared *Cave Wall*; "Halloween Moon over Huddle Knob Creek" in *Shenandoah*. **MICHAEL CHITWOOD:** "Heat," "Transport in Early Spring," "Woodpile," "Those Dying Generations," and "The Great Wagon Road. . ." appeared in *Gospel Road Going* (Tryon Publishing Co., 2002); "Hatchet" originally appeared in *The Southern Review*; "Black Locust" in *Appalachian Journal*. **CATHERINE PRITCHARD CHILDRESS:** "Portrait" and "Polysemy" appeared in *Outside the Frame* (Eastover Press, 2023). **JIM CLARK:** "Handiwork," "Loveless You Wander," and "Sunday Dinner" appeared in *Handiwork: Poems by Jim Clark* (St. Andrews College P, 1998); "Black Dog Shadrick Mayhew" originally appeared in *Notions: A Jim Clark Miscellany* (Rank Stranger P, 2007). **GERALDINE CONNOLLY:** "Blue Bridge" originally appeared in *West Branch*. "Lightning," "Mendon," and "Regrets" appeared in *Province of Fire* (Iris P, 1998). **DONNA DOYLE**'s contributions to this anthology were previously published in *Heading Home* (Finishing Line P, 2008). **DIANE GILLIAM:** "Pearlie Tells What Happened at School" appeared in *Kettle Bottom* (Perugia Press, 2004). "Where I'm From" from *Dreadful Wind & Rain: A Lyric Narrative*. Copyright © 2017 by Diane Gilliam. Reprinted with the permission of The Permissions Company, LLC on behalf of Red Hen Press, redhen.org. **JESSE GRAVES:** All poems from *Tennessee Landscape with Blighted Pine* (10th Anniversary Expanded Edition) (TRP, 2022). **CHRIS GREEN:** "A Tree for Everything" and "Playhouse" appeared in *Rushlight: Poems* (Bottom Dog P, 2009). **CONNIE JORDAN GREEN:** "Boss" and "Late January Letter to a Retired Friend in Florida" appeared in *Household Inventory* (Brick Road Poetry P, 2015). "Coal Mining Camp, Kentucky, 1935" and "Of the Wild" appeared in *Slow Children Playing* (Finishing Line P, 2007). **RICHARD HAGUE:** "Time Lapse Photography: A Mouse Corpse Devoured by Maggots" originally appeared in *Poetry*, then in *During The Recent Extinctions: New & Selected Poems 1984-2012* (Dos Madres Press, 2012). "Talking Togther"originally appeared in *Appalachian Journal*, then in *Lives of the Poem: Community and Connection in a Writing Life* (Wind Publications, 2005). **CATHRYN HANKLA:** "Bee Tree" and "Ghost Horses and the Morning Sky" appeared in *Galaxies* (Mercer Uniuversity Press, 2017) Reprinted by permission of Mercer University Press. "Brush Fires" and "Taking Pictures" appeared in *Great Bear* (Groundhog Poetry Press, 2016). **PAULETTA HANSEL:** "The Road" appeared in *Coal Town Photograph* (Dos Madres Press, 2019). "Facts About Grandmothers" originally appeared in *Still: The Journal*. **MARC HARSHMAN:** "Small Town, West Virginia"appeared in *Woman in Red Anorak* (Lynx House Press, 2018). "Not All That Much" appeared in *Following the Silence* (Press 53, 2023). **RAYE HENDRIX:** "Any Coyote"appeared in What Good Is Heaven (TRP, 2024).

JANE HICKS: "Deep Winter" and "Felix culpa" appeared in *Blood and Bone Remember: Poems from Appalachia* (Jesse Stuart Foundation, 2005). "A Poet's Work" and "Dust" appeared in *Driving with the Dead* (UP of Kentucky, 2014). RON HOUCHIN: "Belief in Soap" appeared in *Museum Crows* (Salmon Publishing, 2009); "Camping at Greenup Locks and Dam" and "The First Christmas I Remember" in *Birds in the Tops of Winter Trees* (Wind Pubications, 2018); "Singing to the Fan" originally appeared in *Kestrel: A Journal of Literature and Art*. DAVID HUDDLE: "Religious Life" originally appeared in *The Southern Review*; "Hilltop Sonnet" in *Redivider*. CHARLIE G. HUGHES: "Where I'm From" and "Lament for Mountains" appeared in *Body and Blood* (Wind Publications, 2010). EDISON JENNINGS: "Rainstorm" originally appeared in *The Nebraska Review*; "Appalachian Gothic" in *Boulevard*; "Apple Economics" in *Slate*. DON JOHNSON: "Grabbling," "Scatology," and "Almanac" appeared in *Here and Gone: New and Selected Poems* (Louisiana Literature, 2009). "Isinglass" and "Going to Chatham" appeared in *More than Heavy Rain* (TRP, 2014). JUDY JORDAN: "Those First Mornings Living in the Greenhouse," "Waking in Winter," and "The Greenhouse, Late September" appeared in *Hunger* (Tinderbox Editions, 2018). Reprinted with permission of the publisher. "In the 25th Year of My Mother's Death" and "Sandbar at Moore's Creek," from *Carolina Ghost Woods*, (Louisiana State University Press, 2000). Reprinted with permission of the publisher. MARILYN KALLET: "Global" appeared in *Packing Light: New and Selected Poems* (Black Widow Press, 2009). LEATHA KENDRICK: "Tonight Weaving" originally appeared in *Shenandoah*; "Brought-On Bride," in *Appalachian Journal*; "Morning of the Heart Test" in *Wind*; these poems were later reprinted in *Second Opinion* (David Robert Books, 2008.) "Lesson in Love Unleashed" originally appeared in *Second Opinion*. LISA KWONG: All poems appeared in *Becoming AppalAsian* (Glass Lyre Press, 2022). JEANNE LARSEN: "Wrong All These Years—It Isn't" appeared in *Poet's Choice* (Washington Post Book World, 2009). "Ardent Things," "Flowering Judases," and "Scar Garden" appeared in *Why We Make Gardens (& Other Poems)* (Mayapple Press, 2010). DONNA J. LONG: "Sago Mine Explosion" appeared in *Traditions: A Journal of West Virginia Folk Culture and Educational Awareness* vol. 10 (Fairmont State UP, 2007). "Hanging Audubon's Flamingo..." originally appeared in *North American Review*. DENTON LOVING: "Under the Chestnut Tree" originally appeared in *Ecotone*. "Feller" originally appeared in *Appalachian Places Magazine*. ROBERT WOOD LYNN: "The River New" originally appeared in *New Ohio Review*. GEORGE ELLA LYON: "Report Card" originally appeared as a broadside by October Press, 2010. JEFF MANN: "Mountain Fireflies," "Creecy Greens," "Digging Potatoes," "Maple Syrup," "Goldenrod Seeds," and "Homecoming" appeared in *Loving Mountains, Loving Men*, reprinted with permission from Ohio UP / Swallow P, Athens, Ohio (www.ohioswallow.com). "Locrian" first appeared in *Appalachian Heritage* and *Coal: A Poetry Anthology*, and appeared in *A Romantic Mann* (Lethe Press, 2013). Reprinted with permission. JEFF DANIEL MARION: "Ebbing & Flowing Spring" originally appeared in *Epoch*; "By the Banks of the Holston" in *Touchstone*. These were reprinted in *Ebbing & Flowing Springs: New and Selected Poems and Prose, 1976-2001* (Celtic Cat Publishing, 2002); "The Lost Nickel" originally appeared in *Letters Home* (Sow's Ear Press, 2001); "The Man Who Loved Hummingbirds" in *Lost & Found* (Sow's Ear Press, 1994). MICHAEL MCFEE: "Robert's Lake" originally appeared in *Cave Wall* and in *Poetry Daily*; "Arcadia Dairy Bar" in *Edible Piedmont*; "Sorry" in *North Carolina Literary Review*. ROSE MCLARNEY: "Realizing" and "Remains" appeared in *Colorfast* (Penguin, 2024). KELLY MCQUAIN: "Dolly" appeared in *Scrape the Velvet from Your Antlers* (TRP, 2023). JIM MINICK: "Her Secret Song," "Clear Blue Spring," and "Waspy Apples" appeared in *Her Secret Song* (Motes Books, 2008); "Ghost Stump, Sun Music" appeared in *Burning Heaven* (Wind Publications, 2008). THORPE MOECKEL: "Bartram's Trail" appeared in *Odd Botany* (Silverfish Review P, 2002); "The August Listener" appeared in *According to Sand* (Mercer UP, 2022). JANICE TOWNLEY MOORE: "Windows Filled with Gifts" originally appeared in *Press 53 Open Awards Anthology* (Press 53, 2009). ROBERT MORGAN: "Prophet" and "November Light" appear in *The Southern Quarterly*; "Burning Spring" and "Apple Howling" in *Bat City Review*; "Horse Fiddle" and "The Years Ahead" in *Appalachian Heritage*; "Translation" in *Smartish Pace*. RICK MULKEY: "High Lonesome," "Toward Any Darkness," "Devolution Theory," and "Homecoming" appeared in *Toward Any Darkness* (WordTech Communications, 2007). "Hunger Ghazal" appeared in *Ravenous: New and Selected Poems* (Serving House Books, 2014). TED OLSON: "The Short Leash," "Displacement," and "Swallows" appeared in *Breathing in Darkness* (Wind Publications, 2006). "River Baptism" appeared in *Revelations: Poems* (Celtic Cat Publishing, 2012). LISA J. PARKER: These poems originally appeared in *Still: Literature of the Mountain South* and *Motif: We All Live Downstream*. LINDA PARSONS: "Driftwood Found on the Greenbrier Trail" appeared in *Home Fires* (Sow's Ear, 1997); "I Dream You Speak the River" appeared in *This Shaky Earth* (TRP, 2016); "Rosemary, for Remembrance" and "Repossessed" appeared in *Mother Land* (Iris Press, 2018); "Hands" and "Jarflies" appeared in *Bound* (Wind Publications, 2011). CHARLOTTE PENCE: "At Opry Mills Mall" and "After Two Weeks Without Rain" first appeared in *Town Creek Poetry*. EDWINA PENDARVIS: "Melee" appeared in the book *Like the Mountains of China* (Blair Mountain P, 2003); "Scarab" and "While We Sleep" in *Human Landscapes* (Bottom Dog P, 1997). PATRICK PHILLIPS: "The Rules" appeared in

Chattahoochee (U of Arkansas Press, 2004). **LYNN POWELL:** "Indian Summer," "Fragments of a Lost Gospel," and "Kind of Blue" appeared in *Season of the Second Thought* (U of Wisconsin P, 2017); "April & Ecclesiastes," "Revival," and "Etudes for Unaccompanied Voice" appeared in *The Zones of Paradise* (U of Akron P, 2003). **RITA SIMS QUILLEN:** "Sunday School Lesson," "My Mother, She Was Very Old-Fashioned," and "Passing Suite" appeared in *Counting the Sums* (Sow's Ear P, 1995). **MELISSA RANGE:** "New Heavens, New Earth" originally appeared in *Poetry London*. All contributions in this volume are included in *Horse and Rider* (Texas Tech UP, 2010). **RON RASH:** "Watauga: 1803," "In Dismal Gorge," and "Speckled Trout" appeared in *Raising the Dead* (Iris P, 2002); "The Corpse Bird," "A Preacher Who Takes Up Serpents," and "Good Friday, 1995" in *Among the Believers* (Iris P, 2000). **GEORGE SCARBROUGH**'s poems all debut in this volume, with thanks to Judy Loest. **VIVIAN SHIPLEY:** "Alice Todd, Outside Cecilia, Kentucky" appeared in *Hard Boot: Poems New & Old* (Louisiana Literature P, 2005). **ARTHUR SMITH:** "Easter" and "More Lines on a Shield Abandoned During Battle" appeared in *The Late World* (Carnegie Mellon UP, 2002); "More Lines on a Shield Abandoned During Battle" from *The Late World*, Copyright © 2002 by Arthur Smith. "Kudzu in Winter" from *Orders of Affection*. Copyright © 1996 by Arthur Smith. All reprinted with the permission of The Permissions Company, LLC on behalf of Carnegie Mellon University Press, www.cmu.edu/universitypress. **JAMES MALONE SMITH:** "First Freeze" originally appeared in *The Atlanta Review*; "Harm's Way" in *Quarterly West*; "Hen" in *AGNI*. **NOEL SMITH:** "Ada's Poem" originally appeared as "Ada to Hank" in *Still*. **R. T. SMITH:** "Mockingbird" and "Mallard" originally appeared in *In the Night Orchard: New and Selected Poems* (TRP, 2014). **DARIUS STEWART:** "My Mother's Hands" originally appeared in *Fifth Wednesday Journal*; "Self-Portrait as Future Third Person" in *Many Mountains Moving* and *Verse Daily*; "The Ghost the Night Becomes" in *storySouth*; "Statues in the Park" in *Callaloo*. **A. E. STRINGER:** "April Snow" appeared in *Asbestos Brocade* (Salmon Poetry, 2017). "My Father Asleep" appeared in *Late Breaking* (Salmon Poetry, 2013). **DAN STRYK:** "The Mountains Change Aspect Like Our Moods" first appeared in *Chariton Review*; "Hawk in the Kudzu" in *International Poetry Review*; "Red-Eyed Cicada" in *South Dakota Review*. "The Mountains Change Aspect Like Our Moods" and "Hawk in the Kudzu" were reprinted in *Dimming Radiance* (Wind Publications, 2008); "Red-Eyed Cicada" in *Taping Images to Walls* (Pecan Grove P, 2002). **ERIC TRETHEWEY:** "Frost on the Fields" appeared in *The Hudson Review*; "Things" in *Cimarron Review*; "Sign" in *Appalachian Heritage*. **SUSAN O'DELL UNDERWOOD:** "Commencement" and "Specter" appeared in *Splinter* (Madville Publishing, 2023). **DOUG VAN GUNDY:** "A People's History of Randolph Co., WV" originally appeared in *Kestrel*. "Hymn for Coal Smoke" originally appeared in *The Guardian*. **ROBERT WEST:** "Presto," "Lullaby," and "Still" appeared in *Best Company* (Blink Chapbooks, 2005); "Oasis" in *Inch*. **JACKSON WHEELER:** "Ars Poetica" appeared in *ASKEW*; "Backhome Story" in *Shenandoah*; "The TVA Built a Dam" in *Swimming Past Iceland* (Mille Grazie Press, 1993). **DANA WILDSMITH:** "Speed" appeared in *One Good Hand* (Iris P, 2005); "Bones" in *Our Bodies Remember* (Sow's Ear Press, 1999). **MATTHEW WIMBERLEY:** "Materials for a Gravestone Rubbing," first appeared on *Poem-a-Day* from the Academy of American Poets. **ANNIE WOODFORD:** "The Four Hundred Angels of Henry County"originally appeared in *Salvation South*. **SYLVIA WOODS:** "What We Take With Us" appeared in *What We Take With Us* (EastOver Press, 2021). "Wearing My Grammar Girdle" appeared in *Appalachian Heritage*. **MARIANNE WORTHINGTON:** *The Girl Singer: Poems* (The University Press of Kentucky, 2021). **CHARLES WRIGHT**'s contributions were reserved specifically for this volume, acknowledged in *Sestets* (Farrar, Straus & Giroux, 2010) as *Appalachian Poetry Anthology*. **JAKE ADAM YORK**'s contributions to this volume appeared in the collection *Murder Ballads* (Elixir Press, 2005). Reprinted with permission of the publisher. **JOHN THOMAS YORK:** All included poems appeared in the chapbook *Naming the Constellations* (Spring Street Editions, 2010). "Brains," "June," and "Puzzle" originally appeared in *Appalachian Journal*. "Egret" was published on Kathryn Stripling Byer's blog, *My Laureate's Lasso*. All four poems appear in *Cold Spring Rising* (Press 53, 2012).

www.ingramcontent.com/pod-product-compliance
Lightning Source LLC
Chambersburg PA
CBHW020909110525
26347CB00025B/22